The Chinook
Short Season Yard

The Chinook Short Season Yard

Quick and Beautiful in the Calgary Region

LYNDON PENNER

Sagebrush
An imprint of

Brush
Education Inc.

Brush Education Inc.
www.brusheducation.ca
contact@brusheducation.ca

Edited by Vanessa Young
Copy edit by Heather Sangster, Strong Finish

Cover design: Dean Pickup; Cover photos, background: Philhillphotography, Dreamstime.com; right: author, left to right middle: Akemi Matsubuchi
Interior design: Carol Dragich, Dragich Design

Printed and manufactured in Canada
Ebook edition available at Amazon, Kobo, and other e-retailers.

Library and Archives Canada Cataloguing in Publication
Penner, Lyndon, 1980-, author
The Chinook short season yard : quick and beautiful in the Calgary Region / Lyndon Penner.
Includes index.
Issued in print and electronic formats.
ISBN 978-1-55059-539-0 (pbk.).— ISBN 978-1-55059-541-3 (mobi).—
ISBN 978-1-55059-542-0 (epub)

1. Gardening—Alberta—Calgary Region.   I. Title.

SB453.3.C2P46 2014   635.097123'38   C2013-907860-6   C2013-907861-4

Produced with the assistance of the Government of Alberta, Alberta Media Fund. We also acknowledge the financial support of the Government of Canada through the Canada Book Fund for our publishing activities.

Government of Alberta ■

 Canadian Heritage   Patrimoine canadien

Dedication

This book is dedicated to all the lovely people (CBC listeners in particular) who, over the years, have graciously and kindly asked me when I was going to write a book. This book is for you. Thank you for bringing me light.

Contents

Part One: Gardening Wisdom

Part Two: Shopping with Lyndon

Introduction

I have been gardening my whole life. Some of my earliest memories are related to gardening. Planting seeds, being in the garden, touching blossoms for the very first time—all of these experiences helped to shape me into the person I am today. Over the course of my life, my garden has been a friend, a sanctuary, and an excellent teacher. It can be those things for you as well. Some of the things I've learned in the garden have been very practical; others have merely been surprising or unexpected. I hope you'll find this book to be the same way!

We should start with introductions. I'm Lyndon. I started working in the garden industry at the age of sixteen, and I've lived a fascinating, strange, wonderful, and complex life as a result. I will become that voice in your brain that says, "Only old people plant geraniums" and "You definitely need that dark red daylily."

Though I now live in Calgary, I was raised in a rural setting just north of Saskatoon. From the time I was very small, I was helping my mother and my grandmother in the garden. An interest became a hobby, a hobby became a passion, a passion became an obsession, and an obsession became my career.

Everyone wants an attractive, functional yard, but not everyone wants to learn the name of every single plant or be enslaved by a vegetable garden. It *is* possible to have a beautiful yard that requires little and gives much, even in a harsh climate like Alberta's chinook zone.

A garden is *a living, breathing work of art*. It is a kind of

This is me, Lyndon.

A short season is defined as anything less than 100 frost-free growing days. We usually get more than that, but not always. Bragg Creek, Alberta, has an average of 62 frost-free days per year.

communication tool. Your garden says something to the world about *you*. That statement can be "I love food" or "I love things that look tropical" or "I'm lazy and can't be bothered to pull weeds." My job is to help you figure out what you want your yard to say and find the plants, flowers, and trees that do this most efficiently. Dolly Parton once said, "The magic is inside you. There ain't no crystal ball." I'm going to help you find that magic.

You don't necessarily need to know the name of that tall thing with the blue flowers (it's a delphinium), but if you know that it blooms like crazy and does well in that spot by the kitchen window, that might be all the information you need.

You do not have to be chained to your garden. You should be able to go away for a week in the summer without your garden completely falling apart.

You should also not be afraid to make mistakes because mistakes help you learn and they are invaluable. Gardening is supposed to be fun.

I am constantly telling people that low maintenance is not the same thing as zero maintenance. You're going to learn a lot, I hope you're

Gardening connects you to the earth and is a great benefit to body, soul, and spirit.

going to laugh along the way, and you're not going to take yourself too seriously. This is just gardening after all, and it should relieve (rather than cause) stress. Going to the local garden centre should be exciting! I'll help you figure out what to spend money on. I'll make sure you choose plants that will work *with* (and not against) the conditions in your yard and will flower over a long period.

One of the first things I hear from people new to gardening is "I don't know what I'm doing." They are frightened, anxious, stressed out, and feel overwhelmed. I understand these feelings, but you must set them aside. You can screw up six ways from Sunday and the right plant in the right place will still find a way to survive. Plants are amazing!

Before you ever plant anything or spend a single dollar on seeds, you must open yourself up to the magic of the earth, the surreal thrill that comes from interacting with leafy green, growing things. Try to see the wonder in it all. To put a seed in the ground and watch it turn into a flowering plant is nothing short of miraculous. To make dill pickles with cucumbers you grew from seed is overwhelmingly satisfying. I should also warn you right now that once you begin to see the magic, it's easy to become totally seduced.

Keep in touch. Visit my blog at www.jadecypress.wordpress.com or follow me on Twitter at @cbcgardener.

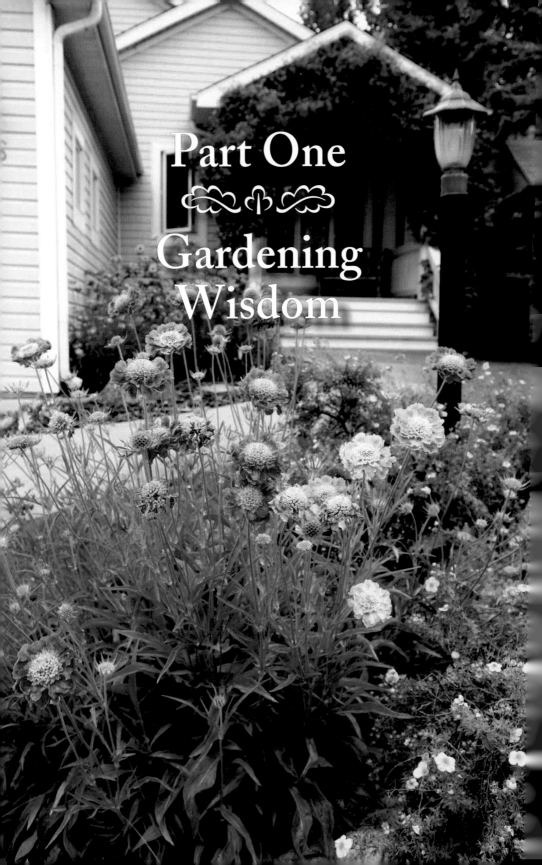

Part One

Gardening
Wisdom

☙ *I* ❧

Location, location, location...

The first rule of success in any field of your life is to understand what it is that you're dealing with. Plants are adaptable and microclimates do exist, but I have no time for a plant that merely "survives." I want something that will *excel*, something that will be rewarding to grow. Any plant merely surviving will need too much of your attention and be more prone to insect or disease issues. If you want a low-maintenance garden, grow something that will be healthy and vigorous in *your* yard.

Survey your area

Before you buy a single new plant for your yard, I want you to really think about where you're going to put it. The spot where your house now stands was once covered with native prairie grasses and entire communities of native plants. What was growing here a thousand years ago? What grew here before your house was built?

Opposite: Scabiosa 'Butterfly Blue' was Perennial of the Year in 2000. Any hardy plant given this award is always a good choice!

I want you to think about the location of your home and how it helps define the plants that will succeed there. Some questions to consider are:

- Do you live in the mountains or on the badlands? Do you live on a flood plain or a rocky slope?
- How close are you to a river? Is your garden in a spot where it could be damaged by flooding? Is your water table very high?
- What type of soil is in your area? Does it drain well? Is your garden sandy or elevated and therefore prone to drought and erosion?
- Are you in a new or old neighbourhood? When they dug your basement, did they simply toss the dirt in your front yard or do you actually have topsoil?
- What sort of trees, shrubs, and perennials do you notice growing in your area? Are there large trees near you that are shading or protecting your garden but capturing water from your property?
- Is your yard sheltered or exposed? How windy is it?
- Which direction does your yard face? Is it mostly sunny or shady?
- Do you hear any birds? Are cats or dogs in your area a problem?

We will talk about your climate, wind, water, and soil in more detail as we continue, but always keep all aspects of your personal space in mind when making decisions about your garden. It's your garden after all; it needs to fit into your space. The better your plant choices suit your space, the less work it's going to be in the long run to keep things healthy and beautiful.

Consider your climate zone, but don't fixate on it.

You may dream of an Asian-style garden with hedges of bamboo, but the fact is, if you live in zone 3, that dream might not be a reality. Most bamboo simply will not grow here because Alberta is absolutely not the right climate. You must always be realistic—just because something survives, it doesn't mean that it is well suited. While it is possible that you may get a magnolia to live, it is never going to perform like it would in Abbotsford. (In fact, "live" is about all it would do, if you were lucky. "Just wait till my magnolia blooms!" said no one in Alberta ever.) It is so easy to forget that we live in one of the harshest climates on Earth until it's −30°C and we are scraping ice off our vehicles.

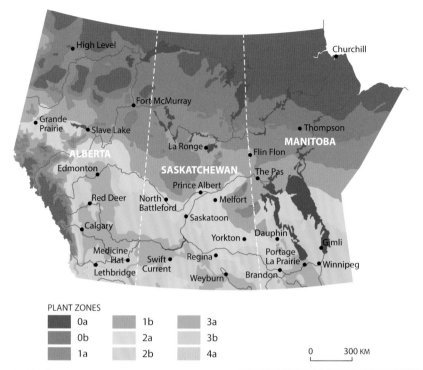

PLANT ZONES

■	0a		1b		3a
	0b		2a		3b
	1a		2b		4a

0   300 KM

Prairie climate zones.

The Canadian zone map differs from the American zone map, so if you are looking at zones in an American gardening magazine, they probably do not relate to you.

The original zone maps for Canada were drawn up in the 1960s by horticulturalist Art Drysdale, along with a climatologist, and were based on the highest possible summer temperatures and lowest possible winter temperatures. Since higher zone numbers indicate warmer climates, zone 6 (on Vancouver Island) is significantly warmer than zone 2 (northern Saskatchewan). Calgary is zone 3.

When you're shopping, always read the plant tags. For example, tags will state "hardy in zones 4–9" or may be abbreviated as "Z3," meaning hardy to zone 3. The idea is that anything with a zone number equal to or lower than yours will survive your winter, and anything higher won't. If you live in zone 3 and you know a wisteria is hardy only to zone 5, you would know instantly that it is not a wise choice. However, a zone 1 shrub would be.

It's worth noting that just because a plant is hardy enough to survive your winter does not mean it is well suited. For example, there are native species of rhododendron that are easily hardy to well below −35°C. However, they are poor garden plants because they require acidic soil and cool summer temperatures, and few of us can really offer that.

A few kinds of scarlet maple and sugar maple selected from the northernmost parts of their natural range are hardy enough to survive here, but our summers are ill suited to them because they have a preference for Ontario's humidity and our growing season is really too short.

The zone map was originally intended to apply only to trees and shrubs, and never to perennials. There are far too many variables to make rating perennials simple, some of which we will go into below. However, if you visit a garden centre these days, nearly every single tree, shrub, or perennial has been assigned a zone rating. It's a place to start, but it's far from the last word.

The stunning blue poppies (*Meconopsis* spp.) often do poorly here not because our winters are too cold for them but because our summers are too warm!

Problems with the zone approach

Zone ratings make me *absolutely insane.* After nearly two decades in this industry, few things frustrate me more or confuse new gardeners more. More often than not, zone ratings are totally inaccurate, and people tend to take them as gospel. They are meant to be a guideline only. We will consider several reasons below, but the bottom line is: Talking to an experienced gardener about what they've had success with in spaces like yours is sometimes more relevant than what the tag says … or just skip ahead in the book to the "Shopping with Lyndon" section.

Wholesalers tend to tag plants hardy for wherever they are located.
Let's say that you are a wholesale grower somewhere in zone 4 in Ontario. Since all the trees and shrubs you sell are hardy where you live, there's no need to put anything otherwise on the tag. Because you know these plants grow well at your location, it's common practice to put zones 4–9 on your tag even though those plants could well be much hardier. Those trees arrive at a garden centre in Winnipeg and new gardeners see the label and say, "Oh, it's only hardy to zone 4. I guess it won't grow here. Why is this nursery trying to sell me something that isn't hardy?"

Labelling regulations mean plants can only be tagged for the lowest climate zone they've been officially trialled in.

Pretend there is a new variety of birch tree that they've grown and evaluated at the Brooks Experimental Farm in Alberta, which is located in zone 3. This tree might well be hardy to zone 2 or even zone 1, but since it has not been *officially* trialled there, they can't put that on the tags. With the recent cutbacks at many of our experimental farms, we're losing the ability to officially trial a diverse selection of plants in lower zones. It is only a matter of time before it becomes problematic finding plants, even perfectly hardy plants, that are labelled hardy for us. This growing trend makes getting gardening advice from experts in your area even more critical.

Many years ago, I became smitten with *Allium karataviense*, a kind of ornamental onion. I read that it was native to the mountains of Pakistan and the Himalayas, which could be a similar climate to ours, so I thought I would give it a try. I grew it from seed, it flourished, and I fell madly in love with its big, strappy leaves and bubblegum-scented flowers. For many years, this plant multiplied in my zone 2 garden in Saskatchewan. Years later, I saw it on an availability list when I was working for a garden centre in Calgary, so I immediately ordered some in. All the tags read "zones 5–9." No amount of me trying to convince people that it was 100 per cent perfectly hardy was effective. After being told my bald, windy prairie farmyard must have had some serious microclimate, or I was mistaken about what I'd planted because the tag clearly stated zone 5, I finally pulled the tags out in frustration and threw them away. The allium sold out entirely, and the following year I had customers asking if I could please bring some more in because they loved it so much.

Wholesale nurseries sometimes have no idea what they're talking about.

I once got in a shipment of Manitoba maple (*Acer negundo*) with tags that read "zones 5–9." Manitoba maple is found throughout the continent, and there is *nowhere* in Manitoba that qualifies as a zone 5. This tree is hardy to at least zone 2 and probably zone 1. But do you think anyone wanted to buy those trees?

Microclimates within your zone

Because the zone maps were based on the temperatures in completely unprotected areas, they don't take microclimates into consideration. What's a microclimate? It's a space in your yard or garden where for some reason things are protected from the very fiercest of the winter elements. These are spaces where you might be able to get away with

Winter injury created by planting in front of heat vent. This is not the type of microclimate you want!

growing something that is not necessarily hardy in your area. Perhaps you have a large stone that helps to trap snow in a certain spot, or you have a south-facing wall on your garage where the ground is sheltered and protected from the winter winds. Maybe you live in the downtown core, which never gets quite as cold as it does in the suburbs.

This doesn't mean that your plant is always going to get to full size here. A good example of this is the butterfly bush (*Buddleia* spp.), which is hardy to zone 4 or 5. In lower zones like ours, it dies back to the ground every year, though the root and crown will overwinter. Butterfly bush will never reach the 2 to 3 metres that it would if I planted it in Vancouver, but since it flowers on new wood, I don't mind this a bit. Just treat it as a perennial rather than as a shrub.

The popular 'Black Lace' elder is another example of a plant that is doable if you have a good microclimate. It certainly survives here, but it will never reach its full size in our climate. Such plants are often referred to as being "marginally hardy." You can get away with it, but not every time and not in every location.

Considering plants that may be marginally hardy is a good idea if you fall in love with a certain plant, you're looking for special design interest, or you want to plant something a bit more challenging. However, if you're a new gardener, you may want to stick with tried-and-true plants. Plants that are constantly stressed tend to be more susceptible to pest and disease issues than plants that are comfortable in your location. Remember, if you want your garden to be vibrant and healthy with little pampering, you don't want a plant that just survives—you want it to thrive!

ZONES: BEYOND THE BASICS

In any city, there are gardeners growing things "out of zone." For experienced gardeners, this is a big thrill and quite a lot of fun. I have a clematis in my garden that is supposedly hardy only to zone 5. It is flourishing. Yes, I give it some extra protection for the winter, but there is a real charge in growing something that you're not supposed to be able to grow! There are immense black walnut trees in Medicine Hat, and I have seen catalpa flowering in Lethbridge. There is a large gingko tree growing in Drumheller and more in Saskatoon. Gingko should not be happy anywhere east of Kelowna.

None of these trees are hardy in these zones, and yet here they are, alive and well, and seemingly having been able to adapt to conditions that are harsher, drier, and more challenging than we typically give them credit for. People forget that trees and shrubs are *living* things, and they have a certain ability to adapt when they are planted young. This is especially true if they are pampered a bit when they are first planted, since they tend to become stronger and more resilient with time.

If I want to know whether something might be worth testing in my own garden, I always look at where it is native. A tree that is native to the mountains of Russia is probably a good candidate for trying in your yard. Many plants from northern China are also excellent because they have similar growing conditions—short, hot summers followed by long, cold winters. If something is native to the jungles of West Africa or the steamy valleys of Thailand, there is a good probability that it will not survive in Alberta. Something native to Great Britain or Chile may or may not survive here but might be worth trying. Remarkably, there are plants native to New Zealand that have survived in Alberta because they come from high altitudes and are accustomed to cold winters and warm summers.

"I tried that plant three times before I figured out how to make it happy" is a common refrain among experienced gardeners. Killing something does not mean you are a failure. It means that conditions did not suit that plant at that time in that particular location. Maybe the plant was unhealthy when you bought it. Maybe a cutworm ate it or it stood in water or it didn't like the soil where it was. Try it in a different spot. Try a different variety or colour, since some cultivars are hardier than others. The trick in all of this is to be optimistic and experimental.

Chinooks: Hot flashes for the prairies

If you live in southern Alberta, as I do, you have to deal with the vagaries of chinooks. While chinooks are great for people, they can be disastrous if you are a plant. I always tell people that in the chinook zone, *any* success is to be celebrated. Why is this? The way a plant survives winter freezing is to move as much water as possible out of its above-ground cells so that when the cells freeze they don't rupture and die. The tree sap is compacted as the long chains of sugar created in the leaves over the summer are packaged into tight molecules of starch and stored below ground with small amounts of water. This allows the plant to have all the supplies it needs to grow vigorously in the spring. While the plant is dormant, as it should be all winter, it can handle long periods of freezing temperatures. The warming temperatures of spring signal the plant to reverse all of these actions until the sap begins to flow again. Chinooks trick the plants into believing it's spring already and time to grow.

The word *chinook* originally meant a warming wind that came from the ocean into the interior regions of the Pacific Northwest. Chinooks can completely obliterate up to 30 centimetres of snow cover in as little as twenty-four hours, and they can last from a few hours to a few days. Chinooks affect all of southern Alberta, the interior of British Columbia, and parts of Montana, Colorado, and Idaho. According to Environment Canada, Lethbridge and Crowsnest Pass get an average of thirty to thirty-five chinook days per winter, so it's something we have to take into consideration if we want to garden here.

Many of my friends in Saskatchewan and Manitoba develop "chinook envy" in February. It can be +6°C in Calgary while it is −25°C in Brandon. Once these plus temperatures have caused the sap to thaw out and begin to flow inside the trunk of the tree, both the existing cells and any new growth will be frost-sensitive. When the temperature plummets again and those sap cells freeze violently, they will rupture. This sometimes leads to significant damage on trees. It can mean tip kill or die back, it can mean ugly lesions or sunscald along the trunk, and it usually means a decline in overall vigour and stamina. A tree in Calgary might be smaller and much less attractive than a tree of the same kind planted at the same time in Edmonton. Chinook damage occurs not just in gardens, but in the wild as well, and trees in these zones are often smaller and shabbier-looking compared with trees in areas with more consistent winter temperatures.

Frost cracking, a kind of winter damage often associated with chinooks, is caused by the living tissue in tree trunks expanding and contracting due to fluctuating warm and cold temperatures.

Bark lesions are a result of chinook damage.

One of the most striking features of this phenomenon is the chinook arch, which is a band of stationary stratus clouds caused by air rippling over the mountains. To those unfamiliar with it, the chinook arch may look like a threatening storm cloud. But these clouds rarely produce rain or snow. They can, however, create stunning sunrises and sunsets.

In February 1992, the temperature in the town of Claresholm in southern Alberta reached 24ºC from a chinook wind. Imagine how confusing that would be to you if you were a tree in the middle of your winter rest!

The downside is that gardening in a chinook zone is not for the faint of heart. Plenty of things simply do not adapt here due to dramatic up-and-down temperatures in the winter. Silver maples, a favourite tree of mine, are rare in Calgary, as they do not adapt well to interruptions in their winter rest. Burr oaks, lindens, Manchurian ash, and many varieties of both apple and apricot refuse to perform well here for the same reason. Why is this? They are easier to wake in the spring—to survive a chinook, you need a plant that wakes up to spring as "quickly" as your average teenager wakes up for 8 a.m. chores on Saturday morning. When you are purchasing a tree at a garden centre here, always ask how well it deals with chinooks.

If a chinook comes along and melts all the snow off your flowerbeds and then temperatures plummet, many of your perennials may die. Inevitably, the first to die in such circumstances are the most expensive plants—meanwhile, the aggressive Chinese lantern that you got for free from a neighbour should come through the winter just fine, chinook or no. To protect your perennial beds, make sure they're well covered with extra snow or mulch, and in the event of a severe chinook, don't hesitate to cover the beds with whatever you have for insulation, such as blankets or burlap, to keep the cold locked in.

Prairie winds both suck and blow.

If you grew up in the chinook zone, you may not be aware of how incessant the wind actually is, but most people around the globe cannot even conceive of prairie winds. On any given day around here, you can probably spit in your own eye. I have Canadian friends who have been living in Hong Kong for more than a decade, and they told me once that what constitutes an average windy day here would be grounds for closing all the schools over there. Hong Kong is located in a protected, sheltered spot and right on the water.

Our biodiversity is significantly less here than it is in places such as Ontario because we have a short, dry, *windy* growing season.

Our winds might actually be one of the biggest factors affecting whether you succeed or fail in gardening here because the wind on the prairies is constant, *constant!* It does terrific damage to things and can be extremely hard on the plants in your yard and garden. It dehydrates both people and the garden. One afternoon, my friend Madison announced that her skin was "just like an alligator purse!" She had been in Costa Rica for a while, a significantly more humid place than southern Alberta. She couldn't believe how rapidly her skin was completely devoid of moisture the instant she got home.

Now imagine that you are tree and it is winter. Your root system is entirely frozen, and you are dormant. You cannot even take up moisture to replace what is lost, so you face a slow death by dehydration. The desiccating wind is why junipers, cedars, pines, and so on are often brown and dead in the springtime and a large part of why it is so important to create some shelter in the garden. No shelter, no garden.

Protection from the wind

Plants in windy sites are often stunted, smaller, and woodier than they are when growing in sheltered places. If you have a very windy, very exposed yard or a plant that isn't doing well in a certain location, one of the first things to consider is creating some shelter. Ideally, you will be able to plant some trees and shrubs to help create some protection.

While you're waiting for your trees to grow, what can you do to provide some quick shelter from the wind? Consider planting:

- annual vines such as runner beans, morning glories, or canary creeper along a trellis or twining throughout that previously ugly chain-link fence;

- large, fast-growing annuals such as sunflowers, lavatera, kochia, or cleome to provide a quick and efficient little "hedge";

- tall or large perennials such as globe thistle, peonies, or Monarda for a more permanent solution; or

- incredibly durable shrubs such as caragana that you can remove later once the more delicate plants have grown enough to be able to handle the elements.

Hardening off your seedlings

The wind is also the number-one reason you need to "harden off" seedlings before planting them. This just means getting them gradually used to being outdoors by putting the containers outside for a few hours at a time until they begin to adapt to fluctuations in temperature and wind. If you take a flat of seedlings that have spent their entire life indoors and plant them, they will be dead in twenty-four hours. The drastic shock of extreme temperature change coupled with the dehydrating winds here will destroy them. Hardening off allows cell walls to harden and the plant to become stronger. Stronger plants are more durable overall. You need to harden things off for only about a week or so, and then it's perfectly safe to put them outside—though you may need to protect them from frost!

Peonies make a beautiful wind block.

Drought.

It's all water under the bridge

Let's talk about water in the garden for a minute. We all know that one house where every time you pass by there's an old guy dragging the hose around. Why should you care about conserving water in the garden? Well, in the first place, water is a finite resource. There is a limited amount of it, especially here. It doesn't rain every five minutes in Alberta like it does on the West Coast.

Water *isn't free.* What are you paying for water? A better question is what was the *cost* of getting that water to you. Great British gardener Anna Pavord once very eloquently said, "Great waterfalls have been silenced so that we can turn on a tap." There is truth to that. Our water is very expensively sucked out of rivers and lakes that more than likely had far better things to do with it than washing our cars or soaking our lawns. Being water wise can save you money, and it's far better for the environment.

What does "water little once established" mean?

All that being said, the number-one reason newly planted trees and shrubs die is lack of water. "I thought it was supposed to be low maintenance" is usually what the homeowner tells the exasperated garden centre staff when he or she comes back looking for a refund.

Anything new that goes into the ground is going to need a lot of water if you want it to establish. "Water little once established" means that in the first season of its life, you are going to have to water that plant very deeply until it has a robust-enough root system to be able to look after itself. If your trees and shrubs don't get roots deeply and securely into the ground, they simply won't have any drought-resistance.

My general rule is that once a plant has doubled in size, it is "well established." For some plants that takes a few months, but for others it may be a season or two before you can reduce your watering. Like a child, a garden can be left alone for increasingly longer periods the larger and older it gets. You can ease up once the garden has started to come into its own but not before.

A drought-resistant flowerbed.

What does "drought-resistant" mean?
Drought-resistant is a term that gets used quite randomly throughout the horticultural world, but what does it really mean? It means that once that plant has reached mature size, it should be able to survive and recover from a drought with little to no trouble. Drought-resistant does *not* mean that you will never have to give it a drink. Be realistic; even plants that are adapted to dry climates are going to need some water sometimes.

Watering your plants
If you know that you have only so much to spend on the water bill or are rationing rainwater, how do you decide what gets watered first? Prioritize your watering based on the needs of the plants, combined with what it is you want to grow the most.

- The younger a plant is, the more water it will likely need. Seedlings, newly rooted cuttings, and newly planted trees will inevitably need the most water.

- If you have a garden full of plants with low water needs but simply had to have that hybrid tea rose, then perhaps this is your first plant to water.

- Plants that produce "juicy" vegetables such as tomatoes and cucumbers tend to need a lot of water if they are to produce abundantly. Make sure to mulch well to prevent your vegetables from cracking.

- Hanging baskets or planters consume a lot of water on a typical summer day. You might have to water them daily or even twice a day on hotter days!

A well-placed water barrel.

Regardless of how well established your garden is, watering is good for all trees and shrubs once in a while and is necessary in summers with low rainfall. Water is especially important for evergreens. Even if they are drought-resistant evergreens such as pine and spruce, they are still going to need to be well watered in the fall. A good soak in the fall helps prevent winter browning and scorching and enables lush green growth when they break dormancy in the spring.

How much water is enough?
With trees and shrubs, a slow soak for five minutes for every 30 centimetres of growth is a good marker. That means if you put in a new tree that is 1 metre tall, give it a deep drink for about fifteen minutes. Some big trees might need to soak for an hour or so. You'll need to water more frequently in drier years. When I was growing up, I remember certain trees we would sometimes soak all morning, and that watering paid off. Those same trees are immense and magnificent, requiring little water now that they are firmly established.

Xeriscaping: Water-wise gardening

If you keep up with recent gardening trends, you'll find much has been said about xeriscaping. All *xeriscaping* means is creating landscapes with an eye toward water conservation and using water wisely. Many people associate being "water wise" with cultivating a desert. They picture a cow skull, cacti, no lawn, and no blooms. This is not the case! The xeriscaped garden can be just as beautiful as any other, but it will require significantly less water. It could also be thought of as the drought-resistant garden or the low-maintenance garden.

A xeriscaped yard means you might reduce your lawn by 30 or 40 per cent, thereby reducing the need for water and creating less run-off. Removing all your lawn and replacing it with gravel is most assuredly *not* a xeriscaped yard. Sure, you won't have to water the lawn, but you are advertising to the world that you're the sort of person who likes to take the path of least resistance.

Xeriscaping means you might choose to plant echinacea and goldenrods instead of roses. It might mean planting a row of portulaca or California poppy instead of ageratum or alyssum. It doesn't mean that your garden won't be *beautiful*—it just means your choices will be modified to make watering less of an issue.

The best suggestion for a truly low-maintenance xeriscaped yard is to put your plants in places where moisture conditions are generally favourable, and to use plants that can handle some dryness. Plants in naturally moist locations are far less maintenance than perennials that you have to water all the time. You should expect that not all plants will survive your first xeriscape plan without a bit of TLC. Like any skill, you will get better at this over time, so do not be discouraged if the first time you attempt a water-wise garden, you make a few mistakes. Mistakes are perfectly acceptable as long as you learn from them.

Designing a drought-resistant yard

For inspiration in designing your xeriscaped yard, look to the natural places around you. Are you finding things in the rose family? The pea and bean family? What kinds of plants are flourishing together, and do they appeal to you? What is growing in low-lying, wet places? When is the peak bloom time? What grows on the barren, windswept high points? You do not have to use exclusively native plants in your garden—just plants that enjoy those conditions.

A grass you find in the wild here might be a terrible garden plant. However, there may be a cultivated form of another species that will give you the same look and require less water or less space. It's important never to take wild plants and transplant them into your garden;

along with a multitude of ethical issues, they simply won't do as well in your space as options meant for the gardener. Look for native plant dealers who ensure their plants are ethically propagated and prepared for a garden space, or try cultivated alternatives like those mentioned below in my Top-twenty list.

Using your run-off wisely

Another fundamental about a water-wise garden is run-off. Before you begin to plant your water-wise garden, you really need to investigate how water moves through your yard. Where does run-off go at your house? Maybe your yard is on a slope—plant more drought-resistant plants on the top, and thirstier plants in the lower spots. Perhaps when you plan your cement driveway, it can be poured to direct rainwater toward your lawn. Adjust your rain gutters so they can empty onto your flowerbeds. There are a lot of opportunities to save water if you look around!

Top-twenty drought-resistant plants

I can almost hear you saying, "Just tell me what to plant, Lyndon!" The following plant choices are excellent candidates for a dry land garden.

1. **Blue Flax (*Linum* spp.)** Blue flax is an airy, feathery plant that is remarkably tough. It grows a little more than a half-metre tall and produces splendid sky-blue flowers from May through October. It is short-lived but will self-sow where it is happy.

2. **Blue Oat Grass (*Helichotrichon* spp.)** There are lots of drought-resistant grasses, but this is one of my favourites. Blue oat grass is a medium-sized, vase-shaped grass with bright blue foliage and large, arching seed heads that resemble oats. It is particularly lovely in the winter, and birds love to eat the seeds.

3. **Cactus (*Opuntia* spp.)** We have several native cacti here on the Canadian prairies, and the prickly pear cactus is an excellent candidate for an extremely hot, very dry area. In places where other plants bake, these flourish! Cactus spines are extremely sharp and can inflict serious injury; they are not to be planted in places where children or pets frequent,

though they are excellent burglar deterrents beneath windows. The flowers are exquisite, and the fruits that follow are sometimes a food source for birds. They are splendid plants for a slope or hillside where the drainage is sharp and they will not be disturbed.

4. **Caragana** Though much maligned and ignored after generations of use as farm shelterbelts, this humble shrub deserves a revisit. Caragana requires nothing in terms of love or attention once established. The globe form ('Globosa') does not produce any flowers or seeds and is ideal for hedging or as a specimen plant. The extremely spiny dwarf caragana is stunning in full bloom, much loved by bees, and an excellent barrier plant. There is also the 'Sutherland' caragana, which is a columnar (very narrow) form, well suited to confined yards where space is limited.

5. **Cotoneaster** Because this shrub is so often used as a hedge, we rarely see it

grown on its own. When left to its own devices, this medium-sized shrub has handsome dark green foliage that turns a blazing scarlet in the fall. Almost no care is required, and it is very fast-growing.

6.   False Spirea (*Sorbaria* spp.) Also called ashleaf spirea because of its resemblance to a mountain ash, false spirea is a large-ish shrub that has white blooms that bees adore and beautiful foliage that turns gold in the fall. It is fast-growing and one of the first shrubs to leaf out in the spring. Willing to grow in sun or shade and under the harshest of conditions, this shrub is an astonishing workhorse in the garden! It has an inclination to form thickets and will sucker freely—this need not be a problem, just something to be aware of.

7.   Gaillardia Usually known by its Latin name, *Gaillardia* is also known as blanket flower. These brightly coloured daisies of red and yellow bloom all summer long and are quick to establish. They are highly attractive to butterflies, and there are half a dozen excellent cultivars to choose from.

8.   Hens and Chicks (*Sempervivum* spp.) The Latin name means "live forever" and it is appropriate! Hens and chicks are one of the few prairie hardy succulents and make a fabulous low-growing groundcover for a very hot, dry area, though sedums are another good choice. Sempervivum (known as semps) produce strange star-shaped pink flowers and will die after blooming. This is not generally a concern, as they produce a multitude of "chicks" and will self-perpetuate well in dry, well-draining areas.

9.   Juniper (*Juniperus* spp.) Junipers are much-planted evergreen shrubs, which come in both upright and creeping forms. They can take up considerable room, and one of the big mistakes that people make with them is crowding. Junipers also have green, gold, and blue-green forms, and they can be extremely beautiful when well grown. Keep in mind that not all varieties you find in your local big-box stores are hardy, so ask pointed questions when purchasing them.

This is me looking almost as snazzy as the blue oat grass.

Cotoneaster, fall colour.

The right juniper will add interesting texture to your garden all year long.

'Slowmound' mugo pine.

The 'James Macfarlane' lilac was introduced by Isabella Preston of the Ottawa Experimental Farm. Unlike many cultivars, it is compact and non-suckering. It is considered the best pink lilac ever developed.

10. Lilacs (*Syringa* spp.) Who doesn't love lilacs? They are hardy, long-blooming, fragrant, beautiful, and rarely troubled by pests or disease. It is not unusual to find old lilac bushes still in flower way out in the country, often at the site of old, abandoned farmhouses. This is a testament to their hardiness and versatility. Lilacs come in a huge range of colours. Some excellent dwarf forms are also available.

11. Meadow Sage (*Salvia* spp.) There are several varieties of meadow sage. Blooms are usually blue or purple, but there are also some good white and pink varieties. Salvia flowers over a long season and acts as a magnet for bees, butterflies, and hummingbirds. If the flowers are not deadheaded, it will also self-seed.

12. Mock Orange These blossoms both resemble and smell like citrus blossoms. Mock orange is a small to medium shrub that flowers profusely in early summer and will endure serious drought once it gets going.

13. Mugo Pine (*Pinus mugo*) Mugo pines come in a wide range of heights and sizes, and, like many pines, they are capable of tolerating the driest, sandiest of soils. Mugos are architecturally interesting, very resistant to winter browning,

and quite happy to have only the skies for water once they are well established. Pines are traditionally the home of spirits, so don't say I didn't warn you if paranormal activity develops in your yard after planting one.

14. Potentilla These are small shrubs in the rose family that are well adapted to dry places and will flower all summer long. Known for their willingness to tolerate abuse and neglect, potentillas can be fabulous. They are excellent shrubs for beginners and very rewarding. Yellow is the traditional flower colour, but they also come in white, pink, red, orange, apricot, and a few double forms. Keep in mind the red forms are the least hardy.

15. Russian Almond (*Prunus tenella*) This gorgeous little shrub grows a little more than 1 metre tall and equally as wide. It flowers with an explosion of pink (or, rarely, white) blossoms early in the spring. In fall, the leaves will often become a plum colour. Once established, this shrub is extremely drought-resistant and low maintenance.

16. Russian Sage (*Perovskia* spp.) Despite its common name, this plant is not a sage at all, though they are related. There are several varieties of Russian sage, and all of them want to be planted in a hot, sunny location with excellent drainage. They are prone to rot in wet, heavy soils, and they do not always adapt here to our harsher, more clay types of growing locations. Generally growing quite tall, this plant is often mistaken for a shrub. It has lovely grey-green foliage and tall spires of blue to blue-purple blooms from

Spirea nipponica.

Yarrow.

Yucca.

mid-August through September. Bees love it, and it is unbothered by pests or disease. Most gardeners kill this plant at least twice before finally succeeding with it.

17. Sea Holly (*Eryngium* spp.) The thistle-like appearance of sea holly is deceiving; it is actually a member of the carrot family! Sea hollies produce extremely spiky, usually blue flowers in mid- to late summer. They are magnets

for bees and happy to grow in the driest, poorest of soil. They will self-sow, but they grow from a taproot and are resentful of disturbance—if you must move them, do so when they are small.

18. Spirea Spireas are charming little shrubs. Most stay quite small, and they are grown as much for their foliage as for their blooms. They make excellent hedges, borders, or specimen shrubs, and they attract both bees and butterflies.

19. Yarrow (*Achillea* spp.) Yarrows are wonderful, inexpensive, fast-growing plants that will fill in quickly and bloom all summer. Depending on the variety, flowers may be white, red, orange, yellow, gold, or several shades of pink. They are highly attractive to butterflies and are also excellent for cutting. Plant yarrow in poor soil and leave it be—too much water turns it into an aggressive thug.

20. Yucca We generally think of yuccas as being native to the American Southwest, but a few do grow on the central plains of the continent. These spiky evergreen plants form distinct rosettes of dagger-like dark green leaves, which sometimes have thread-like filaments on the leaf edges. Yucca is slow to establish but structurally interesting. Though it takes time to reach flowering size, the yucca's cream or white blossoms are fragrant and very beautiful.

Soil: Tilling it like it is

Healthy plants can only grow in a healthy environment. If you truly want to have a successful garden, especially a low-maintenance garden, it begins with your soil. *Everything* begins with your soil. It is hard for me to write about how complex and important soil is without getting caught up in the romance of it. Once I fully learned the secrets of soil, it was like being ushered into a dark and secret club. The ground beneath my feet is alive! This was revolutionary; it changed how I see the world. Once I began to understand that everything in gardening is linked to soil, I began to respect it—and then I began to love it.

Opposite: Healthy soil.

This page: Good soil is the foundation of great garden beds.

Why does a forest smell so good in the spring? What is it about the scent of the earth? There is an empire beneath your shoes, should you have the inclination to investigate it. Lying on the ground with my face pressed against the soil and pondering all its mysteries is humbling and beautiful. Lyrical even. One could write songs and poems about it. I love soil so much I can't promise I will stick to straight science in this chapter, but I'll share with you the most important lessons I know about soil.

Soil is life

Many different citizens are living in both my soil and my compost heap. Once you start to figure out how they are all working together, you will start to see your garden not merely as a project to be finished but also as a way to connect you to something ancient and primal and wonderful. This is a nutrient cycle and lifecycle. It is a dance that began long before you were born, long before there were people living on this continent, long before dinosaurs were grazing on cycads.

The earthworms and other small creatures in my soil all live fascinating lives. There are centipedes and snails and slugs. There are beetles and crickets and small things I can't always identify. Mushrooms

Earthworms aren't just for kids!

show up sometimes—the fruiting bodies of fungi living deep in the ground. Who knew they were even there until they appeared so suddenly? Then there are all the things I can't even see, such as mycorrhizal fungi and microbes and bacteria that break organic material down into even smaller elements that can be used by plants.

Healthy soil is alive, and only healthy soil can grow healthy plants. If you want to keep pest and disease problems away from your garden, ensuring the life of your soil is the absolute best way to start.

How our soil works

Plant diversity, soil fertility, and water are all interrelated. When you are out and about, you will observe that plant diversity changes as the soil changes. The farther west and into the Rockies you go, the more plant diversity increases. This is because the soil becomes more fertile as you go west or east (away from the prairies), and even locally, between people's yards, you will notice great changes in plant life based on the soil alone. The same plant in two different yards will look very different depending on soil health.

What sort of soil are you working with? Many parts of the prairies are blessed with wonderful farmland and good topsoil. Other places have large areas where the soil is primarily glacial till—wet, heavy, sticky clay that randomly births pebbles, rocks, and stones. This means few plants have been able to adapt here, and not all of those that have are particularly garden-worthy.

Most of Calgary, and in fact much of southern Alberta, is "blessed" with alkaline clay soil. Alkali soils have a high pH, generally around 8.5. They are sticky, heavy, and somewhere between annoying and impossible to deal with. They have poor infiltration capacity, which means water doesn't trickle down like it should and often puddles on top. Alkali soils occur naturally in some places, but they can also become that way due to humans. Soil alkalinity is associated with the presence of sodium carbonate in the soil either by natural weathering of the soil particles or by irrigation and/or floodwater. It's often seen where surface water evaporates and leaves behind salts. When the underground water contains high salts, it leads to serious salinity problems.

Coal and power plants that use coal or lignite (which is rich in limestone) will produce an ash containing calcium oxide. This ends up in rivers, and through the magic of chemistry, this also ends up affecting soil pH. Chemistry was never my strong point and, honestly, you don't need to know the chemistry to make it work *for* you rather than *against* you.

What you do need to know is that alkaline soils are difficult to grow things in. They drain poorly when it rains and they turn into concrete in times of drought. Grasses seem to be fairly tolerant of this, which is probably why the North American plains were primarily colonized by grass. It also explains why crops such as wheat, barley, oats, and rye have been able to do quite well here.

What kind of soil do you have? You can pay for a professional soil test, and it will cost you about the same as the do-it-yourself kits, but having a lab test your soil will be far far more accurate. That's likely not necessary though. *All* soil contains some sand, some silt, and some clay. Do you really need to know that you have 37.62 per cent clay in your yard when it's just as useful to know that it's *mostly* clay? Ask a gardener in your neighbourhood. Look at how the water moves when it rains. If it disappears into the ground rather quickly, then it's sandy; if it lingers, it likely has more clay in it.

Realize that regardless of what kind of soil you have, be it sand, silt, or clay (and it's likely mostly clay), the steps to fixing it are exactly the same. You have two choices: you can work with the soil you have and plant things that are accustomed to that type of soil or you can amend, amend, amend! Digging in as much organic matter as you possibly can will encourage microbes and earthworms and a whole host of other important little creatures to move into your garden. Soil needs to be *alive* in order for plants to do well. Organic matter will capture water and hold plant nutrients from your soil like a buffet table for the plants to enjoy. Plants generally grow better in rich soil than poor soil, just as well-fed children are healthier than children who go to school hungry.

Working in clay soils
Under a microscope, clay is shaped like wee thin dinner plates so small that a hundred million of them would fit in a 1 millimetre x 1 millimetre grain of sand. This unique shape makes it behave uniquely. Because clay stacks like plates, the addition of water acts like a glue

Plants suffering from chlorosis have pale green or yellow-green leaves with very dark, pronounced green veins. It is common in prairie soils where the iron is often in an inaccessible form for plant roots.

that makes the clay plates almost suction to one another. Try walking on solid clay after a rainstorm; you'll get taller with each step. In addition to holding tight to one another, clay soils also hold on to nutrients so tight that plants have a hard time accessing them. All this makes clay soils almost impossible to germinate seeds in, and because they hold on to nutrients so well, they are prone to causing iron deficiencies such as chlorosis.

Clay's shape also means that the soil becomes compacted easily. Many gardeners try to "fluff" it up or break up the hardpan with a rototiller, especially in the vegetable garden. This is terribly counterproductive. Because the particles are so thin, clay soils are especially sensitive to mechanical disturbance. Rototilling will shatter them into bits and, in the end, make everything sink and pack even harder. Ask any builder—mixing clay, sand, and water is exactly how concrete is made. You must work clay soil as little as possible, by hand with a shovel whenever you can, and add in as much organic matter as you have available when you do. What do you do with alkaline clay soil in the garden? Deep plowing before planting, and digging, digging, digging is the word of the day.

PLANTING DAY

When you plant a tree in clay, you don't really have the option of improving the soil a bit each year because you could damage the roots. On planting day you must remove as much of the gross clay soil as you can and replace it with good soil. Many trees die here because they try and try but just can't get a foothold and succeed in these heavy soils. Wherever the clay boundary of your tree hole is, make sure it's jagged and neither smooth nor shiny. Don't waste your time perfecting it with the back of the shovel; this only aligns the clay particles into a more uniform barrier, making it even more difficult for roots to break through.

Chemical improvements

Your garden is no place to create a chemistry lab, but a lot of people are trying to do exactly that. It is possible to reclaim alkali soils by adding acidifying minerals such as pyrite or cheaper alum or aluminum sulphate. It's also possible to add gypsum (calcium sulphate) or calcium chloride, but many variables factor in here and you must be extremely, extremely careful when you start playing with the pH

When tree roots become girdled from being root-bound, the tree will look healthy for a few years but will eventually fall over.

scale. Soil has a certain resistance to change, known as a buffering capacity, which works to keep the pH consistent despite your efforts. The minute you exceed the buffering capacity, pH levels will spike at an unknown rate. This can be absolutely disastrous if you're fiddling on a yard-sized scale, since you've now effectively nuked your soil. I've seen more than one person make terrible, heinous errors in this department, and it's not like planting an annual in too shady a spot—this is something that is bordering on *impossible* to fix.

Since amending soil is so much work and needs to be done on an ongoing basis, most people only pay attention to the first 10 to 20 centimetres on top. It is not uncommon for trees to die here after going along nicely for several years because their roots get in past the good soil you worked so hard to put in and they start sucking up toxins and salts.

Caragana is one of the few shrubs that can endure this and may have singlehandedly saved the prairies as we know them from being eroded to nothing in the 1930s. The noble shelterbelt (windbreak) has been protecting soils from buffeting winds for decades, and if not for the caragana, I might not be sitting here writing these words right now.

Adjusting your soil pH

It's not unusual for people to mess with the soil pH to control the colour of their hydrangeas, but you should never try to adjust your pH in anything other than the immediate area you're planting in. Realize that the effects of changing the pH are not permanent. The blossoms of certain hydrangeas can be adjusted in colour based on alkalinity or acidity. This is important information if you live somewhere other than the Canadian prairies. We do not have a long-enough growing season for that here, nor do we do well with the hydrangea species that can be thus adjusted.

MYTHS ABOUT SPRUCE

A prevailing belief suggests that spruce, fir, and pines acidify the soil with their fallen needles. **There is absolutely no truth to this whatsoever.** Every year, people tell me they want to purchase chemicals to fix the soil under their evergreen since nothing will grow there. This is proof that "a little knowledge is a dangerous thing."

Do you know why nothing grows under your spruce? You're *not supposed* to grow anything under a spruce tree. Spruce are the dominant tree in the northern hemisphere. Do you know how they got to be so successful? Spruce have evolved over millions of years to be able to suck every last drop of water out of the soil. There is basically nothing that can outcompete them. Their branches are designed to shed snow. Little kids know that plants need water and sunshine. It is dry and dark under a spruce. Why then do adults insist on trying to grow something in so foolhardy a place? Anything failing to grow under a spruce has *nothing* to do with acidity and *everything* to do with dryness and competition. Oh, sure, I can send you home with things like goutweed and lily of the valley that will *survive* there, but nothing will *flourish*.

Since I'm already ranting about spruce, you should know that in a perfect world, all of us would have spruce trees that had branches right to the ground. These branches are meant to keep the soil cool and moist and to protect the tree's root zone from drying winds. In most cases, people take the bottom branches off of a spruce tree because the tree is too big for where it was planted. This is especially the case in older neighbourhoods. People planted Colorado spruce because that was what was available back in the day, not because they necessarily wanted a tree that grows 27 metres tall. Once these spruce started intruding on sidewalks and driveways and parking lots, we decided, in our wisdom, that they needed to be pruned instead of replaced with a more appropriate tree.

The worst reason of all to remove the branches is "so that we could get the lawnmower under there." Grass does not grow under a spruce tree so you are wasting your time while turning a beautiful, elegant tree like a spruce into something ugly. *Let me be clear on this*: cutting the lower branches off of a spruce is bad for the tree. It dries out much faster, which leads to winter kill and drought stress. It also makes the tree almost unspeakably ugly. Don't even get me started on pruning spruce into ridiculous shapes. If you don't have room for one in its natural, healthy shape, you shouldn't have a spruce tree there at all.

Poorly pruned spruce. Just chop them down!

Organic products

Despite what marketers would like you to believe, the word *organic* doesn't mean "safe." It simply means "This contains carbon." Things that contain carbon decompose and return to the earth once they are no longer alive. Technically, you and I are totally organic. Plastics are not. This word has come to be affiliated with being Earth-friendly. Many people think it means chemical-free. Did you know that organic produce is frequently sprayed with pesticides more often than non-organic produce? The difference is, they are using organic pesticides! As far as I am concerned, a chemical is a chemical—it doesn't matter to me whether that chemical was derived from a root or processed in a factory. When I worked in garden centres, I was frequently asked for "organic" potting soil. *All* soil is organic … that's part of what makes it soil. Be ye not deceived by this word!

Improving your soil

Soil is *old*. If you tend the soil by feeding it, you are *contributing*. You are, in a very real way, making the earth better, more livable, and infinitely healthier for those who come after you. You may have heard the saying, generally believed to have originated in our Canadian First Nations community: "When the last tree has been cut down, the last fish caught, the last river poisoned, only then will we realize that we cannot eat money." There are things in life far more valuable than money, and your soil is one of them.

You will never lose by feeding your soil. Your soil is the framework from which all your other successes (or failures) will be born.

Improving your soil is worth the effort.

Tell people that their new home will cost $450,000, and they hand you all sorts of money. Tell them that they should spend $1,000 on their soil and they get all up in your grill about how you have no idea what you're talking about. Let me assure you; soil has *value*. It has *worth*. I dream about soil. I dream about a world where the soil is like freshly ground coffee and just as richly scented.

To improve clay soil is simple: Amend, amend, amend! Despite what most people think, clay soil already contains plenty of nutrients. You need something in there to give the plants a chance to pry these nutrients away from the clay. Their added structure will also allow water to drain properly. Digging in as much compost, manure, grass clippings, shredded leaves, and organic waste as possible will help immensely. We'll go through the pros and cons of these and other amendments below.

Compost

Compost is basically decomposed, fully rotted organic matter. Every Canadian should be composting their kitchen scraps and anything else that will break down and feed the soil. New gardeners are often anxious about starting to compost, believing it to be some difficult mixture you have to balance perfectly to make it work. Like anything, it can get as complicated as you'd like to make it, but at its simplest it's really just throwing dead stuff in a pile and letting it rot until you can't tell what it is. Composting is really impossible to screw up regardless of what you do (or the Earth would still be littered in dinosaur bodies), but the following simple guidelines will make your compost pile work more efficiently.

- Keep it moist like a damp sponge at all times if you want it to decompose faster. Yes, you may need to water it in the summer.
- Don't add dairy products or meat to it or you'll attract unsavoury creatures.
- Grass clippings, plants, and food scraps compost well, but they'll break down faster if you also add leaves, paper, or a little straw too. Try to keep a bit of everything in there.

Many different compost bin designs are available.

In a larger area, homemade bins from bent wood are quite lovely.

- For bonus points: whenever you're feeling particularly energetic, feel free to stir up your compost.

There are lots of good books about composting available to help you get started, and many of the larger garden centres have composting courses available. If you're not quite there yet, you can certainly buy compost from any good garden centre. Compost can be expensive to buy, but it is fabulous for the plants in your garden. The more of it you mix into the soil, the better your results will be.

> Microbial action will heat up a compost pile, but it isn't likely to catch fire. The grey "ash" people sometimes find at the bottom of the pile is usually a fungus.

Fungi

While you are digging in the garden, you will sometimes come across a line of white or grey mould-like filaments winding through the soil. This is *mycelium*, part of one of the great fungus species that live in our world. Fungi can be beneficial, harmful, or neutral. Mushrooms showing up in your garden are not a bad thing; many of them are as interesting and beautiful as flowers. Many kinds of fungi can cause infection and disease (in both humans and plants), and quite a few more go about their day quietly minding their own business, posing no threat to anyone.

In recent years, the role of fungi in managing healthy soils has become more and more apparent. Studies are proving again and again that healthy forests and healthy ecosystems are built on fungi-based foundations. Mycorrhizal fungi form symbiotic relationships with the roots of living plants. The fungus requires a place to live, which the roots provide. Once established, the fungus forms vast networks of branching threads of tissue through the soil. This tissue absorbs nutrients and water and pulls them to the tree, essentially doubling the size of the tree's root system and thus its ability to take up water. In exchange, the fungus receives some of the sugar produced in the plant's cell tissue.

Studies have shown that birch, Douglas fir, eucalyptus, oak, pine, willow, and many plants in the rose family use mycorrhizal fungi. Studies have also shown that many trees fail to establish without these special little helpers. A few trees have even become extremely specific, and can only host certain species of fungi and vice versa. Since fungi are extremely sensitive to chemicals and disturbance, there are many places where the population of healthy soil fungi is severely depleted.

You can now purchase mycorrhizal fungi as an inoculant at many garden centres. It appears as a white, chalky powder that you have to spread liberally over the roots when you take your tree or shrub out of its container to plant it. One such company selling these products is Mykes, which actually offers to extend the warranty of your tree or shrub if you use its product (www.usemyke.com).

I have little experience in using these kinds of products, but I would say that it can't hurt to give them a try. If you are interested in learning more about mushrooms, moulds, and fungi, I highly recommend the book *Mycophilia* by Eugenia Bone. This excellent and highly readable book will take you into the fascinating world of mushrooms and subterranean fungi, giving you a better understanding of what they're doing down there and why they are so desirable.

Manure

Sometimes I hear people say, "I don't want to use manure in the garden because it will smell." If manure smells like it just came from the barn, it is too fresh to use in the garden! Manure should smell like compost before you dig it in with your plants—a rich, earthy smell. You should have no qualms about being elbow deep in it. Whether you use cow, horse, or sheep manure does not really make much difference to the plants, but it might make a difference to you. Sheep manure tends to be a little more expensive than steer manure because sheep are smaller and don't create the same quantity of waste as cattle do. Like compost, manure can be purchased from garden centres. Unlike compost, manure should not be added as frequently.

Manure is very high in nitrogen, and if you dig in a good quantity of manure every three to five seasons (depending on what you are growing), that is generally plenty. It is fine to mix manure with compost, or you can use it separately. Just dig it in with your topsoil or loam and off you go!

Mushroom manure is horse manure that has been cycled (broken down) by mushrooms. It is excellent for your garden. I once had to explain to someone that "mushrooms don't poop," as she was extremely baffled about what this product was and how it was being obtained.

Peat moss

Peat moss is dried, shredded sphagnum moss. It is usually compressed into a bale and available for sale at most supermarkets, hardware stores, and garden centres. Peat moss has been used to amend prairie soils for several decades, and like so many other things in gardening, this is yet another item we have been lied to about. Gardens with lots of peat moss dug in generally retain water better, and peat moss is generally inexpensive, but this really isn't the whole story. There are a few things you should know about peat moss before adding it to your garden.

Peat moss can hold up to thirty times its weight in water. It is great for adding to dry, poor, or sandy soils. It is not fantastic for mixing with clay soils. Clay already holds enough water. More importantly, people don't realize that peat has little to no nutritional value for plants; it merely makes the soil lighter and fluffier and easier to dig in. Yes, it will help improve your soil simply because it is organic matter, but there are better choices available. Shredded newspaper is a better choice nutrient-wise, and leaves are even better still. But since you don't actually pay money for them, some merchants don't recommend those options.

> I no longer purchase peat moss for any reason, and I don't recommend it for my gardening clients either.

Beyond the wholly practical considerations of peat's effectiveness, there are environmental considerations as well. Peat is harvested from bogs in Labrador, Newfoundland, New Brunswick, and Quebec. It takes thousands of years for a bog to replace what has been stripped from it—and this is assuming we don't disturb it repeatedly during that time. The peat moss industry is "regulated" in much the same way as the oil sands are "regulated"—these companies have to comply with a lot of rules and regulations in the name of "environmental consideration," but I, for one, have not found the evidence compelling.

Peat moss, once fully dried, is also highly flammable and can be considered a fire hazard if stored in garages or garden sheds. Some insurance companies will not cover you if you store it in your garage and it happens to burn down.

So what is the alternative? Coconut fibre, also called coir, is being marketed as an excellent alternative to peat. It is a by-product of the coconut industry and is actually *more* absorbent. I have used it in my garden and I love it! It is only slightly more expensive than peat but considerably more sustainable. Beats Peat is a line of compressed coconut fibre bales that are being marketed as a peat moss alternative. I have found them to be extremely effective in my own garden, and it is my hope that within a few years peat moss will be off the market entirely.

Leaves

That's right, leaves. Leaves are free! Every year, the trees drop their leaves in the fall and we rake them up and bag them and burn them or throw them away. Why? Leaves are great for the garden! There is little nutritional value in fallen leaves (some, but not lots), so what is the value? Shredded and dug into the garden or added to the compost heap, leaves can be very effective for improving the organic matter content in dry, tired gardens. Some people like to rototill them into the veggie garden in fall; others like to use them for mulching. Either way, it's a cost-effective way of helping your garden out.

Zeolite

Zeolite is made from crushed volcanic rock, and although it is expensive, I find that it is another excellent alternative for helping to fluff up our sticky "gumbo" soils.

Other soil amendments

You may have noticed that I haven't once mentioned perlite or vermiculite, even though these are commonly offered for sale in garden centres and greenhouses. The reason I haven't mentioned them is because I don't use them.

Perlite is a granite-like volcanic rock that is crushed and heated to become a lightweight, pH-neutral white soil amendment that is used almost entirely in soilless growing mediums. It helps to improve aeration and drainage. Vermiculite is made by heating raw mica into an inert, lightweight substance used in soilless mixes to improve moisture absorption. This is great if we're talking about germinating seeds indoors.

Both of these items are useless in the garden—and a waste of time and money. Neither of them has sufficient mechanical strength to endure outdoor conditions, and they will quickly collapse once introduced to your soil. Once this happens, they can actually impede rather than enhance drainage. Leave these two items on the shelf.

Fertilizers

Fertilizers help feed your plants. They make up for whatever nutrients plants are unable to pull from the soil. Whenever you buy fertilizers, there will *always* be three numbers on the package. It doesn't matter the brand name or where it came from, these numbers are legally required. These numbers (often called the N-P-K) refer to the *minimum* amount of nitrogen, phosphorus, and potassium in the fertilizer. These nutrients are not the only things plants require, but these three are the most critical.

Nitrogen (the first number) is what stimulates lush, verdant foliar growth. Manure tends to be quite high in nitrogen. If you pick up a bag of lawn fertilizer, it will probably say 20–10–10 or 30–15–10 or something like that. Since the first number is the highest, you know this fertilizer is primarily nitrogen. Nitrogen makes plants green and vibrant, so nitrogen-rich fertilizers are also suitable for any plant that you're growing for its green parts—think lettuce, hosta, whatever. Plants lacking nitrogen tend to become a yellow-green, and they lack vigour and look sickly.

The second number is phosphorus, which does two things. First, phosphorus helps to establish really thick, strong root growth and should be used for plants that need to become well established. It is also responsible for stimulating buds and blossoming. Plants that fail to flower well are often getting either too much nitrogen or not enough phosphorus. If you go into a garden centre and say, "I have a clump of liatris and it doesn't seem to be blooming well. What have you got to help me?" they will probably recommend a high phosphorus fertilizer. Some common ratios for high phosphorus fertilizers include 10–30–15 or 10–20–10.

Finally, the third number is potassium. Plants don't need a lot of this, but they definitely need it. Potassium is associated with the hardening of cell walls (which affects winter hardiness and survival) and is also associated with plant immune systems and fighting off disease. Few plants have a very high need for potassium, but tomatoes are an exception. Tomato fertilizer is often 10–15–18 or similar.

Notice that if you add these numbers up, they do not equal 100. Remember, those numbers are minimum guarantees; there is quite possibly a bit more of any of them in that bag. So what's the rest of that

It is important to remember that fertilizer is nutrition, not medicine. Many people never think about feeding their plants until they become sick or ailing. It is healthy plants that need fertilizer, not just sick ones!

bag of fertilizer made up of? Inert filler. This filler provides something to bind the nutrients to, helps delivery, and makes the bag look impressively full. In slow-release fertilizers, this extra stuff also acts as a control agent so, like a jawbreaker slowly dissolving in water, the layers of fertilizer melt away to release nutrients in a more controlled manner. For any fertilizer, aesthetics aside, the filler helps on a practical level too—it's much simpler to spread a cup of fertilizer evenly over your flowerbed than it is to spread a teaspoon.

Applying fertilizers

Nitrogen is something you have to be careful with because it can "burn" your plants. Watch what happens when a dog pees on your lawn—the spot turns yellow. Why does that happen? Urea is very high in ammonia, and ammonia is in part made up of nitrogen. In this case, the nitrogen is too strong a dose for the grass to handle, so the grass "burns." It becomes yellow or brown, and this sometimes kills it completely. This is why fertilizers come with mixing instructions. The "recommended dose" is not merely a guideline! Fooling around with fertilizers can be harmful to your garden if you don't use the right amount.

Many people think that if less is more, just think how much more *more* would be! My friend Vanessa relays her family legend of how her notoriously cheap uncle "helped" her grandmother one summer by barely sprinkling her lawn fertilizer on her lawn, then he stole it, ran home, and gleefully used up the rest of the bag on his lawn. Everyone in the family enjoyed driving past both lawns all summer—his was fried, hers was quite lovely. Always, always, *always* follow the instructions on a package of fertilizer, down to the letter.

Quick versus slow release

Fun items such as kelp meal and guano are "slow release," meaning they break down at a rate that plants can handle and you don't have to worry that you will "burn" anything. Water-soluble fertilizers are your quick-and-easy fix. They provide a blast of nutrients that is immediately available to the plant. There is nothing wrong with using these, and they are neither superior nor inferior to slow-release fertilizers. Miracle-Gro is an excellent water-soluble fertilizer. Simply mix it with water according to the directions, and water your plants with it.

Fertilizer options

There is nothing quite so nutritious as compost, and I've already talked about manure, but you should also consider the following options:

Bloodmeal/bonemeal

Bloodmeal is a by-product of the meat industry and is essentially baked and powdered blood. It is quite safe to use, though it does have a bit of an odour and I recommend wearing gloves when you apply it. Bloodmeal is very high in nitrogen and breaks down quickly. It is an excellent fertilizer for a quick "greening up," to stimulate lush growth, and is particularly useful to evergreens. Although it is sometimes recommended for pest control, this is a bad idea.

Bonemeal is also a by-product of the meat industry and is made in the same fashion as bloodmeal. It is dried, baked, powdered bones. Whereas bloodmeal is high in nitrogen, bonemeal is high in phosphorus. Bonemeal is a gentle yet effective fertilizer, and for years it was the "go to" product when planting bulbs or new plants. Studies have shown that although bonemeal feeds over a long period, it breaks down extremely slowly at a speed that does not stimulate immediate root development.

Over the years, I have had several people express their concerns about possibly contracting mad cow disease (bovine encephalitis) through the use of bonemeal in their gardens. Let me assure you, people, that this is an absolutely impossible scenario. Have no fear about using bonemeal in your garden. You're not going to contract any diseases from it.

Fish fertilizer

Fish fertilizer, often sold as "Alaskan fish fertilizer," is a product that was much favoured in the 1970s and 1980s and is still available. It could alternatively be sold as "what the bears didn't eat." It is made from the bodies of dead fish, usually salmon, and that's exactly what it smells like. In fact, fish fertilizer smells so fishy that it has been known to attract neighbourhood cats! It is, however, extremely effective. Most of us know at least one elderly gardener who swears by this stuff, and I have to concede that if you want results, fish fertilizer is an excellent means of doing so. It's also inexpensive, and the smell does dissipate in anywhere from a few hours to a few days.

Guano

Guano is another fertilizer that works beautifully, albeit more expensively. Guano is the composted crap of fruit bats and/or seabirds. That word *composted* is key; otherwise, it would just be bat crap. Guano from fruit bats is the richest known natural source of phosphorus in the world. I buy a kilogram of this in the spring, and I like to work a bit into the soil—about a tablespoon (15 grams) or so—specifically for blossoms. This includes dahlias, daylilies, delphiniums, gladioli, irises, lilies, peonies, and poppies.

Kelp

Kelp meal is an excellent slow-release fertilizer that plants love. Kelp is a kind of seaweed, and it grows amazingly fast—about a half a metre a day! Kelp absorbs huge quantities of nutrients from the ocean to do this, which it slowly releases back into your garden. After a storm, thousands of tonnes of kelp wash up along beaches in BC, Washington, and Oregon. This seaweed is dried and powdered and sold across the continent. It can be expensive, but you won't burn anything with it and working it into the garden at any time of the growing season is a terrific practice.

Other plants

Did you know that you can enlist other plants in the manufacture of fertilizer in your garden? There are some plants that actually "fix" nitrogen. This means that they take nitrogen out of the atmosphere and put it into the soil in a form that plants can use. All legumes (plants in the pea and bean family) do this. The endless hedgerows of caragana that we see across the prairies are all fixing nitrogen and enriching the soils around them. This ability to create their own food means that many legumes can grow in soils that are too poor for many other plants. It really is astonishing!

On the roots of these plants are special nodes on which very specific types of bacteria live. Each legume hosts a different kind of bacteria. In exchange for a place to live and using some of the plant's sugars, the bacteria manufacture nitrogen, which in turn benefits the plant and the soil around them. In many cases, entire fields of legumes are grown to help rejuvenate the soil after a particularly high-nutrient crop has been grown. After several years of growing canola (they called it rape seed for a reason), many farmers grow a "green manure" crop such as alfalfa or lentils to help replenish the soil.

You can even buy inoculant to coat the seeds of peas, beans, and sweet peas before you plant. Plants that are inoculated tend to be more vigorous and bloom more heavily, and you can find inoculant anywhere that you can buy seeds. As it is a living product, inoculant will not keep from one year to the next, so buy new stuff every year.

A few common legumes that you can put in your garden include, of course, peas and beans but also alfalfa, broom, buffalo beans, chickpeas, clover, lentils, licorice, lupines, milk vetch, sainfoin, soybeans, sweet peas, sweet vetch, and wisteria. A very *few* other plants outside the pea and bean family have stolen this trick, including sea buckthorn, alders, and the beautiful mountain avens, the official flower of the Northwest Territories.

Scarlet runner beans fix nitrogen in your soil.

Mulching

So, now that you've been amending away and have your soil holding as much moisture as possible … what are you going to plant? Actually, let's set that question aside for just a moment. Let's assume that you've already done a design and have all your plants in. How are you going to *keep them* moist? How are you going to keep unwanted plants away? Well, one of the best ways of doing both is by mulching. In a natural grassland setting, old leaves from the previous season's growth naturally form a thick, heavy mulch. In a forest setting, spring blooming plants will burst forth from underneath last year's fallen leaves. We replicate this in the garden using mulch. Mulching is where you place a layer of something on top of the soil to keep water in and weed seeds out, but it also helps out in many other ways. How thick this layer is really depends on what mulch you're using and why you're using it.

Mulching helps your soil retain moisture for longer because the soil cannot dry out as fast. Because mulch helps keep water levels steadier, water-sensitive plants like tomatoes and cucumbers get an extra benefit—a mulched plant means less stunting overall and fewer cracks in your tomatoes. Whatever expense mulch might be, it will ultimately save you money on watering.

Mulch also helps deter weeds from germinating. As it breaks down, organic mulch feeds the soil by adding organic content. Mulch will help reduce soil compaction and stop mud from splashing on your plant leaves. Mud splash sounds like a minor inconvenience, but keeping mud off leaves is a big help for disease prevention. If it's organic mulch, it will also improve your soil while still doing all the work

A well-mulched garden looks finished.

mentioned above! I cannot say enough good things about the benefits of mulching.

Organic mulches

Shredded cedar, bark nuggets, or wood chips all make excellent mulch. In some parts of the world, shredded peanut shells are used. A good tip is to keep your organic mulch anywhere between 5 to 10 centimetres thick. You don't want to leave mulch up against the stems of really soft plants or they may rot or be prone to slugs. Do not make "mulch volcanoes" around tree trunks.

You may want to contact your local tree companies and arbourists, as some of them will give away shredded wood to anyone willing to haul it off their lot. These are generally from soft woods, so they make excellent mulch because they break down much faster than cedar, which is a more durable hardwood. Why on earth would you want your organic mulch to break down so quickly? Doesn't this mean that you'll have to replace it more often? Why, yes it does. But realize that as the mulch is breaking down, it's adding organic content directly into your soil. Topping it up every few years is a small price to pay for that luxury.

Sheets of cardboard and sections of newspapers are also beginning to be used as sheet mulch, especially in areas where people are planting vegetable gardens or permaculture installations. Of course, since these items are more solid-shaped, you only want a few layers. They will impede water movement a bit more than loose mulch will but are

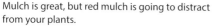

Mulch is great, but red mulch is going to distract from your plants.

Rock mulch may be natural, but it doesn't necessarily look natural.

very effective at weed control either along a garden path or beneath your new sod.

Regardless of what type of mulch you use, make sure you water your garden very deeply before installing it. Mulch will lock in moisture, so it's a good idea to start with the moisture actually there!

Inorganic mulches

Plenty of inorganic options are also available. They can work just as well as organic options in some ways, but while you will gain durability, you will lose any soil benefits. Plastic sheeting is one example. Stones can also be used as mulch, but as they do not break down and weeds will grow between them, they are a much less-effective option. Heat can also be reflected off of stones and this isn't good for plants either. There is even rubber mulch made from recycled tires that is being used in playgrounds and schoolyards, though this tends to be more of a safety consideration than a horticultural one. Please resist the urge to use brightly painted rocks or plastic; just because they're available doesn't make them a good idea.

⁓ 3 ⁓

Maintaining your garden

Even a low-maintenance garden is going to involve *some* maintenance. Over time, trees and shrubs will get larger, and eventually they may cast shade that causes some problems for your more sun-loving plants. This might mean you need to do some light pruning or replace those plants with something more shade-tolerant. Some plants are naturally short-lived, and some of them will grow and bloom well for several seasons and then vanish. You may or may not need to replace these.

Daily maintenance

Tending to your garden every day means things won't get out of control. It is relaxing and lovely to be in the garden. A little bit of daily work is the way to do it. People who say things such as "I have

Opposite: A tool shed is practical, but can also be quite attractive.

This page: Goutweed is an aggressive spreader, but also very attractive and only a problem if grown in the wrong location.

Thursdays for weeding" soon find out how insanely fast weeds grow, especially if it has been raining, in which case weeding can be a very onerous task indeed. Simple daily maintenance is how to keep your garden easy and enjoyable to look after.

Step 1: Walk through

The first step in maintaining your garden is to do a walk-through. I start by doing nothing. I just wander on through, enjoying the garden, and I try to notice things. Dew on a spiderweb here, that plant developing a bud over there, maybe a bird nest somewhere … the point is, if you become familiar with your garden, you'll likely notice a problem before it starts.

Usually the first thing to do is watering. Did you notice any plants wilting? Was there anything limp or starting to look sad? If so, that would be a good place to put the sprinkler or turn on the irrigation first. If there are containers, especially hanging baskets or plastic pots, these likely need to be watered—especially if it is July or August and temperatures have been high. Those pots go through a lot of water!

I go to the rain barrel, fill up the watering can, and I soak all the planters. How do you know how much water to give? Well, I often lift small containers. If they are quite heavy, they are probably wet. If they are very light, they are probably dry. I soak until I see water coming out of the drain holes. Then I check them again the next day. Watering the planters is enjoyable; I do not see it as being a lot of work.

Step 2: Tidy

If the first walk-through is to keep everything healthy, the next one is to either make everything pretty or prevent future ugly. I usually have a small pair of snips with me in the garden, and if there is a plant that is looking shabby or past its prime, it might be necessary to do some deadheading or just cutting the plant back a bit to tidy and clean up.

Deadheading

If you're going to have plants in bloom, you're also going to have plants that have finished blooming. A great deal of debate takes place among gardeners about whether to remove spent blooms. This is called deadheading, since you are removing the "dead heads" of the finished blossoms. In many cases, deadheading helps to create a tidier, nicer-looking plant. Preventing a plant from forming seeds can also encourage it to keep flowering for longer than it normally would. Seed production requires a great deal of nutrients, and removing the seed heads from plants such as lilies and irises can help them remain more vigorous and flower even better the following year.

Poppy seed head.

Deadheading has a downside for some plants, however. Both Siberian irises and martagon lilies have seedpods that can be quite decorative in the winter months, and removing the seeds prevents them from forming. So really, it's up to you. If you want to save seed from a particular plant, or you want it to self-seed, obviously you will have to leave the seed heads to develop. Some plants, such as dittany and nigella, have truly attractive seedpods, and some, such as globe thistles and sunflowers, have seed heads that are a huge draw for songbirds. Deadheading is not essential, and over time, you will learn which plants you prefer to clean up and which ones you prefer to leave standing. Some perennials, including columbine, valerian, and 'Johnson's Blue' geranium, produce such copious amounts of seeds that if you don't deadhead them, they make weeds of themselves. Clipping the seed heads off prevents this. A sharp pair of small shears is the ideal tool for this job.

A dandelion seed head.

Think about how many nutrients are being sucked out of the ground by a plant with a root like this dandelion!

Step 3: Pest control

Did you notice any plants in the garden that have holes in the leaves or are looking chewed or bitten? Look closely. Maybe holes in the leaves are from a recent hailstorm. Then again, they might be from caterpillars. Examine the plant. Look around the buds and under the leaves, and up against the stems. Find any caterpillars chewing away? Squish them. Congratulations! You have just done pest control. Are there ants crawling all over a particular plant? You probably have aphids. A strong blast from the hose should fix 'em!

Did you see any plants with mildew or yucky spots on a leaf or two? That could be a disease. Pluck those leaves off and throw them in the garbage, not the compost.

Step 4: Weeding

Do yet another walk-through. If you see any weeds growing, especially teeny-tiny ones, pull them out. Three to five minutes a day of weeding is all that I usually do. If the garden is well mulched, weeds are less of a problem. Dandelions will, of course, find ways to survive. They are sneaky buggers.

You will often find a large weed such as a thistle that has miraculously appeared growing out of one of your shrubs and is suddenly a metre tall. "How embarrassing!" you say. Then you yank it out. That's it. That's "maintenance."

It's important not to let the weeds get away on you. "Isn't there something I can spray?" *No, there is not!* There is not a single thing you can spray to keep weeds from growing. There is no magic wand that will do that for you. People would love a product that miraculously kills weeds but not desirable plants, is totally earth-friendly, works for long periods, and costs practically nothing. That product simply does not exist. If you stay on top of your weeds, weed control will become much less overwhelming. Why? Because you're removing the weeds before they go to seed so you'll have fewer and fewer to deal with every season.

Lawn care

We all know people, usually men past the age of fifty, who spend insane amounts of time obsessing over the lawn. Having a nice lawn is not a reasonable goal for a quick-and-easy garden. Why? Trying to keep lawn alive and green consistently in this climate is like trying to nail Jell-O to a wall.

Lawn requires copious amounts of water. If you want lush, thick, beautiful lawn, you have to water accordingly. Have you ever noticed how golf courses turn on their sprinklers practically every single night? That's not just for kicks; that's a necessity if you want to maintain a great lawn. Lawn that is lush and verdant is usually too thick for weeds to penetrate or mushrooms to grow in. Lawns that are inconsistently watered become host to dandelions and fairy rings and clovers and God knows what else.

I suppose I should tell you what to do with lawn that you have decided to keep. Well, the first thing to note is that if you want a nice lawn, it needs to be in a sunny spot. Any lawn that is not in full sun becomes patchy, ugly, and often gets powdery mildew. This might be how you go about getting rid of 30 per cent of your lawn: get rid of the parts in the shade.

> Grass should not be allowed to grow right up to the edge of your tree trunks. If it does, you may damage the tree with the lawn mower.

Lawn has high nutrient requirements, so you will have to fertilize in spring and/or fall. Most people do both. You'll also have to mow it and aerate it to get oxygen to the roots. You may also want to get a special thatch rake to tidy it up in the spring.

Keep a garden journal

This is of the utmost importance because it creates a living record of what you've created. If you plant a variety of bean that you really like and it gives you good results, you may not remember that name next year. You're far less likely to remember the variety of rose you planted when it really starts flourishing, five years later, unless you wrote it down when you planted it. Your notebook need not be elaborate or fancy (though it can be if you like). Things you should record include the following:

1. The dates you planted everything, especially vegetables, and what specific variety you are trying. It's also handy to draw a map so you know where it's supposed to be when you can't see it.

2.   Record seasonal changes. Keep track of when the last spring frost and the first autumn frost occurred. This becomes invaluable information when you're doing winter planning. Keeping track of rainfall is helpful too, especially if you are considering irrigation or xeriscaping.

3.   Make notes about what birds (good or bad) or pests you've had in your garden. If they became a problem, note what you did to discourage them and how effective it was.

Your journal is your reference point. When someone says, "We've never had so little rain," you can grab your journal and say, "Actually, the spring of '97 was far drier than this one . . ." With your journal, you can begin to anticipate problems before they take over your garden—maybe you're going to lay down that mulch on everything this year to help lock in the moisture before it's all gone.

If you should ever sell your house, consider giving your garden journal (possibly with before and after photos) to the person who buys your home. This is legitimate proof of the value and worth of the garden, and the person you are selling to will likely appreciate this very much. Once you start keeping a garden journal, you will find it invaluable and wonder how you ever managed without one.

SPRING CHORES CHECKLIST

- Cut back last year's growth on your perennials down to where the new shoots are emerging.

- Check for plants that did not survive the winter. Be patient; some plants take much longer to break dormancy than others. Do not assume anything is dead until after June 1 at least.

- Top-dress your garden with compost and/or manure. This can also be done in fall, if you prefer.

- Check your tools. Make sure they are clean and sharp and everything is functioning.

- Certain perennials can be divided now, if you so wish.

- You should be fertilizing regularly in the spring. The specifics of this will vary, but feeding your plants is important.

- Prune out any deadwood on your roses.

- Mid-March is usually a good time to begin sowing seeds indoors. Always ask yourself, "Is this something I can direct-sow?" If the answer is yes, don't bother starting them inside. Things to start now include petunias, snapdragons, salvia, heliotrope, nicotiana, peppers, tomatoes, cabbage, cauliflower, broccoli, salpiglossus, certain melons, and some herbs.

- In May, when it begins to get nice, hardening off young plants and seedlings becomes an important task.

SUMMER CHORES CHECKLIST

- Daylilies and bearded irises are best divided in late summer. August is the perfect time for this.

- Gather seeds from the best annuals and heirloom vegetables. Store the seed in carefully labelled envelopes and keep them in a cool, dry place.

- Weeds! Staying on top of your weeding is probably the most important task for this season.

- During a heat wave, be sure that nothing is wanting for water.

- Monitor carefully for pests and diseases.

- If you've planted beans, cucumbers, zucchini, and so on, you'll be busy with harvesting.

A well-mulched garden needs less maintenance.

FALL CHORES CHECKLIST

- Some people like to cut back perennials in the fall; I don't. I do it in spring. The only things I cut back in the fall are delphiniums, irises, lilies, and peonies. These plants can have both pests and diseases that overwinter on the foliage. Don't cut them back until they are well and truly dormant. This usually means mid- to late October.

- Top-dress your garden with compost and/or manure. This can also be done in spring, if you prefer.

- Apply a good layer of mulch to the garden.

- Dig root vegetables such as carrots and parsnips, as well as tender tubers such as dahlias.

- Pull out annuals and seasonal plants that are past their prime or have been claimed by frost. Unless they are diseased, they should go in the compost bin.

- Be sure to keep your evergreens well watered right up until the ground freezes. Watering well in the fall helps to prevent winter browning.

- Buy an amaryllis bulb so you have something fabulous blooming to keep you company in winter.

- Fall is an excellent time to be planting trees and shrubs, along with bulbs.

- In fall and early winter, you should be planning your garden. Getting magazines and seed catalogues at this time, putting your order together, and sending it off early will ensure you get what you want and that you'll have the seeds by the time you're ready to plant.

WINTER CHORES CHECKLIST

- Educate yourself. Use winter to learn as much as you can. Are there any universities, colleges, and so on in your area that offer gardening classes? Check into it.

- Look at the bones of your garden. Examine bark, twigs, shape, spines, fruits, and such. Take a good inventory of what offers winter interest and where winter interest is lacking.

- Celebrate solstice. For thousands of years, this was the critical day for those who tend to the earth. Not everyone celebrates Christmas or Hanukkah. Many of us have friends who are Hindu or Buddhist or atheist or otherwise. Everyone can celebrate solstice. The return of lengthening daylight is a fabulous reason to host a party. Daylight lengthening and shortening is critical to plants, and it is important that we recognize this.

- After a particularly heavy snowfall, you might want to knock the snow off some of your tree branches and shrubs so they don't break under the weight. If branches do break, grab your pruning shears and clean this up promptly.

- Late winter or spring is a good time to do some pruning, though keep in mind that this rule does not apply to everything. Mock orange, forsythia, and dogwoods can all be shaped and clipped at this time of year, as can spireas.

- There are few things that want to be seeded in January, but some things that need a very long season can be started now. Artichokes and 'Foxy' foxgloves can be started in the middle of the month, and while most people would prefer to buy begonias and geraniums as plants, you can start them from seed now if you are so inclined.

❧ *4* ❧

Nuts and bolts of gardening

You can learn as much as you want to about gardening. The more you pursue it, the more you'll learn. Some people only want to know what they *need* to know. Others want to know *everything*. Here I offer some of the wisdom that I've gathered along the way, and I hope it will be of some use to you.

Getting started

Do you have everything you need to start gardening? Is there anything more satisfying than crossing multiple items off a "to do" list? Of course not. So let's make a checklist of the fifteen most important things you need when starting a garden.

Opposite: The theme here is late-season colour: amur maple, echinacea, goldenrod, joepye weed, tall phlox, and rudbeckia. These are all great plants for late summer and autumn interest.

This page: Perennials such as this bugbane (*Cimicifuga*) are slow to establish and resentful of disturbance. Choose a planting site with care as they will not want to be moved!

1. Theme: Have you got a theme picked out for the garden? Just a few options include historical, woodland, winter interest, meadow, or tropical.

2. Budget: Have you figured out how much you want to spend on your yard? Do you have the willpower to stay within this budget?

3. Colour Scheme: Do you know what colours are going to be best in your theme?

4. Tools: Check the "Must-Have Garden Supplies" section to see what tools should be on your list.

5. Book: Do you have a copy of this book somewhere nearby for handy reference if you get lost? Take it with you when you go shopping.

6. Directions: Do you have a Google map to that garden centre your friend keeps raving about?

7. "Must-Have" Plants List: As with grocery shopping, apply the "only buy things on your list" rule. You might have peony, daphne, and lilies on your list, so only buy those things. The exception

to this rule is that sometimes you meet a plant you didn't know about. For example, you were unaware of the existence of Queen Anne's lace, but you know it would be absolutely perfect in your cutting garden. Check the price. Does it fit within your budget? Do you have space for it? Excellent. By all means purchase it.

8. Time: Have you cleared your schedule? I mean it. Having the time to play in the garden is very important. Be sure to budget time to do this. Nursery-grown plants in black plastic containers dry out very quickly and if forgotten will usually dry up and die, and now you've wasted your money and you've wasted time because now you have to go back to the nursery and buy replacements.

9. Weather Forecast: You did download that app about weather, right? Or you've bookmarked a link to it? You need to make yourself aware of possible frosts, coming storms, high winds, and so on so you can protect your plants.

10. Mentor: Do you have a good gardening friend? Like everything else in life, there is no reason to go through this alone. Most gardeners love sharing their knowledge and expertise. If you're at all unsure of what you're doing, pick up the phone and call Susan and say, "Hey, can you make yourself available to come to the garden centre with me this week? I want to buy some lilies and I want to make sure I buy good ones." Susan will be thrilled to go with you, and flattered that you hold her gardening knowledge in such high esteem. Susan can also help you choose sites in your garden to plant your new treasures.

11. Amendments: Have you picked up some compost/manure? It's important to work organic matter into your soil as often as you can.

12. Focal Point: Have you figured out what the jewel of your garden is going to be? This isn't a decision to make lightly.

13. Transportation: Do you have a means of getting all your supplies, especially a large item such as a fountain or a tree, home? Buying a 2-metre tall tree when you drive a Honda Civic becomes a challenge. Many garden centres offer delivery; check beforehand. Do not show up to make physically large purchases without means of transport; many garden centres are short on space and will not be pleased to "hold on" to an item until you are ready to pick it up.

14. Positive Attitude: This is important. Gardening is supposed to be fun.

15. Sun Protection: Fashionable hat and sunscreen? This is also important.

FOCAL POINT

What is not always immediately apparent is the garden focal point. When you look at a yard, your eye will subconsciously focus on *something*. You need to make a deliberate effort to control what that focus will be or your yard may feel busy and uninviting. Generally, you don't want your house to be the focal point. More effective focal points include statuary, a specimen tree, a pond, an arbor, or unique pottery. Sometimes, it is very clear what the focal point *should be* but there is too much else going on! Competing focal points aren't comfortable to

The statue is a clear focal point in this yard.

look at. Practically speaking, you don't want to spend seven hundred dollars on a fountain only to have it be ignored because you put it next to an incredibly large and ancient tree. To make your garden beautiful, focused, and welcoming, make sure you choose a specific focal point and plan your design to showcase it.

Competing focal points don't work.

Must-have garden supplies

Even before you buy plants, you need to have the tools to work with them.

A gardening education

Your first vital tool is education. Here you are, reading a book written specifically for gardening in your zone. Well done! There is a *lot* of gardening advice available online. Just remember that any idiot can make a website, and many do. Also, even the good advice is not necessarily good advice for your area, so it's important to find local information.

Compost fork

These are lightweight and somewhat resemble a pitchfork, though considerably smaller. They are for turning over and aerating compost heaps. They are inexpensive but should be well made and of high quality.

Containers add life to a large deck.

Containers

If you're going to have planters or containers on your deck, clearly you will have to obtain said planters and containers. You can purchase these from most garden centres with plants already in them if you like, but these are usually at best colourful and at worst tasteless. For the sake of successfully keeping to their budget, most people who are new to gardening will use plastic pots. This is all right while you're learning, but don't use plastic long-term. Every year, you should buy yourself at least one nice ceramic pot.

Gardening gloves

I never used to wear gloves in the garden, but after years of my skin drying out, never being able to get my fingernails clean, and being scratched, scraped, and gouged by thorns, splinters, rocks, and broken branches, I have converted. Get gloves that feel comfortable and are breathable while still allowing you to have a good grip. Machine-washable is also important. I tend to buy high-quality gloves for around $25, and they usually last me a season, sometimes not even that. I am, however, a professional gardener. I don't expect you to do the same volume of gardening as I do. For you, a single pair might last several years, and I will surely be jealous of you. Regardless of what kind you buy, gardening gloves should be used for typical gardening activities only. They will shred quickly if you wear them when rearranging the stones in your flowerbed and are completely unsafe for handling chemicals (which I encourage you never to use anyhow).

Hoe

These are great for making little trenches for sowing seeds, and they can get into places that your spade might not be able to reach. A winged weeder or stirrup hoe is absolutely fantastic for getting into tight spaces when weeding between plants and in hard-to-get-at spaces. I don't know where I would be without mine.

Hoses and sprinklers

If you are going to use a sprinkler, I highly recommend buying one of high quality. Cheap, low-grade sprinklers from big department stores frequently chip, crack, leak, and need to be replaced. It is better to buy one that you can trust to distribute water more evenly. If possible, buy a sprinkler made of brass, iron or any other really strong material.

One of the best investments you can make in terms of sprinklers is a soaker hose. These are great for watering newly planted trees and shrubs because it is better for these guys to get a deep drink every three to seven days rather than small amounts of water daily. Trees and shrubs that get a small quantity of water daily frequently produce suckers and are not as drought-resistant overall.

Get a water wand. These handy watering devices create a gentle shower that waters effectively without washing your seedlings out of the ground or creating great torrents of water that flow from one end of the bed to the other.

Plastic watering cans are okay (and inexpensive), but I prefer metal or aluminum watering cans. If you leave plastic watering cans outside on a freezing night when they have water in them, they almost always crack.

Try to do your watering in the early morning if possible. Watering in the evening means plants can go to bed cold and wet, which can facilitate the spread of fungal

A water wand.

diseases. Watering in the afternoon (especially if it's hot) means that you can lose a lot of water to evaporation.

Kneepads
One of the facts of life that we all have to deal with is aging. Some of us are starting to notice that the "old grey mare ain't what she used to be." Gardening involves a lot of bending and kneeling, so getting a decent pair of kneepads or a kneeling pad is a very good idea and can really save your knees.

Pruning shears
The quality of the shears you buy should be based on the amount of pruning that you do. If you only do some very light pruning once or twice a year, a $20 pair from your local garden centre will probably do you just fine. If you garden professionally, you might need to buy a $100 pair of high-end secateurs.

Pruning shears need to be kept scrupulously clean, and they should be disinfected after each use, as it is quite easy to spread disease with dirty pruning shears. Essentially, they are surgical tools for trees and shrubs. Besides being kept clean, they need to be kept extremely sharp. You are never allowed to "chew" through a branch—all incisions need to be purposeful, precise, and clean.

Rain barrels
Rainwater is better for your plants because it doesn't have any of the chemicals that treated water tends to contain. Every home should have at least one rain barrel—and probably more. Rain barrels can be very heavy and sometimes they are expensive. Check with your local municipality or waste reduction council to see whether financial support for purchasing one is available. They can also be difficult to hide in the yard because they need to be accessible without being highly visible. This is a fine balance to achieve.

Ideally, rain barrels should have a cover to keep mosquitoes out and should be made from a durable material. Plastic rain barrels are okay as long as they don't leak. These barrels should be emptied for the winter, ideally onto your evergreens to help prevent winter browning, and they should be stored upside down or in a shed for the winter.

Spade
Probably the most important thing you can own is a really, really good spade. A shovel is used for moving snow, hence the term *snow shovel*, or mucking manure out of the barns. A spade is shaped like the ace of spades and is meant for digging. It should be the right height for

your body, be very strong, and be lightweight. A little known fact for the gentlemen is that it doesn't matter how facially challenged you are, if you can work a spade in the garden and dig like a badger, you'll be widely revered as devilishly handsome.

Don't buy junky metal spades that will rust if left out in the rain. Stainless steel is good and will slice through the earth like a pre-heated knife through cold butter. You also don't want something whose handle will snap when you exert a bit of pressure on it.

Like your pruning shears, your spade should be kept meticulously clean. Wash dirt and clay off of it after every single use. Always put it back in the same place when you're done using it. You should also have your spade sharpened regularly because routine use will dull it over time. You can have this done professionally, often at the place where you bought it, or you can do it yourself if you have the proper tools and equipment.

Equally important is the trowel, which is basically a tiny, handheld version of the spade. The trowel is infinitely useful for planting small things such as seedlings and annuals, and the same rules as the spade apply.

Sunhat

When gardening, you should always wear a high-quality sunhat, lots of sunscreen, and, if you can bear it, long sleeves while you are actively working. The sun is not your friend. In fact, it is trying to kill you. I write as someone who has lived in Queensland, Australia, the skin cancer capital of the world. Take breaks to sit in the shade, drink copious amounts of water, and be alert to any signs of sunstroke, such as dizziness or nausea. Wear high-quality sunglasses and try not to be in the garden during the hottest part of the day.

A sturdy wheelbarrow is worth the price.

Wheelbarrows

Buy a sturdy, lightweight wheelbarrow as they are great for mixing up compost and topsoil or hauling bags of mulch or prunings or whatever. You'll really wonder how you lived without one. You might want to drill a tiny hole or two in the bottom so that if you leave it out in the rain, it won't fill up with water. If you have difficulty pushing a wheelbarrow around, a garden wagon may be simpler to manage since they often come with ball-bearing wheels and rack and pinion steering to make turning easier.

The basic rules of gardening

Gardening is not a set of hard-and-fast rules, nor is it the same for every person. I am the first person to encourage you to dive right in, to be bold and courageous in your garden, but we all know at least a few gardens where horrible botanical atrocities have occurred. While there is a lot of flexibility, we all must adhere to principles of responsible gardening. I have created a list of rules that should apply to all gardens everywhere. Now, as much as I like to boss people around and tell them what to do in the garden, sometimes it's just a lot easier to tell you what not to do.

Rule #1: Do not neglect the mature size of whatever it is you are planting.

Do not think in the short term! A tree or shrub is a permanent feature in your landscape, so you need to plant one according to the space you have available, not according to the space that you wish you had. If a tree is genetically programmed to reach a certain size, do you honestly think you are going to thwart it with a pair of pruning shears? You,

The tree fits here now, but in ten years that fence is in trouble.

dear gardener, will not win against 40 million years of evolution. Furthermore, trees that are butchered and pruned into "size" look awful, particularly in winter. They lose all of their natural shape and dignity. It is like trying to make a teenager wear children's clothing.

Rule #2: Your garden choices must coordinate with your home.

Think of your garden as an extension of your home. Like any good accessory, your garden needs to look like it belongs with that house. As Clinton and Stacey, the hosts of the television show *What Not to Wear* always said, "The earrings do not need to match the necklace, but they do need to 'go.'" It is much the same in a design. A garden that does not coordinate with its house looks and feels unnatural; it is jarring and discordant. If you have a sleek, ultramodern-looking house, it is probably not going to look right with an English country garden border. If you have a century-old farmhouse with an old wooden fence, it may not look right with a very minimalistic, super-chic modern planting scheme. A white house backing an all white planting scheme will lose its punch.

Rule #3: You can't plant everything.

Sometimes we buy shrubs because they are on sale, not because we really need them. Sometimes we become fond of lilies or irises or hostas and start to feel like we must grow all of them. Do not allow your garden to turn into a botanical zoo! A garden is a kind of art; it is a tool of communication. You must be discerning and set limits and boundaries. It is perfectly acceptable to be fond of roses or peonies or spireas. Just be sure that your garden continues to feel like a garden, and not like a trial plot for a major nursery.

Be realistic about what you are working with. If your garden is entirely shaded by immense spruce trees, you may have to put your dream of growing prize-winning dahlias on hold. If you don't have full sun, don't plant things that require it to look good. If your garden is poorly drained and prone to flooding, you may have to abandon designs that include native cactus. Be flexible and be real with yourself.

Rule #4: Never be a "plunker."

Plunkers are gardeners who simply "plunk" things in, with no thought of design. If they have a gap in a sunny spot, any plant that catches their eye and might survive there is considered suitable. This makes the garden feel jumbled and incoherent. After a few years of this, it begins to look like you are having a yard sale. There is no sense of thought or reason in plunked gardens—they are at best colourful. Good gardeners incorporate planning and design. Plants that are plunked down haphazardly rarely end up in the best place for them, and you're setting yourself up for failure. Stressed-out plants are susceptible to pests and diseases.

Rule #5: Remove all tags and labels attached to plants, especially trees and shrubs.

My friend Madison loved fashion. If she bought a Louis Vuitton bag or a sexy little black dress to wear to a party, do you think she left the tag with the brand name and price attached? Of course not, she would have removed that before leaving the house, as would any sensible person. Do the same in the garden.

There are two types of tags, and you don't want either left in your yard. Tags are labels that are tied on, often with elastics, to trees and shrubs usually. Sometimes these can cut into the bark of the tree as it grows, injuring it. Labels are also printed on tiny stakes, usually plastic, and say what variety of allium or artemesia you have just planted. When you keep these with the plant and the plant it marks happens to die, the tags start to resemble tombstones. "Here lies Bergenia. Beloved spring bloomer. RIP."

Now, I hear you protesting, "But if I remove the tag, I'll never remember the name of it!" That is an excellent point, but I remind you that those tags are usually plastic. Plastic chips, fades, cracks, and blows away. You are served not at all by a tag that you cannot read. Take those tags and labels inside. Wash them. Put them in a shoebox labelled "tags." Keep your box of tags with your garden journal so you know not only what you planted and when, but also where you planted it. That way when you need to know its name, you can go back and find it, instead of rooting through tiny, broken plastic chips in the shade garden, saying, "I know the tag for this astilbe has to be in the ground here somewhere . . ."

Rule #6: You are not allowed to take the easy way out.

"I need something really fast-growing; I don't want to have to wait ten years for something to grow." If ever there were a mindset that led to bad landscaping, this is it! People want instant; they don't have the patience to wait for anything to grow. This means that people will plant five Swedish aspens when they would be much better served by planting two willows or one large shade tree. People do this with junipers a lot too. The 'Prince of Wales' juniper has a mature spread of more than 3 metres. People, including bad landscapers, will plant three where one is more appropriate, all in an effort to have a fuller effect sooner. This is bad in the long run. Make the right choice for the right location.

Recognize that some things grow faster than others. Recognize that planting a tree is an investment, and although you may not sit in its shade, your children or grandchildren or nieces and nephews might. Never make any choice in your garden based on "this was the cheapest tree available" or "this is the fastest-growing thing I could plant."

Carefully selected objects can add interest to your yard.

Rule #7: Do not put flimsy plastic crap in your garden.

It is perfectly acceptable to have art in the garden. A well-placed sculpture, a wooden trellis, a fountain—these are all lovely and often fabulous pieces to include. But plastic breaks, chips, cracks, and fades. That cute little plastic frog you bought at the garden show won't be so cute in two years when the prairie sun has bleached him from bright green to pale yellowish white. And you get what you pay for; that flimsy trellis you only paid $20 for is going to snap like a dry twig in our first windstorm. You do not serve your landscaping or the planet by putting cheap plastic lambs on your front steps.

Whatever city you live in, there is likely a whole litany of local artists who would be very pleased to make you something out of ceramic or stoneware. Maybe you could take a class and make something yourself. You might even meet some other gardeners in the process.

Rule #8: Learn how to prune *before* picking up the shears.

People like pruning. But if you are unsure what you are doing, do some research first or contact a qualified arbourist. You would not attempt to do surgery without first being trained as a doctor or surgeon—why should you get to just prune anything in the yard if you don't know what you're doing?

Some goal has to be met by your pruning. Sometimes you have a tree where branches are crossed and they are rubbing against one another, possibly opening up a wound and inviting disease and infection. Are you trying to rejuvenate an elderly shrub or maybe want your tree to produce more blossoms? Or are you pruning simply because you feel this tree has gotten too big? Different goals require different approaches and different timing. In some cases, such as apple trees, a good pruning job when they are young helps them to support the weight of the fruit when they get older. They need to be shaped and sheared when they are young. Dogwoods produce the best winter colour on new growth, so they need to be cut back hard every few years to produce those brilliant red stems that we love so much.

You cannot prune whenever the mood strikes you. Most trees and shrubs can be pruned either in fall after they drop their leaves or in spring before they leaf out, but this is a generalization. Some trees, such as birch and maple, will bleed profusely when cut and so should only be pruned in full leaf. Many fruit trees and things like lilacs should only be clipped when they are finished blooming for the year. Your municipality may have rules for when to prune your elms. It's generally a matter of determining what it is, why are you pruning it, and who should do it. If you take too much off, you can't put it back on again, and a bad pruning job can be visible for years.

Your tools need to be very sharp and very clean. You can spread disease easily with a pair of infected pruning shears. You are *not* allowed to chew off a branch with a rusty pair of dull secateurs. Pruning should be quick and painless for the tree.

Rule #9: Once it is planted, you still have to take care of it.

A garden does not grow all by itself. Be realistic about how much time you have to spend in your garden, and don't make it bigger or grander than you can feasibly take care of. A neglected and overgrown garden can be worse in some ways than a garden that was never planted at all. Make sure if you go to the trouble of planting a garden, that you look after it. Plant things that are suited to your climate. Avoid pesticides and herbicides at all costs. Use compost. Pull weeds. Water during dry spells with water from your rain barrel. You have a rain barrel by now, right?

Rule #10: Do not plant fruit trees in places where they will be a problem.

Most people think of fruit trees as trees from which they will be harvesting a crop, but this is not necessarily so. Flowering crabapples, mountain ash, nannyberry, 'Schubert' chokecherries, and many others are all trees that produce fruit that isn't going to be eaten by people. Birds love these trees; do not plant them where bird droppings are going to be a problem. Planting mountain ash along sidewalks is a terrible idea—the fruit is going to smear all over the pavement and be tracked inside to nearby buildings. Planting a chokecherry or crabapple, even an ornamental variety, around a parking lot is foolhardy.

The fruit will drop on both vehicles and pavement, creating a mess. Always be cautious about where you are putting these trees. They are sensational, but they need to be planted in the right location.

Rule #11: Remember that your decisions matter.

Your decisions matter very much. The garden you plant could have long-reaching effects, both for your community and for local wildlife. Be wise, and be aware. Take your time when making big decisions regarding the garden.

Rule #12: Learn from your mistakes.

Every gardener makes mistakes, regardless of where and how they started gardening. You will too. This is okay! In fact, this is very important. If you make a mistake in the garden, the most important thing to do is to learn from it. Try not to repeat your errors. The second most important thing is that once you recognize an error, you must fix it. If you realize that the shrub you have chosen is simply going to get too large, remove it or relocate it. If you plant something really aggressive, and getting rid of it proves a huge deal of work,

A row of flowering crab looks beautiful in full bloom, but you may not want it beside your driveway.

you will hopefully learn to be more discerning with spreading plants in the future. Planting bulbs too late in the fall results in a poor show in the spring? There's a lesson there too! Try not to lose the lesson. Each experience in the garden, whether good or bad, is meant to shape and teach us on our gardening journeys. Learn from your errors, and be a better gardener because of them. The only way to get really good at something is to really suck at it for the first little while.

THE ETHICS OF NATIVE PLANTS

I am a huge advocate for having native plants in the garden. What could be better suited to the conditions where you live than plants that are indigenous to your area? Many of our native plants are extremely beautiful, but we need to be responsible and we need to be ethical about having them. When I was a teenager and didn't know better, I dug many wildflowers from the wild. Sometimes they succeeded in the garden, and sometimes they didn't. Often I introduced new weeds in the process.

Keep in mind, not all native plants are good garden candidates. Some plants behave very differently in cultivation than they do in the wild. For example, the prairie wild rose, Alberta's provincial flower, is beautiful and fragrant when it blooms in the ditches in early summer. However, under garden conditions it can become extremely aggressive and very difficult to eliminate should you change your mind about having it there. I always thought wild rose was a great name for a political party for this reason. Fireweed is another good example—it often grows more than 2 metres tall and refuses to flower under cultivation, despite flowering madly in places where competition is high.

Do not ever dig native plants from the wild! It is unethical and, in many cases, illegal. If there is a native plant that you like, the first thing to do is identify it. Take a photo. Go to a local garden centre or nature society and find out what it is. Go to a library and get a good field guide for your area. Once you have identified

The lady's slipper orchid is among our most beautiful native flowers, but make sure yours is responsibly sourced.

it, you can find out if it is available from garden centres in your area. In many cases, the garden forms of native plants are superior to the unrefined species. The hybrid forms of prairie crocus have stronger colours, larger flowers, and often a longer bloom time than the one that grows in our pastures and ditches. The garden forms of goldenrod are more vigorous, longer blooming, and far more disease-resistant than the wild forms.

If a plant you like is not available locally, perhaps you can gather some seeds from it. This is all right provided that you never take more than 10 per cent of the seeds. You don't know how many years it has been since that plant had enough nutrients to produce those seeds. You don't know how many birds or small creatures are dependent upon those seeds for food. Never take more than you need, and be respectful of the ecosystem you are in.

Sometimes you can take cuttings from native plants. This won't hurt them and can much benefit your garden. I have taken cuttings from native penstemons and also certain shrubs, and this is far more successful than trying to dig one out of its native habitat. Many native plants simply won't transplant well, or at all. A cutting eliminates a lot of those issues.

Hard-won wisdom

You can learn a lot of technical things when you garden. Things like how, when, where, and what to plant or learning the difference between botrytis and mildew or if a flowering crabapple is more suited to a certain spot than a dogwood. I have learned so many important lessons from my garden, and as much as I have put into gardening, it has always given me back more. Some things I've learned from my garden include:

Patience

If nothing else, my garden has taught me there are rewards to being patient. I have no patience for standing in line or for being put on hold; yet I have no problem waiting three years to see that penstemon that I grew from a cutting produce flowers. There are shrubs I have grown from seed that took five years to bloom; nurturing them and watching them mature has been delightful. Every year, I must wait for the lilacs to flower. I must wait for the tulips to emerge. I must wait for the berries and fruit to ripen. I must wait for the return of the birds. Everything has a time, a season, and a proper period in which it does what it does. My garden has taught me to slow down, not to expect instant gratification, and to be grateful when it all comes to fruition.

Just because it dies does not mean you've failed.

The truth is, you are going to kill plants sometimes, perhaps often. This is only a worthless experience if you don't learn anything from it. Many times I will hear a new gardener say, "I tried planting that, but it died so I never planted it again." And that is perfectly okay—working with your garden and focusing on what does well there is a very reasonable approach for a low-maintenance garden, but it is worth asking the question why, especially if it's a plant you see others having success with.

Flower beds and borders are always more appealing with curved lines rather than straight.

What happens when you fall in love with a plant that isn't cooperating? Garden for long enough, it's going to happen. Realize that a lot of very good gardeners may have killed that plant many times before they succeeded with it. Ask anyone who has gardened for a long time if they have a plant they find "difficult." They will say something like "I finally realized it wants to be in a drier location" or "I figured out they go dormant if temperatures get too high."

Ask yourself, "What is different from my location and theirs?" If something dies the first time you plant it, try it in a different location. Try a different variety. Try planting it at a different time of year. Try getting it from a more local source if possible because this really does matter.

Figuring out how to work with nature to grow that one plant you really can't give up on is part of the fun of gardening, and the fruits (or flowers) are that much sweeter once you succeed.

If you listen to your garden, it will tell you what to grow.

The old saying "You've got to work with what you've got" holds especially true in gardening. If something does well for you, plant lots of it. What plants do well for your neighbours—don't be afraid to snoop! What plants frequently die?

If you notice that ferns do especially well in your border, plant lots of ferns and investigate plants that like similar growing conditions and plant those too!

Perhaps you have large deciduous trees. There are probably spring blooming bulbs that would do really well beneath them if you're careful not to disturb the tree roots when you're planting.

If you have a slope, look at what is growing on slopes in your area and plant accordingly. Juniper and native cactus are probably just the plants for you.

Listen to your garden. Be aware. Tap into the natural forces that are at work there. Always work with nature, not against it. This is especially important advice if you're looking for a low-maintenance garden.

It's not just about you.

The fact is, when you create a garden, you are creating change in the landscape. In some cases, such as when you plant a tree, you are making a permanent change. That tree could be there for the next eighty to one hundred years. We have to be responsible and wise about how we go about this. In many cases, I will tell someone that a particular tree or shrub is going to grow too large for the location they have in mind. The usual response to this is "oh, that doesn't matter. We are only going to be in this house for two years … by the time it gets that big, it won't be my problem." Gardening professionally has taught me that people see plants and trees as products—as things. Trying to get them to understand that a tree is a living, breathing organism is very difficult.

We have to put down the pesticides and herbicides! When you put flowering plants in your garden, you will be attracting small insects, which will be attracting birds. Wildlife will make use of your garden. If you have a pond, small creatures like frogs and salamanders may take up residence there. We have to realize that when we put food out for them, they will come. A garden changes and evolves, and you have the power to make a difference. Planting the host plants for native butterflies is an excellent thing to do, but it's pointless unless we stop using pesticides. What kills the tent caterpillar will also kill the monarch.

We need to be really aware and clear that our gardens are so much more than we realize—they are homes for the creatures we share the Earth with, and we need to be kind to them and respect them. We need to stop putting poisons in our environment, and we need to teach our children about the great gifts we have been given in this country! Emily Dickinson once said, "The problem with nature is that if we pull the smallest of threads, everything else unravels." Gardening has taught me this first-hand—how everything is connected. We need to use this simple fact to motivate the decisions we make, both in our yards and in the greater picture of things.

5

Plant diseases

Plants can get diseases just like people can. Just as there are hundreds of diseases that can infect humans, it's the same with plants and often difficult to tell when to worry. Some diseases are merely cosmetic, meaning they are ugly but don't really harm the plant, and some can be fatal. Many plant diseases are also host-specific, meaning they only infect certain kinds of plants.

Not everything can be blamed on disease.

Sometimes environmental damage can resemble a disease. For example, sun can damage a plant or a nutrient deficiency can mimic a disease. I've included several photos of different environmental damages throughout the book, but keep in mind that your plant could be ailing from soil or pest issues as well. Make sure you know what you're dealing with before attempting to address the problem, especially before you even consider any kind of chemical action. It's sometimes very difficult to diagnose problems, even for experts. If in doubt about the problem, take a photo of the suspected disease and bring it or email it to a local expert at a garden centre, university, or horticultural society.

Opposite: The higher moisture levels from a water feature can make plants more prone to disease.

Sunscald.

If all your plants are touching each other, you are setting your bed up for mildew and disease. This is particularly true with things like asters, goldenrod, monarda, and phlox. Try to allow a little "breathing room" between plants.

Prevention

Providing plants with healthy growing conditions and making sure they aren't wanting for water or nutrients is a good way to prevent diseases from starting. Certain plants are prone to specific plant diseases and so sometimes when purchasing a plant, it's a good idea to ask, "Is this plant disease-resistant?"

With our rather dry climate and cold winters, we are not as prone to illness as our more humid Ontarian and West Coast gardening friends. Better growing conditions favour more diseases. Roses might flower longer in Kelowna, but ours stay healthier!

The main culprits

Naming plant diseases is sometimes confusing for beginners since diseases are often named to describe the

Black knot on a trunk.

problem they create (e.g., blight) or by a specific host (e.g., Dutch elm disease) or by the agent causing the problem. Though this list is by no means exhaustive, it includes the most common ones you are likely to encounter.

Black knot

Black knot is a fungal disease, and it is extremely host-specific. It infects chokecherries (including the ornamental varieties with

Black knot on branches.

purple foliage), mayday trees, and pin cherries. It's not altogether noticeable in the summer but is very visible in winter when the branches are bare. Dark black, crusty lesions that look exactly like dog crap appear on the branches. Over time, black knot weakens the tree and can eventually kill it. It also makes the tree extravagantly ugly in the winter. Infected branches should be pruned out at least 15 centimetres below the infection. This will control the disease, but it is impossible to eliminate since it is present in the native populations of chokecherry. Birds eat the fruit of these trees and spread the spores in their droppings.

Blackspot

One of our most common diseases is blackspot, another fungal disease that primarily infects roses but occasionally certain perennials as well, such as the tall kinds of phlox. Many varieties are resistant, but those that are prone to it will develop yellow and then black spots on the leaves, which look like cigarette burns, and then the leaves drop off. Basically, your plant becomes defoliated and yucky-looking. Blackspot favours cool, wet conditions and is generally not as much of a problem in drier, warm summers. If it occurs several years in a row, it can weaken the plant enough to compromise winter hardiness, but usually it's more of a nuisance than anything else. Rake up all the fallen leaves and burn them. Do not put them in the compost heap or you will merely spread the spores through the rest of the garden. If you grow weary of an especially disease-prone plant, you might like to remove and replace it with a more disease-resistant variety or a different kind of plant altogether. Most of the 'Parkland' and 'Explorer' series of roses are little bothered by blackspot.

Botrytis

Botrytis is yet another fungal disease, and while there are several plants it can infect, lilies seem to be especially prone to it. Leaves turn from yellow to brown and then die. Botrytis is fatal, and there is no cure for it. Dig out infected plants and burn them. Avoid planting lilies in that location for at least two or three seasons following.

Damp-off disease

Damp-off disease affects seedlings. You can have a flat of healthy, robust seedlings, and suddenly they seem to all fall over and die. Damp-off appears as a fluffy pale white fungus at the base of the stems. Providing good air circulation, not overcrowding your seedlings, and ensuring that temperatures are not too warm can help to deter it. It primarily attacks seedlings indoors. Direct-sown seedlings rarely become infected as damp-off dislikes inconsistent temperatures. For many years a fungicide called No-Damp was widely available and very effective at controlling this problem. It was pulled from the market two years ago (I have yet to find a satisfactory answer as to why).

MY VIEW ON FUNGICIDES

People who know me know that I am not a fan of using pesticides. Some might wonder why I would be willing to use a fungicide. Both are chemicals, but pesticides and fungicides are two very different things. Fungicides are chemicals that are specifically designed to kill fungal tissue—if you have ever had a yeast infection or athlete's foot and have seen a doctor about it, you have been treated with a fungicide. I am confident that you have never been treated for anything with a pesticide! Starting seeds on a windowsill in the middle of March in a soilless growing medium is just about as far removed from a "natural" setting as I can think of. I used No-Damp for years because a tiny amount went a very long ways, and it kept my seedlings alive until they were large enough and strong enough to be able to handle themselves. I had no worries about using minute amounts of a very specific anti-fungal toxin in very specific conditions according to very specific manufacturer's instructions. I also use a preventative fungicide sometimes when storing dahlia or canna roots for the winter—a light smattering of "bulb dust" (available at any garden centre) helps to keep moulds and mildews from taking hold while these plants are in their dormant state. Would I ever use a fungicide in the garden? Probably not. Most fungi in your garden is benign or even beneficial, so using a fungicide is unnecessary or even harmful in the long run.

Dutch elm disease

Dutch elm disease (DED) is probably the most famous plant disease in the world, responsible for killing millions of elm trees. Remarkably, Alberta and Saskatchewan have been able to keep it at bay! Dutch elm disease is a fungal disease caused by two different fungi—*Ophiostoma ulmi* and *Ophiostoma novo-ulmi*. This fungus is carried by several species of elm bark beetle, most specifically *Scolytus scolytus* and *Hylurgopinus rufipes*. DED is believed to have originated in Asia, and most Asian species of elms are partially or nearly totally resistant to it. The disease arrived in Holland in 1921 via imported timber and slowly began spreading throughout the rest of Europe.

The fungus works by interfering with the tree's ability to take up and move water. The first symptom is usually a single branch that turns golden several weeks before autumn colour is expected. Other branches soon follow, and then these branches begin to die. Death takes several seasons, and cause of death is essentially dehydration. There is no cure for it, and it is 100 per cent fatal.

The disease eventually reached Great Britain, and during the 1970s, it killed an estimated 25 million elms there. DED arrived in the United States in 1928 and quickly devastated North America's elms. Ohio was the first state to identify it, and it arrived in Canada in 1944, entering Ontario through infected wooden crates. Just fifteen years later, in 1959, it had killed an estimated 700,000 Canadian elms. It was in Manitoba by 1975 and first recorded in Saskatchewan in 1981.

Both the Dutch and American governments worked tirelessly to stop the spread of DED. It started with powerful insecticides to kill elm bark beetles. This seemed to help; unfortunately it also killed millions of beneficial insects and thousands of birds. Then attempts were made to focus on the fungus itself, and equally powerful fungicides were used to treat trees all over the continent. Anti-fungal inoculants were also developed, but these were only semi-successful and very expensive. It was found that not only did beetles spread the fungus but also that it was transferred via the root systems where large groups of elms were growing together, such as along boulevards and streets.

When it eventually became clear that no amount of poisons were going to work, efforts were focused on isolating and removing infected trees. These trees have to be destroyed; even their timber is worthless as the fungus can wait for years to re-emerge when conditions suit it. Since a 1-metre-long elm log can carry more than a thousand elm bark beetles, strict protocols were developed regarding the transportation of both elm timber and firewood.

St. Joseph's elm in Medicine Hat, Alberta. Planted in the early 1900s, this is the most magnificent American elm specimen I have ever seen, anywhere, in my entire life.

Saskatchewan and Manitoba have been very successful at keeping DED to a bare minimum, and both provinces employ scouts to monitor and maintain elm health. Alberta has had the most success keeping DED out; in fact, Alberta has the healthiest population of mature elms in the world. There are more mature, healthy elm trees in Edmonton than in any other city on Earth. There are an estimated 60,000 elms growing on city property, to say nothing of the vast numbers of them on private land.

With the exception of a single isolated specimen in 1998, DED has been kept out of Alberta entirely. Calgary, Red Deer, Medicine Hat, and Lethbridge have healthy, flourishing populations of elms. Saskatoon, Regina, and Winnipeg also claim solid, healthy populations. Newfoundland also claims to be DED-free, but elms were never as important a tree there as they were on the prairies.

Despite our success, most growers and garden centres no longer propagate them or offer them for sale. As a general rule, they are also no longer recommended. This is due in part to the fact that elms are very large trees and are increasingly unsuited to urban yards, but also because the stigma associated with DED has never left the public consciousness. Attempts to develop resistant elms have been reasonably successful, but they are not yet widely known or widely available.

Fireblight

Fireblight is fairly common in some years, but unlike a true blight (which is fungal), fireblight is actually a bacterial disease. It usually enters the tree through a wound, and it is often especially bad in years when there is hail damage. Fireblight is host-specific, and it only affects the rose family. Apples are a favourite victim, but cotoneaster, hawthorn, mountain ash, pears, saskatoon berries, and a few others are also susceptible to it. It appears very quickly, almost overnight, and usually presents itself as burnt- or scorched-looking foliage, normally on new growth, bent over in a distinctive "shepherd's hook" shape. Black marks, lesions, and cracks may also appear.

Fireblight is usually carried by insects, including honeybees, though wind and rain may also be responsible for disseminating the bacteria. Infected trees often exude a substance from wounds that attracts insects, thereby spreading the disease further. In hot and wet weather, fireblight will spread exponentially. Antibiotics such as streptomycin or terramycin are available to large-scale growers (such as you find in California and British Columbia) to treat infections before they get out of hand. If caught early enough, sometimes infected parts can be pruned out and burned. As a general rule though, there is no cure, and fireblight is almost always fatal. The best thing to do is to be diligent about watching for it and making an effort to grow disease-resistant varieties.

Fireblight.

Fusarium

Fusarium wilt is a common fungal disease that often occurs in annuals. It likes cool, wet conditions, and there are many different types of it. If you have a plant that just suddenly turns black and dies for no obvious reason, you are probably dealing with fusarium wilt. I seem to lose at least one basil plant to this disease every single year. If this happens, replace the plant, and move on with your life.

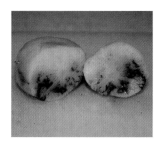

Fusarium.

Powdery mildew

Powdery mildew is probably the fungal disease I get asked about the most. It usually shows up in mid- to late summer, appearing as a milky-white or grey-white dusting of powder on leaves. It often looks as though the plant has been sprinkled with icing sugar. Powdery mildew does not kill a plant, but it can severely weaken it and it looks awful. Cool, wet conditions favour its spread. The best thing to do is try to prevent it. Good air circulation (meaning not crowding the plants) and not allowing water to sit on the leaves overnight will help. Plants that want full sun that are forced to live in partial or full shade often become mildewy.

Being aware of what plants are prone to powdery mildew can help keep it out of your garden. Many asters and goldenrods get mildew, as do several monardas, roses, and spireas. Although some people insist on trying to kill off mildew with fungicides such as copper sulphate or sulphur, there really isn't much point. Treat it the way you would blackspot, or remove the plant entirely. A few infected leaves here and there you can simply remove. A plant that is entirely coated with it can and should be yanked out. The exception to this is caraganas. Anyone who has a caragana hedge knows that by late summer, the leaves are often coated with powdery mildew. Not to worry, they leaf out again in the spring and everything's fine.

Powdery mildew.

Root rot

Root rot is what happens when plants stand in water for too long. Like you and I, plants need oxygen to breathe. Trees that stand in water for too long will drown. Root rot happens in planters that have no drain hole or very heavy, continually wet soils. It is often characterized by a bad smell.

Shoestring fungus

Shoestring fungus is a disease that primarily affects Amur cherries and mountain ash. Basically, it interferes with the tree's ability to take up water, and as a result large sections or branches of the tree die. It is 100 per cent fatal, but it often takes several years to kill the tree. It doesn't seem to matter whether the tree is old or young, but trees that have experienced chinook damage or sunscald seem more prone to infection.

∽ 6 ∽

Creepy crawlies

Anywhere you are in the world, a healthy garden will have insects. If there are no bugs at all in your garden, something has gone terribly wrong somewhere. Many people are afraid of insects, but this is unnecessary and means that you will miss out on the fascinating menagerie that will call your garden home.

Most insects are either benign or downright helpful. A few are problematic, but for the most part you need to adopt a "what the insects are doing is none of my business" attitude. Buying a good local field guide is an excellent way to help you learn to identify the insects in your yard, but the general rule is that if in doubt, leave it alone. The probability that the bug in question is one of the good guys is pretty high.

Opposite: Monarch butterfly.

This page: Lilacs are among the first shrubs to bloom and are excellent forage for honeybees.

A healthy garden must have a healthy bug population, so your goal is never going to be to eliminate bugs (even the bad bugs). The idea is to keep things from getting out of control.

Pesticides in your garden

You need to ban pesticides from your garden, and I mean it. Pesticides are indiscriminate and will kill *all* the bugs—both good and bad. Whether you use organic pesticides or not, the effect will be the same. What will kill the caterpillars eating your currant will also kill butterflies. Malathion, for instance, is exceptionally toxic to bees and fish. My advice is to control insects in your garden through good gardening techniques and encourage a healthy, balanced ecosystem. For the most part, if your system is healthy, the good bugs will take care of most of the bad bugs, and any stragglers are usually easy to deal with or ignore. If your plants are already healthy because you put the right plant in the right spot, a minor pest problem is really no problem.

I can honestly say that I have not used a pesticide in my garden in well over a decade. Very often an explosion of pests indicates poor growing conditions. For example, aphids prefer to feed on the newest growth (which is the softest) or on plants that are poor, weak, or stressed out. Aphids rarely attack healthy, happy plants in the prime of their life. When they do, their populations are generally kept in check by healthy populations of predators such as ladybugs. It takes time to achieve this balance in your garden, but eventually it will come. Using a pesticide always, *always* disturbs the balance! I am diligent about watching for pests. I will remove and squash caterpillars by hand. I will sometimes prune out or cut back plants that have been badly affected. And I have simply stopped growing a few plants that I know are pest-prone. For example, if you live near a canola field, you are going to have issues with flea beetles. You may want to avoid growing things that are in the cabbage family, which are the targets flea beetles are after.

Local bugs

Some of the bugs you will encounter in your garden include the following:

Ants

I'm not sure what the big hatred for ants is all about here, but for the most part you don't really need to worry about them. First of all, ants are diggers. They like warm, dry soil because that is where it is easiest to build their tunnels. This is why ants love south-facing slopes and locations beneath spruce trees—it's generally nice and dry there.

Ants *are* useful in the garden. In moderation, their digging actually helps to aerate the soil and allows much-needed oxygen to reach plant roots. It is only when their numbers get excessively high that things become problematic. Keeping your soil cool and moist will help to keep ant populations manageable. This means mulch. Mulch is almost always a brilliant idea.

When I lived in Saskatoon, I had a greenhouse with a dirt floor built on to the garage. This meant that by April, the ants were becoming a huge nuisance in my greenhouse. Not about to spray a chemical, I scoured the Internet for a solution. An organic gardener in Virginia told me that ants hate cinnamon. I thought that was worth a try, so I bought a bulk tub of cinnamon from the grocery store and cinnamoned the living bejeesus out of my greenhouse. The greenhouse smelled great, and the ant numbers dropped dramatically. They didn't disappear, but they definitely went down to manageable levels. Over the years, I have shared this information many times, and many people have told me that cinnamon was a very effective ant-deterrent in their gardens.

Another thing to be aware of is that if you notice ants very busy on any particular plant, it probably indicates an aphid infestation. Aphids, when physically stimulated, will secrete a drop of sugary liquid called honeydew. Ants love eating this and will actually "farm" the aphids. In exchange for giving them a free meal, the ants will defend the aphids from predators such as lacewings and ladybugs. If you see ants all over a plant, check for aphids and deal with the aphids, preferably with a garden hose.

I have been swarmed and repeatedly bitten by nasty little red ants, and so I do understand why some people try to get rid of them. If you know you have a big ant hill in a site where you need to do some work, give it a slow, deep soak for an hour or so before you have to work there. This usually sets the balance in your favour and you're less likely to be swarmed.

If you're still not convinced that ants are useful, it may interest you to know that there are several plants that can be pollinated by ants, though there are no known plants that are dependent upon them. Several sedums and the much-loved annual alyssum have both been observed to be occasionally ant-pollinated. There is also at least one species of dicentra (bleeding heart) whose seeds are dispersed by foraging ants.

Aphids

Also called plant lice, these small, soft-bodied insects usually appear in large numbers in a heat wave. Aphids do not cause huge amounts of damage in and of themselves, but they can weaken a plant and cause it to decline in vigour. They are a key link in the food chain, and every healthy garden will have them at some point. Hopefully, by the time they appear, you've also built up healthy populations of predators such as ladybugs and lacewings. The real issue with aphids is that they can transfer viral diseases and also attract ants and wasps. A strong, sharp stream of water from the hose can help to knock them from their perch, and like many pests, they favour weak or sick plants. It is more important to worry about control than elimination, which is true for many pests.

Black aphids.

Aphid damage on honeysuckle.

Honeybee.

Bumblebee.

Bees

It is terrifying but true that we live in a world where bees are in a great deal of danger. Bee populations have been steadily declining all around the world for a few decades, and this has been directly attributed to pesticide use. If these trends continue, it is possible that we will be living in a bee-free world as early as 2050. Alison Benjamin, a British scientist and beekeeper, is the author of the tremendously frightening book *A World Without Bees*, which I think everyone should read.

Why should we care about bees? Whether we realize it or not, we live in a bee-driven economy. Bees pollinate the crops that make our medicines and feed our livestock. They pollinate the cotton that makes our clothing. They pollinate 90 per cent of the food you buy at the grocery store—the only non-bee-pollinated crops of major commercial significance are corn and rice. Without bees, nothing would set fruit or produce seeds. In parts of southwest China, where pesticides have eliminated the bee populations, pollination of both apples and pears is being done by hand. It takes a person five to nine days to accomplish what a hive of bees could do in a few hours.

Plants that attract bees include: agastache; asters (fall); bee balm; borage; buffalo bean; cranesbill; echium; fruit trees, including apples, pears, plums, and cherries; giant impatiens; globe thistle; hollyhocks; joepye weed; lamb's ear; lavatera; lupines; nasturtium; phacelia; potentilla; Russian almond; Russian sage; roses (single-flowered); salvias (perennial); snapdragons; spirea; sunflowers

What can you as a gardener do to make the world a better place for bees? First, recognize their importance. Nobody wants to be stung by a bee, but it is absolutely essential that you have bees in your garden. Plant as much as you possibly can for them to forage in, and as with butterflies, it is crucial that you eliminate pesticides. It is especially important to eliminate Malathion, a pesticide that is horrifically toxic to them.

Bees forage best in warm, sheltered areas, so planting some shrubs to create a bit of windbreak is a good idea. Ideally, use shrubs they enjoy, such as single-flowered roses and potentilla or spirea, and plant seasonally. Many fruit trees provide an early and welcome source of nectar for foraging bees, and lots of perennials will flower well into October for them.

Bronze birch borer

A rather notorious insect across much of the prairies, the bronze birch borer is blamed for the deaths of hundreds of paper and weeping birches. What is often not mentioned is that this insect is native here and plays a key role in managing birch forests. The birch borer favours old, weak, and stressed trees. Many of the birch trees in all three prairie provinces were planted in the 1950s and 1960s, and in recent years many of them have approached the end of their life spans. Several successive years of drought in the nineties further stressed these trees. This provided a veritable buffet for bronze birch borers. The best thing to do is to prevent them; they dislike young, healthy trees. Plant birch in good soil and keep them well watered. An increasing number of cultivars, most of them coming from the University of North Dakota, are at least partially resistant to infection.

Butterflies, non-destructive

Gardening for butterflies is easy and rewarding. If you are planning a garden specifically for butterflies, you need a warm, sheltered area with lots of places for the butterflies to sun themselves, such as clumps of grasses and large, flat rocks. Butterflies are attracted to flat, fragrant flowers and feel most welcome when plants they like are planted in large groups. They also do not want a neatly manicured or immaculately groomed place to play; they like a messier sort of feel. Have you ever noticed that butterflies are very abundant in ditches and meadows but not so much in gardens? They need wide-open, wild-feeling spots where they can easily hide from predators if they need to, as well as find shelter in rough weather. Butterflies (and their offspring) are among the most sensitive of all creatures; if you want butterflies in your garden, eliminating pesticides is a *must*.

Use grasses and daylilies if you can, and try to create a "meadow" look. It is also important that you plant for the seasons and have things in bloom from spring through fall. Use a mix of annuals, perennials, trees, and shrubs. You may also want to find a place to create

Flowers that butterflies want include the following:
ageratum, allium, alyssum, asters, astilbe, bee balm, butterfly bush (*Buddleia*), delphinium, echinacea, goldenrod, heliotrope, joepye weed, liatris, lilac, lilies, marigolds (single-flowered), milkweed (*Asclepias*), phlox, roses (single-flowered), rudbeckia, sedum, shasta daisy, sunflowers, yarrow, zinnia

Butterfly puddling.

Spring-blooming flowers are important food sources for butterflies.

Tiger swallowtail butterfly.

a permanent "mud puddle," as butterflies like to suck minerals from wet sand or earth, a habit called "puddling." A few people go so far as to leave a few pieces of soft or rancid fruit in the garden, which will further entice butterflies. While providing butterflies with food (nectar) is easy, you should keep in mind that butterflies start out life as caterpillars and will need suitable host plants. Most butterflies are host-specific and will lay their eggs only on certain kinds of plants, so I've included suggestions for these below.

The prairies are home to a good many native butterflies, and some of them are extremely beautiful. My favourite butterflies that live here include the following:

Tiger swallowtail *(Papilio canadensis)*
This is a gorgeous black and yellow, rather large butterfly that is usually found along the edges of woodlands. It is a difficult butterfly to attract to a garden, as it favours places with large trees. Eggs are laid singly on birch, poplar, or apple. Their caterpillars are quite formidable-looking and have been known to cause some alarm.

White admiral *(Limenitis arthemis)*
This is a medium-sized, pretty butterfly with attractive, lacy white markings on dark wings. It is easily attracted to your garden. Birch, chokecherry, and willow are its most common host plants, but it is also known to lay eggs on apple, elm, hawthorn, linden trees, and saskatoon berry.

Milbert's tortoiseshell *(Aglais milberti)*
This beautiful butterfly is often one of the first attracted to a butterfly garden. It has a preference for wet areas and can most often be found in damp pastures, marshes, along hiking trails, and in ditches. It uses stinging nettle exclusively as the host plant for the caterpillar. Milbert's tortoiseshells are also well known for puddling in wet manure. It is a very quick butterfly, relying on its speed to escape from would-be predators.

Milbert's tortoiseshell.

Monarch caterpillar.

Monarch *(Danaus plexippus)* The monarch is the largest butterfly native to the prairies and easily recognized by its bright orange and black patterning. Monarchs are more common some years than others, and they are well known for being migratory. They overwinter in great numbers in coniferous forests in central Mexico. *Four Wings and a Prayer*, by biologist Sue Halpern, is an excellent and highly readable book if you want to learn more about them. Monarchs exclusively use milkweed as a food source for caterpillars, and several of these plants are quite garden-worthy. Conveniently, if you happen to live around Brooks, Medicine Hat, or Lethbridge, milkweed is fairly common. Look for them around coulees, in ditches, and on sunny slopes. Gathering seed is easy and is an excellent way to obtain this plant for your garden.

Mourning cloak *(Nymphalis antiopa)* Another butterfly of the woodlands and mountains, the mourning cloak appears to be almost brown in colour, but closer inspection reveals that it is actually a very

Monarch butterfly.

dark red with yellow and blue markings. Like the tiger swallowtails, these are butterflies of the woodlands, although they are more likely to make an appearance in the garden than the others. These are usually the first butterflies to awake from hibernation, and on rare occasions, they have even been seen on warm days in February! They lay several dozen eggs at a time, and the spiky red-brown caterpillars are quite fierce-looking. The caterpillars feed primarily on willow, but they will also use elm, poplar, or birch.

Cabbage butterfly

These white butterflies are very familiar to prairie gardeners, and they will feed on nearly any plant in the cabbage family. The caterpillars tend to feed on the undersides of the leaves at night. It is an introduced species that can destroy an entire crop in very short order. They are best protected against with floating row covers, which are available from most garden centres. These are cloths specially designed to cover a row of vegetables. They allow air, sunlight, and water to penetrate but not insects.

Cabbage looper damage.

Cabbage looper

While they do indeed feed on cabbages and their relatives, the cabbage looper feeds on a wide variety of other crops as well. They are bright green "inchworm"-type caterpillars but are rarely present in large enough numbers to be a big concern as they are much preyed upon by small birds and other foragers. The ones who survive become moths.

Columbine worm

Closely related to the currant worm (see below), the columbine worm is the larvae of a sawfly and the damage it can do is very similar to that done by the currant worm. Unlike the currant worm, however, this species is not native here but was introduced from Europe. Although columbines are the most common victims, plants with similar foliage (such as meadow rue) are also some-

Skeletonizers make short work of an alder leaf.

times affected. The columbine worm appears at the same time as the currant worm and can skeletonize a leaf or entire plant the minute your back is turned. Be on the watch for them and remove as necessary. Some people will cut back plants entirely and give them a shot of fertilizer to help encourage fresh growth. Healthy columbine usually come back pretty strongly.

Currant worm

The terms *worm* and *caterpillar* are often used interchangeably, but true caterpillars turn into butterflies or moths. The currant worm is actually a species of sawfly, and the larval stage closely resembles a true caterpillar. They are small, green chewers that eat the leaves of currants and gooseberries from the outside in. They are the exact same shade of green as the leaf, and they are difficult to observe unless you are watching for them. They will generally strip a currant or gooseberry of all its foliage overnight. They appear in early summer, and as they are so voracious, you must be very diligent watching for them. There is only one generation per year, and they are best controlled by hand-picking. A healthy currant or gooseberry will be able to survive this and will releaf.

Cutworm

There are dozens of different varieties of cutworm, which are the larvae of several kinds of moths. These are soft-bodied, rather delectable caterpillars that avoid predation by feeding at dusk and at night. They are usually found in the first 5 centimetres of the soil and are not specific in what they will devour. Any soft plant tissue will do, which is usually the roots or the point right when the stem and the roots meet. This can cause plants to mysteriously topple over and die almost overnight. Frequent tilling around plants helps to reduce their numbers yet may damage plant roots. Mulching will also help since cutworms prefer warm, dry soil over cool and moist. Encouraging birds to forage in your garden is good. If you live on a farm, chickens and guinea hens are especially good at scratching out cutworms. Bats will also feed on the night-flying adults.

Close up of cutworm damage.

Delphinium worm

The delphinium worm, a rather horrid little creature, is the larvae of the golden plusia moth. It feeds on delphiniums of all kinds, as well as larkspur and sometimes globe flower or monkshood. There is only one generation per year, which makes them somewhat easy to control. Adults emerge in late spring or early summer, usually right when the delphiniums are budding. Small green caterpillars that blend in beautifully chew the tips and leaves and can cause the whole plant to take on a ragged, shredded appearance with no buds. The caterpillars overwinter in the hollow stems and pupate in early spring, emerging in late spring or early summer as adults. Crush and squish them as you find them, and cut back delphinium in the fall, thereby eliminating the worms' wintering grounds.

Delphinium worm.

Dragonfly.

It is physically impossible to sneak up on dragonflies. They have excellent vision and can see forward, backward, sideways, up, and down simultaneously.

Dragonfly

Dragonflies, along with their close relatives the damselflies, are easily attracted to your garden if you provide just one thing for them … *water!* They are semi-aquatic (their larval stage remains underwater for up to two years). Dragonflies will essentially eat anything smaller than they are, with mosquitoes making up the bulk of their diet. In turn, they themselves provide food for birds, frogs, fish, and a variety of other creatures. Despite what you may have heard, dragonflies are completely harmless and will not bite you or threaten you in any way.

Fireflies

Few creatures are more ethereal than fireflies, but not many people know they exist all through the prairie provinces. Fireflies are actually a type of beetle, and an excellent guest to have in the garden since the non-flying larvae are 100 per cent carnivorous. They favour moist, cool places and generally feed on snails, slugs, and insects. Adults are omnivorous, but most of them are mysterious and difficult to study.

If you see fireflies on the prairies, it is almost always on warm, calm nights when the humidity is high, most often just before or after a rain, and generally between sunset and about 2 a.m. June and July are the most frequent times for sightings, but they can sometimes be seen in August as well if conditions suit them.

The truth is, it is quite difficult to lure fireflies to your garden. They seek fairly large areas with a significant abundance of tall grass to hide in, and our gardens are generally too bright for them. They want places that are very dark, so if you happen to have a farm or an acreage garden, you are more likely to attract these little creatures. If you have a secluded corner where you can let the grass grow long, and there will not be any light from porches or garden lamps, and there are perhaps some low, overhanging trees where the adults can find cool shelter during the day … you *might* attract some fireflies. Having them one year does not guarantee you will have them again. If you know of a place where they like to hang out, cherish it!

Flea beetle

Beetles are one of the most successful life forms on Earth; some are good for your garden and some are bad. Dozens and dozens of species of flea beetle exist, many commonly found in prairie gardens. They are tiny, about the size of a sesame seed, and have dark, metallic bodies. Although they can normally both walk and fly, they are great leapers, which is where the name comes from. Flea beetles feed on leaves, stems, and petals and are happiest in warm, dry weather. They have a preference for cruciferous plants (the cabbage family) and are particularly fond of mustard and canola. They tend to travel in large groups, feed, and quickly move on. Flea beetles are very difficult to control but generally don't stay very long.

Ground beetle

Ground beetles are large, fairly common beetles that are primarily active at night. If you move a large flowerpot, you may see them scurrying away to avoid the light. They are often (but not always) shiny, handsome things that are dark brown or black and can be found setting up shop in compost heaps, under rocks, beneath logs, and so on. At night they emerge to hunt, and they are extremely effective killing machines. Ground beetles are fast-moving for a large insect and have voracious appetites. You want them in your garden. They will devour endless quantities of snails, slugs, caterpillars, crickets, grasshoppers, and really anything they can find. Ground beetles can be encouraged in your garden by using wood mulches and lots of compost—they favour cool, moist places. They are often more common in shady, well-watered parts of the garden than they are in hot, dry places. Although they have wings, they are clumsy flyers and prefer to travel on foot if they can.

Hoverfly

Hoverflies are small insects that hover on wings moving so quickly that they appear to hang motionless in the air. Like hunting wasps, they feed on nectar and protein and favour umbelliferous flowers such as dill and coriander for their sugar needs. Hoverflies feed on anything smaller than they are, and do great service for the gardener!

Japanese lily beetle

The lily beetle first showed up in Alberta in 2007 and is believed to have come into the province with lily bulbs that were shipped (legally) from Holland. Although lily beetles have traditionally been a problem only in warmer climates, Alberta's winters have not been harsh enough over the last decade to kill them off. They are voracious devourers of lilies and occasionally other plants in the lily family as well, such as fritillaries. They are attractive red and black insects that should be

Ladybug larvae.

Ladybug visiting hawthorn flowers.

picked by hand. A few "good" beetles resemble them, so if in doubt, trap some in a jar and have them identified by insect experts at the zoo, a horticultural society, members of the horticultural department at the university, the parks department, a reputable garden centre, or gardening friend. Keep in mind that Japanese lily beetles are excellent fliers, and you need to be really diligent about monitoring for them.

Ladybug

Most people are familiar with ladybugs, which are insatiable predators of aphids, though they will eat other soft-bodied insects as well. Red and black are "warning" colours in nature, and birds prefer not to eat them. Ladybugs release a foul-smelling defensive fluid from their joints when harassed. Their larvae are especially voracious predators and look more like tiny black alligators than they do adult ladybugs. Both the larvae and adult beetle are very sensitive to pesticides, so if you want ladybugs in your garden, you will have to act accordingly. Adults overwinter primarily in leaf litter, and unless you absolutely can't bear it, don't rake away fallen leaves until it has warmed up in the spring. The ladybugs will thank you.

You can now purchase ladybugs, and in my opinion, this is mostly not worth your time or money. Ladybugs are best released early in the morning or late in the evening, and most of them will not care that there might be a few aphids in your garden. Ladybugs want there to be *thousands* of aphids, as they are looking to start families and want to be sure of a food source. A caragana shelterbelt teeming with aphids is appealing to a ladybug; one infected plant in your garden is not. As there are many different species of ladybug, if you *do* decide to purchase some, make absolutely certain they are a species that is native to your part of the country.

Lacewing

Lacewings are great hunters of aphids, scale, and a variety of soft-bodied insects. They are usually green in colour with large, lacy-looking green wings. Though lacewings look delicate, they are actually quite resilient.

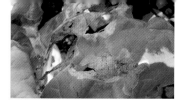

Beet leaf miner on swiss chard.

Telltale railroad tracks indicating a leaf miner as the culprit.

They are not often observed, but they are definitely a gardener's friend.

Leaf miner

Leaf miners are the larvae of yet another kind of sawfly, and they are generally host-specific. The larvae feed on the tissue inside a leaf and leave telltale "railroad tracks" or unsightly, dehydrated-looking patches across

Leaf folders at work.

the leaf surface. They are very difficult to control. The best thing to do is to remove and destroy the infected foliage, and just keep plants as healthy as you can. Be diligent and try to remove the larvae before they become an issue.

Leaf rollers and leaf folders

Leaf rollers and leaf folders are very common, and there are many kinds of them. They are particularly common on ash and aspen, but they can affect almost any tree. The adults are smallish moths that overwinter in bark crevices on trees. They emerge in the spring and lay eggs that hatch into small caterpillars, and generally they go unnoticed. However, when it comes time to pupate, they roll themselves up in a leaf and soon emerge as adults. The problem with leaf rollers is that by the time you notice them, they have probably already left! The leaves stay rolled up long after the insect has departed, which is unsightly. A healthy tree can withstand a leaf roller infection with little problem.

Sphinx moth

While it is true that most moths are not that pleasant to look at, a few kinds are worth attracting and some are quite beautiful. Most notable is the sphinx moth, also known as the hummingbird moth or the hawk moth. This is a day-flying moth of which there are many species, in several different genera. It ranges from small to quite large and will hover at flowers and feed on nectar in the same way as a hummingbird. Its long tongue resembles a beak and gives the moth an even more bird-like nature. Although sphinx moths are most active at dawn and at dusk, they can be seen at any hour of the day.

They start out life as immense, muscular green caterpillars known as hornworms, and although they are quite scary-looking, they are harmless. Sphinx moths are a delight to watch (they look just like hummingbirds with antennae) and also play a role in pollination. Flowers that attract them include bee balm, columbine, cranesbill, fireweed, fuchsia, heliotrope, hesperis, lilac, lupines, petunias, and sweet peas.

Root maggot

Root maggots are the larvae of a small species of fly. Though they can affect other plants, they feed primarily on the roots of radishes and turnips. Adult flies lay their eggs in the soil near the plants, and the larvae quickly chew through the roots of host plants, ruining their quality. They will pupate in the soil and emerge as adult flies. Plants are best protected with floating row covers.

Snails and slugs

Although they are not, of course, true insects, snails and slugs are an increasing problem in prairie gardens. These creatures favour cool, moist locations and are very sensitive to light. They will emerge at dusk or on rainy days to feed on the soft tissue of plants. They are ravenous eaters, chewing immense ugly holes in leaves, and can destroy a fern or hosta in a matter of hours. They also leave behind a telltale trail of slime that serves as a "chemical map" for other slugs and snails. Slugs and snails are important food for a variety of small creatures, including toads, salamanders, frogs, birds, and insects. Because they are slow-moving, they are easily controlled by hand-picking. This, however, is time-consuming and needs to be done frequently. It is often simpler to lay out a piece of untreated lumber, bread, or citrus peelings on the soil for the slugs and snails to hide under. Flip these over in the morning and step on whatever had the nerve to threaten your plants!

Slug.

Spiders

Spiders are the gardener's friend in every sense of the word. They create magnificent webs (free art) and eat more insects than almost any other creature. A true spider will never, ever eat your plants. They are 100 per cent carnivorous in all species. Spiders are usually nocturnal and will eat almost anything they can catch in their webs. If you have a large number of spiders, what it really means is that you have a large number of insects since they only appear in large numbers where prey is numerous.

Black widow spider

In Canada, only two species of spider are poisonous: the black widow and the brown recluse, and only the black widow is found in the chinook zone. Black widows favour out-of-the-way, dark, enclosed spaces. You are highly unlikely to find one in your garden, but since they are defensive biters, leave them alone if you do. Even if by some wild stroke of misfortune you were bitten by one, the chances of you actually dying are very small. Don't be afraid of spiders and don't discourage them!

WASPS

It may seem strange to want to attract wasps to your garden, but did you know there are many different kinds? Not only the hornets and yellow jackets with which we are so familiar but also a variety of parasitic and hunting wasps do great service in your garden. Even the familiar paper wasp will help to rid your garden of unwanted caterpillars and various chewing insects. Hunting wasps, along with their close relatives the hoverflies, spend their day seeking out food for themselves and their young. In most cases, that food is anything smaller than they are. Some are prey-specific and will find a suitable insect and lay an egg (or eggs) upon the hapless creature. When the eggs hatch, the wasp grubs will feed on the still-living insect. This is gruesome but effective. In other cases, the wasp will merely gobble up the intended victim.

In addition to needing the protein insects provide, wasps need sugar. This sugar comes from nectar, and many kinds of umbelliferous plants provide this for them. This means angelica, coriander, cow parsnip, dill, lovage, Queen Anne's lace, and all other plants in the carrot family. Long, slender hunting wasps are often dark in colour.

Paper wasp nest.

While you should ignore wasps flying in the garden, no one wants them nesting on the deck or in the hedges. Grey fabric bags that mimic nests can be purchased and placed in potentially problematic areas. Since wasps are territorial, this discourages other wasps from setting up shop. If at all possible, try to live in peace with them.

⋙ 7 ⋘

Gardening with animals

As gardeners, we must recognize that our gardening does *not only affect ourselves*. A garden, although unnatural in many ways, can and does have an effect on the environment. Creatures small and large will take up residence in your yard and garden, whether you will them to do so or not. You can take steps to ensure that your garden is a hospitable refuge and place of sanctuary for the small, fragile little beings that you want to attract. In addition to these beautiful creatures, we will also look at ways to reduce your encounters with the beasts you don't want.

Opposite: Fences can be beautiful and are often the simplest fix to your large animal issues.
This page: Birds are usually a welcome addition to gardens.

You are not Snow White!

The first thing we have to do when dealing with unwanted animals in our gardens and living space is to stop "humanizing" them. Not all pests that appear in your garden are going to be insects. In recent years, deer, jackrabbits, squirrels, and even elk and moose have become increasing problems in urban gardens. There is no room for romantic notions or sentimentality here. An animal in your garden is a potential threat to your family since they can carry ticks and diseases. It can also be a threat to your pets; for example, if deer are rutting or are protecting a fawn, they will attack dogs. Since unwanted wildlife will also eat all of your vegetation, they are a threat to your finances as well; greenhouses and nurseries are certainly not giving their products away!

It is time we took some responsibility for our actions. Animals are excellent at adapting to new situations when they have to, and deer and rabbits are learning to live in our cities and towns very comfortably. We have eliminated all their known threats, we have provided a steady food supply, and we have offered them no other option of where to set up house.

Local animals

Some of the wildlife you're likely to encounter in your garden may include the following:

Amphibians

Amphibians are fabulous in a garden! Salamanders, frogs, and toads, by virtue of the fact that they are amphibians, need to be reasonably near to a water source. In exchange for the happy home you provide them, they will patrol your garden for insects.

Salamander.

Salamanders

Salamanders are nocturnal but will venture out on warm summer nights, usually after a good rain, to hunt for insects, grubs, and beetles. They are charming and completely harmless. I remember a colleague telling me of a student in her class who went into great detail about how she "poured salt" on salamanders and tried to "sweep them to the road with a rake." My colleague was appalled, and so were the other students in the class. Cruelty to animals, whether they are warm- or cold-blooded, is not acceptable. If you don't want wild creatures living in your yard, you don't really want a garden. You can't have a sanitized, bug- and creature-free garden and have beautiful flowers and plants at the same time. As for this woman pouring salt on salamanders, I believe in karma, and some day she just might too.

Frog.

Frogs and toads

Frogs and toads, like songbirds, will charm you with their singing in the spring. Both will often take up residence in a garden. Both like moisture and are largely nocturnal. They will feed on an infinite number of insects, and toads are especially fond of eating slugs, so encourage frogs and toads to live in your garden. They are highly sensitive to chemicals, so that's just one more reason there are no pesticides or herbicides allowed! A dark, moist place where they can hide during the day is also helpful. "Toad huts" are available from garden centres, but it's easy to make your own out of a shallow, partially broken clay pot. Just turn it upside down and bury the rim. As long as there is a place where the toad can go in and out, your toad(s) will be happy.

Bats

You may not want bats in your attic, but you definitely want them in your garden. Why? Well, for one thing, watching bats emerge at dusk to feed is really quite magical. If you've never experienced it, I encourage you to do so. Second, bats will devour huge quantities of insects every night, notably mosquitoes and many of the night-flying moths whose offspring cause us issues—cutworms being an excellent example. Bats can often be found near water sources because water attracts insects. Bats are surprisingly clean creatures, and although much is made of the fact that they can carry rabies, their infection rate is no higher than that of coyotes or foxes. That being said, if you should ever find a bat that appears to be sick or injured, it is best not to touch it. If you don't happen to have an old, dead hollow tree in your yard, the best way to attract bats is to put up a bat box. These are available at most places that sell birdseed and birdfeeders, and you simply mount them on the side of a building or a nice big tree. Be patient; bat boxes are known to sit empty for several seasons before bats will move into them, but once they do, they will use them for years.

Birds

A lot of people hate birds. People often say to me with great hostility, "I don't want anything that attracts birds!" A prevailing belief among some people is that if you have birds in your garden, it is the equivalent of a chicken farm, with bird droppings hither and yon, all over the freshly washed car, all over the fence, all over the sidewalk, and it's going to be impossible to be outside without being pooped upon or dive-bombed. Unless you have a gaggle of geese back there, this is usually not case.

Birds give a garden *life*! Birdsong is a critical element to enjoying the garden. It is soothing and beautiful, adding a cadence and vitality to a garden that is missing otherwise. Learning to differentiate among birdsongs can further enhance your gardening experience. Buy a good field guide to birds of your area and take it with you on the bus or read it on your coffee break at work; it is an excellent way to spend your time. It's easy to become a bird watcher—birds are lovely souls and they do an invaluable service in the garden. Martins and swallows are not only pretty but also wonderful to watch—they do enormous work keeping the mosquito population down.

Many strategies will attract birds, but your primary goal is to cater to the needs of the birds you want. Birds feed at different levels, so it is important to have plants of varying sizes. Try to have some shrubbery for shelter and protection from the wind as well as an easy hiding spot. The feeling of safety is critical for birds to be comfortable enough to forage and nest. Spiny things like sea buckthorn, hawthorn, and roses make excellent nesting places for birds because these plants offer them safety from predators. A water source such as a pond or birdbath is also critical—a garden with a water feature will attract infinitely more birds than one without it.

Birds are drawn to the food and shelter conifers provide.

Birds are often more effective than pesticides at ridding the garden of unwanted insects and weed seeds.

Conifers such as spruce and pine are also excellent. In addition to being evergreen and providing shelter from the wind and invaluable nesting habitat, they produce cones that provide a rich abundance of nutrient-filled seeds. Cedar, fir, juniper, pine, and spruce are magnets for birds of all kinds.

To attract seed-eating birds, try plants such as purple coneflower (*Echinacea* sp.), globe thistle, and bee balm (*Monarda* sp.). Goldfinches in particular are fond of seeds. Sunflowers and safflower are also excellent choices. Ornamental grasses, particularly some of the annual varieties, will produce lots of seeds for birds as well as provide winter interest. Canaryseed, hair grass (*Deschampsia* sp.), millet, panic grass (*Panicum* sp.), and sorghum are all excellent for providing a food source for hungry birds.

For fruit-eating birds, you have an almost infinite number of choices. Some excellent fruit-producing trees and shrubs that you might like to try include buffaloberry, chokecherry, cotoneaster, cranberry, hawthorn, honeyberry, mountain ash, Nanking cherry, nannyberry, prensepia, saskatoon berry, and sea buckthorn.

Since this is not an ornithology book, I can give only the briefest of overviews regarding birds, including:

Ducks

Most birds are great, but you really don't want ducks in your garden. Both ducks and geese are very messy and quick to sully everything, especially if you have a water feature. I would discourage them from nesting in your garden or being in your yard at all. If you have been to Wascana Park in Regina or Prince's Island Park in Calgary, you know just how foul fowl can be. Every square centimetre of these parks is covered in goose and duck poo. Ducks and geese do not belong in your garden, so don't let them feel at home.

Great blue herons

If you have a pond in your garden, great blue herons may also make an occasional appearance. Herons are so elegant and deliberate in their movements that it is easy to forget they are predators. While small fish and frogs make up the majority of their diet, they will eat anything they think they can swallow. There are some incredible videos online of herons eating baby ducks, but I don't expect anyone to find this is as fascinating as I do.

Hummingbirds

No gardener ever forgets the thrill of seeing his or her first humming-bird! Plenty of myths and misconceptions surround hummingbirds, but there are a few important things to know. Three species of hummingbird are found in the prairie provinces. The ruby-throated is the most common, but the rufous can be regularly found here as well. The calliope hummingbird is an occasional visitor. Hummingbirds are very tiny, very quick, and spend more time perching than they do feeding. Hummingbirds are scrupulously clean, and when they are not feeding, they spend most of their time either preening or watching for other hummingbirds. They generally arrive here in mid-April to early May and depart for warmer climates around the second week of September.

Hanging out a hummingbird feeder is a good idea, but the solution needs to be changed daily or it will spoil. It also needs to be hung in a very sheltered area; otherwise the solution will slosh out and attract wasps. Hummingbirds should only be fed sugar water—do not give them carbonated drinks, artificial sweeteners or honey or anything else. One cup of sugar to four parts water is the correct ratio. Do not put red food colouring in the water as this has been found to cause kidney issues for them.

Hummingbirds are curious and brave little birds and are not intimidated by hawks, humans, or anything else for that matter. They are extremely aggressive toward other hummingbirds, as well as any other bird that enters their territory. While reds, oranges, and bright colours seem to be a major attractant for them, anyone who watches hummingbirds for any length of time knows that they will investigate most flowers of most shapes. They do not instinctively know which flowers will yield the most nectar, and studies have shown that they learn from experience. Bright, tubular-shaped flowers often yield the most nectar, and these tend to be what they go for first.

Hummingbirds make more effective pollinators than insects in many cases because being warm-blooded means that they can be actively pollinating in temperatures that are too cold for bees or butterflies. If you want hummingbirds in your garden, you will need plenty of places for them to perch and "survey." Planting lots of red, orange, yellow, and pink flowers will get their attention. If they like what they find, they will often stay.

They are also most active at sunrise, and this is frequently the best time to observe them. Always choose single- rather than double-flowered varieties when gardening for hummingbirds—double-flowered varieties rarely produce nectar. Hollyhocks and fuchsias are good examples.

Hummingbirds also love bathing and will often use a sprinkler to wash in. In addition to being charming to watch and providing a valuable pollination service, hummingbirds eat a wide variety of tiny insects, even being known to pilfer them from spiderwebs!

Flowers that attract hummingbirds include the following: agastache, apples, bee balm, bleeding heart, cherries, cleome, columbine, coral bells, daylilies, delphinium, fuchsia, hibiscus, hollyhock, honeysuckle, lilac, lilies, nasturtium, nicotiana, passionflower, penstemon, petunia, pulmonaria, salpiglossus, salvia, scarlet runner bean, tithonia, weigela, and zinnia (single-flowered varieties)

Hummingbird.

Owls

The great horned owl happens to be Alberta's provincial bird and is the only predator that routinely takes down skunks. These birds are to be encouraged, and if one should take up residence in your neighbourhood, consider yourself lucky.

Raptors

Raptors (birds of prey) are also of immense importance. It might surprise you to know that large birds of prey are adapting to living in cities easily. Peregrine falcons nest on buildings in downtown Calgary, where they feed primarily on pigeons. Hawks are also becoming more commonplace. These often-maligned birds play a vital role. While they will eat some songbirds if the opportunity comes up, they will also eat gophers, mice, voles, and other small creatures that are otherwise difficult to remove from your garden.

Songbirds

Songbirds include chickadees, crossbills, finches, grosbeaks, nuthatches, orioles, robins, warblers, waxwings, wrens, and so on. Songbirds can either be seed eaters, as is the case with finches; insect eaters such as wrens; or fruit eaters, as is the case with waxwings. These birds have charming, lovely little songs. If you don't want songbirds eating your fruit, buying some bird netting is a good idea. Cedar waxwings, while handsome and charming, will obliterate a crop of saskatoon berries pretty quickly.

Woodpeckers

Woodpeckers are another important bird because they eat immense quantities of insects. Their drumming on tree trunks is distinctive but rarely damages a tree. Of all the species of woodpeckers in North America, the only ones that can actually cause any real tree damage are sapsuckers. You can tell if you're dealing with a sapsucker by the distinctive circular pattern of holes it drills as it works its way around a tree trunk. Sapsuckers

Orioles love oranges!

Sapsucker.

Sapsucker injury.

seem especially fond of birch and alder. The rest of the woodpeckers out there are actually helping you by feeding on often-problematic insects.

Deer

Deer are becoming an especially bothersome creature. The first rule of warfare is "know your enemy." The deer in question is almost always the white-tailed deer (*Odocoileus virginianus*). This deer is the official animal of Saskatchewan and ranges throughout North America.

In addition to the wildlife dangers mentioned at the beginning of this chapter, recognize that the average deer consumes 4.5 kilograms of vegetation in a single day. Deer can also be very destructive when they are rubbing velvet off their antlers—they have been known to completely devastate trees and shrubs by scraping off all of the bark! To make matters worse, these "rubs" are scented with a rich assortment of pheromones, encouraging other deer to use the same tree.

Deer are also very social, so it's not unusual to have a herd of deer roam through your neighbourhood and destroy everything in their path. Even if you only see one, it is safe to assume its herd is nearby. Deer are spreading through our cities at an alarming rate—it is estimated that there are between 300 and 400 deer now living within city limits in Winnipeg and 400 to 500 deer living in Ottawa. Estimates have not been done in other Canadian cities, but they are definitely on the rise in Saskatoon, Regina, Edmonton, Calgary, Medicine Hat, Lethbridge, Brandon, Vancouver, Victoria, and even Toronto and Montreal.

Deer antler damage.

Unlike rabbits (which have a clean bite), deer lack upper incisors. They will grasp tender new growth or branches in their mouth and tear them away from the plant in a single, swift jerking motion. Deer positively love to devour annuals (which are tender and succulent) and new growth on trees and shrubs, but they will also eat almost any other perennial, vegetable, legume, shoot, leaf, bark, acorn, grass, fruit, berry, or even birdseed they encounter. No matter where you live in Canada, roses and hostas seem to be a much-loved deer delicacy. These plants are often expensive, and I think that the deer instinctively sense this.

Deer have very occasionally been known to eat meat—one was observed in the United States plucking a small bird off its nest and eating it, then eating the nest! A deer killed in Ontario was found to have the remains of a mouse in its stomach, which no one could really explain.

Deer find hosta delicious, especially expensive hosta.

Deer are very much creatures of routine and habit, and if they find your yard hospitable, they will return again and again. The first thing you must do, before deer *ever* get to be a problem in your yard, is to make your yard unwelcoming to them. Every time you see a deer in your yard, you must give the deer some indication that you are a threat. Spray it with the hose if you have to!

Gardeners will often say the best way to keep deer out of the garden is by having a dog. There is some truth to this, but be wary. The scent of dog droppings or urine is not enough to shoo away deer; nor is the presence of a dog in the yard enough. The deer must believe that the dog is truly a threat to its safety. If the dog angrily barks at deer and aggressively chases them out of the yard, the deer will learn to associate danger with *that* dog—but not necessarily with dogs in general. If a deer feels cornered, is rutting, or is protecting young, they may not run even if they are chased. In fact, they may lower their antlers or kick at the dog.

Build it and they won't come.

The only sure-fire, guaranteed, environmentally friendly way to keep deer out of your garden is to build a fence that is more than 2 metres tall. This is not an ideal or feasible solution in most gardens, but it really is the only way to keep them out. Many gardeners become so exasperated trying other methods that they finally realize it's cheaper and less stressful to simply build a fence. I'm willing to bet most of them wish they'd done it sooner. Since fences can cast shade and be undesirable in some areas, some gardeners may discreetly use electric fencing. If deer know the fence is there and don't simply leap over it, this is effective (but ensure it is legal in your area before you install one).

Deer repellants

If a barrier isn't an option, maybe a deer repellant is. Deer repellants are generally grouped into two categories: physical or chemical. Physical deterrents include lights, sprinklers, and noisemakers, while chemical deterrents are just that, usually a spray or powder that repels by scent. Most of these scent-based chemicals use blood, urine, or hot pepper.

PHYSICAL REPELLANTS

Noisemakers are readily found in stores and are pushed as being eco-friendly and highly effective when, really, this is only partly true. People will often tie pie pans or metal cans together and hang them in the trees as homemade noisemakers. This does not bother deer in the least, and it is also unattractive. Gas-propelled noise devices are frequently expensive. Motion-activated ultrasonic noisemakers are also available. These make a sound at a pitch too high for human ears to hear but detectable by deer.

Noisemakers are best in rural rather than urban settings—in many cities, they may violate noise bylaws.

Deer are highly adaptable and quick-witted, so they will quickly become accustomed to an unusual sound if they determine that it is no harm to them. These devices are most effective when used for short-term protection from deer rather than for long-term and if they are used with another deterrent such as a chemical or motion sprayer. Regardless, any deterrents should be put into place before the deer do serious damage. If they know your garden holds tasty treats, deer are willing to risk considerable safety to pillage it.

Visual deterrents for deer are often made of Mylar, which is a highly reflective and shiny plastic material that makes a peculiar buzzing noise as the wind moves over it. Mylar ribbons, streamers, and "scare eye" balloons are often recommended for deer repelling. Like noises, deer can easily become accustomed to these, and they may work longer if they are frequently moved around the garden.

Motion-activated sprinklers detect when deer (or humans) step into a certain parameter, and they emit a quick, sharp burst of water in the direction of the movement. This can be quite effective at deterring deer, but deer are also smart enough to figure out that after the initial burst, they are undetectable if they stand still, so it's often not enough to keep them from eating your plants.

CHEMICAL REPELLANTS

Those who know me understand how reluctant I am to use chemicals in most situations (the exception being fertilizers). Many gardeners will hang bars of soap or dryer sheets from trees, branches, and twigs in hopes that the unfamiliar scent will deter deer. Deer will simply eat around your soap. Many a hairdresser has tried using human hair as a deer deterrent, as well as for rabbits, and found it effective for a few hours at best.

Perhaps the most common means of trying to deter deer and rabbits is bloodmeal. This needs to stop, and stop immediately! People seem to forget that bloodmeal is a *fertilizer*, and any time you use a product for something other than its intended use, you are asking for trouble. Bloodmeal is a by-product of the meat industry and is essentially dry, powdered blood. It is very high in nitrogen and has a distinctive odour. It breaks down quickly in the garden and is an excellent fertilizer for evergreens, lawns, and vegetable gardens ... when used in moderation. The scent of bloodmeal is a deterrent to most foraging animals, but because it begins to degrade extremely quickly, particularly in wet or rainy conditions, it is effective for only a few hours to a few days. Gardeners are throwing this into their flowerbeds several times a week, and plants are not doing what they should be doing as a result. Stay away from bloodmeal as a pest-deterrent; it's not going to be effective in the long term and it's going to affect your garden negatively.

Cayenne pepper is the herbivore version of pepper spray, and many gardeners liberally sprinkle cayenne, paprika, or chili powder all through the garden and on the plants they don't want eaten. While studies show that this can be effective in the short term, cayenne breaks down rapidly in the garden. Several name-brand products use capsaicin, the active component of peppers that makes them "hot," to deter browsing animals. One such product is Critter Ridder, which claims to be effective for up to 30 days and be both earth- and animal-friendly. I would advise caution with this, but it is available for you to use. Ingesting a mouthful of cayenne is painful for both deer and rabbits. While I do not want them in my garden, I do not believe in being cruel to them either.

Perhaps the best known and most widely tested product for getting rid of deer is PlantSkydd, which was developed in Sweden by a team of scientists who found a way to sterilize and pulverize dried blood. PlantSkydd is a combination of this, mixed with water, and uses vegetable oil as a binding agent. It has to be applied when temperatures are above freezing and the plants are dry, but it will set as rain-proof in 12 to 16 hours. Deer and other animals smell this stuff and believe that a predator is in the area and a kill has taken place. When you spray, it comes out red. To be effective, spray till the tree or shrub you are protecting also appears red. The colour fades and eventually disappears after a few hours, and it will be effective for several months.

Studies have shown that PlantSkydd works best when used in combination with other deer deterrents, but it *is* effective. It also works against jackrabbits.

DEER-PROOF PLANTS DON'T EXIST.

Many people try to plant "deer-proof" plants that are unpalatable to deer, in hopes that deer will browse elsewhere. Lists and lists of plants that deer won't eat are showing up in gardening magazines and books more and more all the time. The problem is that deer are not reading these lists. It is *very* hard to find plants that deer won't eat because what deer will eat this year they may not eat next year or what deer refuse to eat in Ontario might be a delicacy to deer in Alberta. Plants that they eat in the spring they may refuse to touch in the fall. Sometimes they will leave the flowers of a plant and eat only the foliage or vice versa. Sometimes they will eat a plant in its juvenile stage but refuse to eat an established or mature specimen. Sometimes they will eat only the bark, leaving the rest of the plant alone. And if all else fails, the deer will trample your "deer-proof" plants on their way to something that they do like to eat.

The following list includes the most *consistently* deer-resistant plants you can put in your garden. Deer will *generally* leave these things alone, but again, this is not a hard-and-fast rule. Deer will usually avoid anything that is very hairy or bristly as well as anything very strongly aromatic. Lamb's ears and pulmonaria are good examples of hairy or bristly plants, and deer usually ignore them. For some reason, thorns are *not* a deterrent, and deer will very happily eat roses and barberries right down to the ground. Deer very rarely touch highly scented plants such as yarrow and herbs like rosemary, which is understandable since strong scents are usually a warning in nature. Deer dislike juniper, but they will eat it if nothing else is available. Just keep in mind that if a plant is labelled deer-resistant, it usually means they will take a few bites and move on rather than eat it in its entirety.

Deer-Resistant Annuals: borage, castor bean, cleome, datura, dusty miller, gazania, geranium, most herbs (this includes rosemary, basil, oregano, thyme, dill, mint, etc.), lantana, marigold, morning glory, tithonia, verbena, vinca

Deer-Resistant Perennials: allium, artemesia, bleeding heart, catmint, columbine, foxglove, daffodil, fritillaries, iris, lamb's ear, lamium, lily of the valley, monarda, monkshood, pulmonaria, rue, Russian sage, sedum, wild indigo, yarrow, yucca

Deer-Resistant Trees and Shrubs: caragana, forsythia, honey locust, juniper, lilac, mock orange, Russian olive, sea buckthorn

Get Off My Garden is a well-known product whose active component is methyl-nonyl ketone, a naturally occurring element that can be found in trace amounts in cloves, ginger, bananas, rue, guavas, and a few other plants. It is manufactured synthetically now and used primarily to train cats and dogs not to defecate in the garden. It is an oily, extremely unpleasant-smelling substance that is available as a gel, spray, or liquid. It is sometimes used to try to confuse deer and rabbits, but as a general rule, it doesn't work against them.

Increasingly, animal urine and urine-based products are being used to try to deter deer. Coyote "urine pellets" are starting to show up in garden centres. How effective these are I cannot say, only that they are increasingly on offer.

A quick scouring of the Internet provides endless entertainment in the form of homemade deer-repellent recipes. All of these recipes are pretty loony. Don't try them—they are a waste of both time and ingredients, and many of them are messy, smelly, and will actually attract creatures. When it comes to deer in the garden, the bottom line is skip the repellants and build a fence.

Jackrabbits

Meet our next enemy, the jackrabbit, or better known as the hare. Jackrabbits are much smaller than deer and are therefore able to hide better. They take quick, sharp, clean bites and will eat a plant right to the ground, whereas deer tend to strip things and browse as they go. Jackrabbits also multiply much faster than deer, and since we've removed all of their natural predators, they will grow from a minor nuisance to a huge problem in as little as a few weeks.

There are now both rabbits and jackrabbits in our cities, and you need to know the difference. Rabbits are generally small and cute. They almost always live in burrows and give birth underground to blind, hairless, helpless babies. Since they are quite shy, they are not generally a problem in most Canadian gardens. Canmore and Victoria are two Canadian cities that are exceptions to this.

Rabbits have forty-four chromosomes, while jackrabbits have forty-eight. They do not interbreed. Jackrabbits are becoming a huge, *huge* problem right across the prairies, but they are still a relatively *new* problem. You will not find any products on the shelf specifically to deter them, but that is changing. They are considerably larger than rabbits, with longer ears, much larger feet, and grotesque, bulging eyes and immense teeth. Look closely at a jackrabbit as it destroys your garden, and you'll see what I mean. I counted no fewer than eleven jackrabbits sitting in the parking lot of the Calgary airport one frosty winter morning, and all I could think of was the film *Donnie Darko*. Jackrabbits are infinitely creepier and scarier after having watched it!

Rabbits, often affectionately known as "bunnies," do not wreak the kind of havoc in urban gardens that jackrabbits do. Jackrabbits have insatiable appetites, yet they never eat weeds, dandelions, or aggressive or invasive plants. They *do* eat expensive heuchera, rare daylilies, and mail-order poppies, including *Meconopsis* sp. Thorns and spines do not deter them. Roses will be eaten right to the ground. Lilacs and young trees will have their bark stripped off down to the core, thereby killing the tree. Jackrabbits are extremely destructive and generally rely on their excellent hiding abilities and great speed to escape danger. They are powerful runners and leapers and can reach speeds of up to 70 kilometres per hour!

Although they can be active at any time of the day, jackrabbits are mostly nocturnal, waiting until you are asleep to eat everything in your yard. Unlike rabbits, jackrabbits give birth to young that are fully furred and have open eyes. They can follow their mother around within only an hour or two of being born. They do not tunnel or burrow, preferring instead to seek refuge under low-lying shrubs such as junipers or in tall grass. Although jackrabbits are considered edible and the pioneers did eat them, they are not worth much as a survival food as they have little body fat. Jackrabbits are well adapted to both freezing and arid environments, and are learning to live very comfortably in our urban settings.

Like deer, you have to make rabbits and jackrabbits feel unwelcome in your garden. Rushing at them with a stick, a broom, or the hose and actively chasing them from your garden is necessary. You have to be alert and watch for signs that they have been around, which usually comes in the form of severely decapitated plants along with a large pile of droppings as further insult.

Most of what I have said about deer is applicable to rabbits and jackrabbits, but there are differences. A fence that keeps deer out will not necessarily keep out a jackrabbit. Many of the repellents that work for deer will also work for rabbits. The list of "deer-resistant" plants can also be applied to rabbits but in a more limited way. Rabbits and jackrabbits are far less choosy than are deer and will eat most anything you have on offer. Since they are generally confident that they can escape, rabbits and jackrabbits are also much less intimidated by dogs than deer are.

Mice
Many people are afraid of mice, and this fear is not entirely unfounded. Ask anyone who ever had a mouse run up a pant leg while hauling

bales. Mice are primarily problems in gardens in the fall and winter; it is unusual that mice will trouble you in the spring and summer months. You don't want mice in your garden for the same reason you don't want deer or rabbits—not only are they destructive, but they can also carry a wide range of bacteria and diseases, including the often-fatal hantavirus.

Voles girdled the base of this tree.

The country mouse or field mouse is more accurately called the vole. Their population moves in three- to five-year cycles but tends to reach an extreme high about once every twenty years, and they are especially destructive on farm and acreage gardens because they chew off the bark of trees. Much of what is said about mice can be applied to voles too, so we're going to include them here.

Good sanitation is the key to keeping your garden mouse-free. Mice are food for many creatures, and mice seem to know this. Therefore, they are always looking for places to hide. A messy, cluttered garden is an open invitation to them. Mice are opportunistic and will eat almost anything that is available. They are known to chew open bags of fertilizers and eat the fertilizer. If you have a birdfeeder in your garden and the birds are messy or you are offering the birds seeds that they don't particularly like, mice will instantly use that which falls as a food source.

Mice are known to chew through electrical wires on occasion (for what purpose, who can say?) and will also find ways to damage or spoil a wide variety of valuable items. In a greenhouse, they are skilled at finding newly planted flats of seeds and digging the seeds out and eating them. In a garage or a garden shed, they will leave droppings that are crawling with bacteria all over your workspace. In short, you do *not* want mice in your garden!

In the autumn, when temperatures begin to drop, mice begin looking for warmer places to spend the winter. They do not hibernate, but they find brilliant ways to come in from the cold. Do not leave anything in your garden that could potentially harbour a healthy mouse population. A woodpile beside the garage, an unheated camper that isn't sealed properly, straw bales being used to protect tender plants … whatever it is, be really aware of anything that could potentially be "mouse real estate" and deal with it accordingly. Mice are never solitary; if you see one, assume you have many!

Obvious mouse-sized teeth scrapings and mouse droppings.

Mouse tunnels can be found once the snow melts.

Many commercial baits are available for mice, but these are also potentially harmful to other small creatures. I prefer to use traps (which work very well if they are checked regularly, kept clean, and used consistently), or you can get a cat (Siamese cats seem to be the best mousers).

The wintertime is when mice do most of the damage in the garden. They make tunnels beneath the snow and will often destroy perennials in their runs. Snow in summer (*Cerastium* sp.), for example, is a perennial that mice are particularly efficient at destroying. They will also chew bark in a manner similar to rabbits, although they take much smaller bites. Wrapping especially tender trees with chicken wire in the fall can really help to deter mice and rabbits from chewing them and girdling the bark. Plastic collars or cones are also available.

Be it in your garage, greenhouse, or wherever, if you see *any* signs of mouse damage, be prepared to clean everything they may have encountered thoroughly. Wear rubber gloves and a dust mask and use an antibacterial spray to make sure that nothing is potentially contaminated. When you are disposing of dead mice from a trap, the same rules apply. Never handle a dead mouse with bare hands, and dispose of it immediately. The only thing that smells worse than a dead mouse is a dead badger. Don't ask.

Moles

What we call a mole on the prairies is actually more technically called the pocket gopher, thanks to their large, pocket-like cheek pouches. These are the creatures that make the mounds of fresh black dirt on golf courses, in ditches and fields, and, sometimes, in our gardens. They are usually 25 to 30 centimetres long, males being larger, and both sexes have immensely huge teeth and strong feet and legs that are well adapted to digging. Moles are generally solitary creatures that feed primarily on earthworms and root vegetables but they can also cause significant damage to tree roots.

The chances of you encountering a mole are minimal, but they are vicious little creatures that can give a human a serious bite or easily kill a cat. We usually see evidence of moles when they are tunnelling near the surface. Moles favour moist soil since it is easier to dig. They are also notorious hoarders. Moles use their cheek pouches to store things they find and take them back to their "hoard chambers." Here they stockpile roots, tubers, and so on and return to eat them after they have finished excavating.

How do you deal with a mole in the garden? You can either put up with it, rake the hills down, and try to live peaceably together, or you can buy a mole trap. Mole traps work on the same principle as mouse traps so they result in a quick, sudden death for the mole. Thankfully, mole populations are relatively low, and they rarely reach numbers here that are significant enough to be worrisome.

Pets

I am often asked about gardening with pets. The first thing you should know is that all the gardening magazines are lying. We always see these photos in books and magazines of a charming little cat sitting between the herbs or a gorgeous big dog sitting elegantly *beside* the perennials. In real life, that cat may have just killed all three birds at your feeder, and the reason that big dog looks so pleased is because it just rolled over all your seedlings, then dug out a perennial so it could lie in the cool, rich earth. The truth is that *untrained* pets are very destructive in the garden.

Garden centres offer no shortage of smelly, slimy products reputed to keep cats and dogs out of the garden, but they're largely ineffective. There are also no plants that adequately repel them, regardless of what you might have been told.

Dogs

Dogs can sometimes be very useful for keeping deer and rabbits out of the yard, but more often they are not. Dogs, especially big dogs or puppies, can be destructive if they have not been taught your expectations for them. "How do I keep the dog out of the garden?" is a question I am often asked, but unless you're willing to put up a fence, it's a question that is likely better asked of a dog trainer.

It's in a dog's nature to dig, and they don't necessarily learn that digging is bad. You can't really fault a dog for being a dog. Often a client will say to me after the design is done, "By the way … how do we keep the dog out of the garden?" Other than a fence, I don't know what to tell you. If there's a part of the yard where the dog insists on digging or lying down, maybe you should stop trying to grow stuff there and just *let it have that spot*. You may also just have to recognize that sometimes dogs dig, and you might lose that perennial or shrub because the dog dug it out while you weren't home and the shrub dried out and dehydrated in the hot summer sun.

What about dogs peeing on your lawn? There are "dog patch" options for lawns available at most garden centres, but wouldn't it be better just to train the dog not to pee on the lawn? Can you devote a space or a small strip of yard at the back that is specifically for the dog to do its business? Many homeowners have had success with this method and will put down a long, narrow strip of rocks or gravel and teach the dog that *here you may go and nowhere else.*

Cats

Cats are less destructive in the garden than dogs, but they create problems in different ways. There is nothing more disgusting than going to plant yourself a new flower, digging into the soil, and finding a pile of cat barf or cat poop. This is especially upsetting if you do not own a cat.

Studies have shown that the greatest danger to migratory songbirds in North America is the common housecat. You can't get upset with a cat for doing what is in its nature to do. I can't tell you how many people have said to me, "Oh, but my cat doesn't kill birds." You might be surprised what your cat does when you aren't watching.

Most towns and cities have by-laws regarding free-roaming cats, and I encourage you to keep your cats supervised while outdoors. I do *not* recommend those cat leash/halter things. One of my clients felt that it was best to put her cat on one of those retractable leash things so that it could spend more time outside. This worked fine for a while. She thought that as long as the cat was supervised and leashed, there would be no problem. She sat outside reading a book one morning, and then the phone rang and she went into the house. When she came back outside, her cat was dead. The cat, presumably chasing a bird, had leaped up onto the outdoor table and then the fence that bordered her yard with the neighbour's. Then the cat tried to leap somewhere else and ran out of leash. The cat hung itself and died. This was very traumatic for my client, and one assumes it was not a nice death for the cat either.

Keep your cat out of the garden unless it's supervised and be *especially* diligent about keeping your cat out of other people's gardens.

Porcupines

Porcupines, along with beavers, are the largest rodents native to North America and among the largest in the world. Porcupines are actually gentle, shy creatures, and I have a certain amount of affection for them. Nose Hill Park in Calgary is home to a healthy population of these remarkable animals, and I have often seen them there. The problem with porcupines is twofold; first, they feed chiefly on bark in the winter months and can do severe damage to trees. Second, they can result in very expensive (and painful) trips to the veterinarian for quill removal if you have a dog that fails to understand that these creatures are not for playing with. If a porcupine shows up in your garden, please contact the proper authorities. It's fairly uncommon, but it does happen occasionally. Porcupines are chiefly nocturnal, spending their day sleeping high in a tree. Think of them as prickly koalas.

Porcupines chew at a 45 degree angle.

Skunks

Occasionally your garden may become home to a creature that you did not expect. Skunks are increasingly more urban than we thought and infinitely more adaptable. A member of the weasel family, skunks are omnivorous, which means that they will eat both animal and plant material. Skunks will eat road kill, eggs, frogs, salamanders, birds, vegetables, fish, and, really, anything that seems edible. They will happily paw through both your garbage and your compost bin looking for treats. Skunks are polite, discreet little animals, and generally they don't want any trouble. They will only spray as a

Porcupines will happily climb a tree to snack on it.

last resort and will actually work very hard to keep their own odour off of themselves.

If a skunk takes up residence in your garden (and I have experience with this), don't panic. Skunks are almost entirely nocturnal and spend their day in a burrow. Mine lived beneath the deck, but beneath a garden shed or beneath the roots of a great tree also makes a fine home for a skunk. You would see them at sunset or at dawn most likely, or if you are in your garden after hours. The most likely way to realize you have a skunk is its tracks, droppings, or slide marks into your pond. Realize that even if you know a skunk is living in your garden, it is not a certainty that you are going to come into contact with each other.

Because skunks are rarely very direct in advertising their presence, you are unlikely to know you have one until they do something destructive. What are they best known for? Tearing up your lawn! Skunks are very fond of beetle grubs, earthworms, and a variety of other subterranean delicacies. If a skunk determines that your lawn is host to these kinds of appetizers, they have no problem absolutely destroying a newly laid piece of turf by ripping it to shreds. They will also do this occasionally in your shade garden while looking for slugs. Skunks may also help themselves to things in the vegetable garden, but it's usually a one-time raid and then they don't do it again.

There are a few ways to discourage skunks in your garden. Be careful what you add to the compost heap, or at least be careful to bury things that might be perceived as edible. Rake up your leaves in the spring from beneath big trees to discourage foraging and digging. My skunk loved the leaves beneath my oak tree. Having a dog in the yard is a big deterrent to a skunk, but there is also always the risk of the dog and skunk having one of those "encounters" you'd like to avoid!

One other problem with a skunk in the garden is something I like to call the "come on over and bring the kids" problem. You will very quickly go from having a skunk in the garden to having a family of skunks in the garden.

If a skunk does move into your yard, you should contact your city's wildlife control or animal services department and let them know. In many cases, they will capture and remove the skunk for you. Skunks are also potentially carriers of rabies, and this isn't something you want to fool around with.

This is potentially very problematic. Skunks are good parents, and I'm not gonna lie ... Mama skunk and her brood of five or six babies (called kits) are ridiculously cute. Mama skunk is also protective and watchful of her babies, and is more prone to spraying you, your family members, or your pet if she feels hers are threatened.

If you are prowling about in your garden and you happen to encounter a skunk, remain very calm. Remember, the skunk does not want any trouble from you either. Do not make any sudden movements, and do not do anything that might be perceived as threatening, such as shouting or clapping your hands or running. Back up very slowly, and when you are a safe distance away, walk away. Carefully watch the skunk's body language. If the skunk does not feel threatened, it will watch you carefully as well but will generally remain where it is. If it feels that you are *really* not any kind of threat, it might even return to its foraging and just ignore you.

If a skunk makes eye contact with you and begins hissing, it's ticked off. Hissing is the first sign that a skunk has a problem with you and is followed by sometimes a baring of the teeth or opening and closing the mouth rapidly. The tail will be straight up in the air. This is how an adult skunk says, "You are pushing your luck!" Baby skunks cannot spray until they are about a year old and will almost always have their tails up as they forage. This helps Mama skunk locate them. If an adult puts its tail up, watch out! Often skunks will even stand on their hind legs briefly before spraying. This is when you run.

Skunks are finding their way more and more into our gardens. There are healthy populations of skunks within city limits in Saskatoon, Regina, Calgary, Edmonton, Medicine Hat, Lethbridge, and Vancouver, and I anticipate that within the next twenty years, they are going to become a huge problem all over.

Snakes

Snakes don't want to be around you any more than you want to be around them. You don't have to like them or get cuddly with them, but you should recognize the role they play in your garden. Snakes are, by nature, rather shy, and while we do have the odd rattlesnake in some parts, it's highly unlikely it will be in your garden. You're most likely to encounter a garter snake. They are easily recognized by their dark colouring and long, rather slimming stripes. Garter snakes may bite if handled, but their bite is more startling than painful and, since they're not poisonous, quite harmless.

Snakes, being cold-blooded, like a nice big stone or sidewalk to sun themselves on. They need places they can escape to in a moment of danger, so a large rock to crawl under, a sizable shrub, or a pond can suit them well. They will feed on large insects, mice, gophers, frogs, small fish, and, in some cases, even smaller snakes. Do them no harm! If you are kind to them, relatively quiet, and move slowly around them, they sometimes become accustomed to your presence and won't disappear right away. If you should be lucky enough to have a snake actually *living* in your garden, consider it a sign from the universe that you are doing something right. This is a thrilling accomplishment and you should be proud!

Garter snake.

Part Two

~~~ ❧ ~~~

Shopping with Lyndon

∾ 8 ∾
The garden market

A quick Internet search will show you an awful lot of information on how to grow, what to grow, and where to grow it, but few websites will explain how the horticulture business actually works. Like most things in life, once you understand the system, it's a lot easier to make decisions about how you're going to use it. Knowing where a plant comes from, why it's in the garden centre, and what you can realistically expect from it should make it easier to decide what type of plant you're going to purchase.

What's with the Latin?

Labels can be confusing, especially when talking about plants that are mass-marketed. Nothing drives me nuts more than finding some exquisite cactus or echeveria, and when I try find out what it is called, a very generic tag tells me "succulent" or "tropical."

People are starting to use the name of the cultivar instead of the name of the plant in question. A woman phoned me once and told me her mint juleps weren't doing very well and she wanted them replaced. I almost suggested she contact a bartender instead of a garden centre. "Oh, you were talking about *junipers*! Yes, I see, the 'Mint Julep' juniper, of course!"

Opposite: Quality is never accidental. If your local garden centre offers you beautiful, healthy plants, it means they are well cared for and have the best chance to start life in your yard.

If you know the Latin name, you always know what plant you're looking at.

I'm not suggesting that you always have to remember the name of the plant, but write it down somewhere, preferably in your garden journal. Many plants share cultivar names, so it's far more important to know what the plant is than what the cultivar is called. 'Pink Ice' is the name of a thrift, a phlox, and a daylily. How will I know which one you mean? 'Innocence' is a lilac, a diascia, a delphinium, and an evening primrose. If you call me and say, "Yeah, my innocence is being eaten by bugs," that tells me absolutely nothing.

Furthermore (and here's something few other garden books will tell you), if you can identify it correctly, garden centre staff will take you seriously. I worked in garden centres for years, and anytime someone came in complaining that their "bushes" had a disease, I inwardly rolled my eyes and sarcastically thought, *Oh, good. Here's someone else who has no idea what they're doing.* However, if that person came in and said courteously, "I seem to be having an issue with my shrubs. I bought some 'Tinkerbelle' lilacs this spring and there are dark spots on the leaves," I immediately would think, *Oh, here is a person who took the time to learn what they were growing*

> "Latin is a language dead as dead can be. First it killed the Romans, now it's killing me!"
> —Author unknown

A good planter will have a balance between interesting shapes, colours, textures, and sizes. It will also drink a lot of water on a hot day!

and is paying attention to what is happening in their yard. Brilliant. You will get stellar customer service in garden centres this way.

What is the difference between a cultivar and a variety?

Cultivar and *variety* are two words often used interchangeably, even though they shouldn't be. When a plant is given a scientific name (Latin name), sometimes there is more than one variety of it. For example, the scientific name for chokecherry is *Prunus virginiana*. Normally it has red or purple fruits, but occasionally the fruits can be yellow. Everything else about the tree is pretty much exactly the same year-round, and this is consistent from season to season, throughout the generations. Therefore, the yellow-fruited chokecherry is not a different species; it is merely a naturally occurring variation (variety). To show this, we call the yellow-fruited form *Prunus virginiana* var. *xanthocarpa*—with *xantha* meaning yellow in Latin and *carpa* meaning fruit. Because it is naturally occurring, it is relatively easy to make more like it since the seeds from these plants will look just like the parent tree it came from. Though not strictly biologically correct, you can almost think of plant varieties like dog breeds—they may look a bit different from one another, but they're all still definitely dogs, and the purebred puppies are pretty predictable.

Cultivated varieties of chokecherry, such as 'Pickup's Pride,' are cultivars. A cultivar is a cultivated variety, which means that someone noticed something special about one of the plants (variegated foliage, double flowers, disease resistance, etc.) and thought we needed more just like it, so they named it, grew more through cloning, and introduced it to the nursery trade and, thusly, the world. To continue the metaphor, you can think of cultivars as fancy mutts—you really never know what the offspring is going to look like, so if you want hundreds of mutts just like this one, you're going to have to fire up your cloning machine. Good thing plants naturally clone fairly easily through cuttings, dividing, or even tissue culture.

Why bother learning to use the Latin names?

Well, first and most importantly, the Latin names are definitive. They help us organize and categorize plants. It doesn't matter what country you are in or what language is spoken there, the Latin name is the same the world over. Latin is also beautiful and poetic-sounding; this alone should be reason enough to learn at least some of it.

Some plants share a common name; soapwort is applied to both *Yucca* and *Saponaria* species. Creeping charlie is a common name that can refer to any horizontal weed. True creeping charlie belongs in the genus *Glechoma*. The only way to be sure you are buying the plant you want is to check the Latin name.

The Latin name is also the only way to be absolutely certain that two people are both referring to the same plant. Giant impatiens, giant balsam, Himalayan orchid, jewelweed, poor man's rhododendron, quick-in-the-hand, and touch-me-not are all common names for *Impatiens glandulifera*. There are more than seventy-five common names for this plant, depending on what part of the world you are in, but the Latin name will always be constant.

Where are all the specific recommendations?

You might notice that I don't often recommend a specific variety or cultivar. I think it's important that gardeners, especially new gardeners, get familiar with a plant before they get too caught up with a specific example of that plant. Once you are familiar with daylily and have grown a bunch of them, then you can start getting specific about different kinds of daylily. Discovering which cultivar you like is part of the fun of gardening. Why should you just grow the ones I like? You might like totally different varieties for totally different reasons.

Listing specific cultivars can also set a bit of a trap. In some cases, it tends to date the material. A cultivar that is popular today may not be popular in ten years. While echinacea is as good a choice today as it was a decade ago, your available cultivars have certainly increased. If I name a specific type, you might go crazy trying to find it and you might pass up a perfectly good plant just because I told you to search for a different one. Also, even if you snap this book off the shelf immediately after it's published (which I highly recommend), some cultivars are still only available at very specific locations.

After having worked in the nursery industry for many years, I have seen the following scenario happen as well. Tina, a new gardener, has just paid a landscaper to help her come up with a design. The designer has recommended 'Royal Standard' hostas. Since I don't have any in stock, I recommend 'Honeybells' since both have green leaves, are vigorous growers, and have fragrant flowers. "Oh no!" says Tina. "The designer said it has to be 'Royal Standard'!" Now I've lost a sale, and Tina has to wait till next spring before I have that cultivar again, thus setting her back by a year. Always ask your designer why they chose a particular plant cultivar so you can make reasonable substitutions when necessary.

How plants get to market

Once upon a time, horticulturists toiled for years and years, often in obscurity, trying to breed a new cultivar—be it a tree, shrub, or perennial—that was far superior to anything else available. They picked the best plants with the traits they wanted and began to cross this variety with that one, raising them to full size to see how they performed, often trying over and over until they were lucky enough to come up with just the right match. They were hoping to find that one plant that would perform very well in gardens and could be propagated easily enough to make it available to the gardening public. Only the very best of these plants were selected, named, and introduced to the market as a new cultivar.

When Canada was a young nation, a great deal of money and effort was spent *supporting* our scientists instead of silencing them. Research stations were opened all across the country, including the Ottawa Experimental Farm (where Isabella Preston developed the world-famous Preston lilacs), the Morden Research Station in Morden, Manitoba (where some of the hardiest roses in the world were bred), as well as stations in Rosthern and Indian Head in Saskatchewan and Brooks in Alberta. Many universities also developed programs to breed and introduce new trees and shrubs for shelterbelts, windbreaks, and food production. Private breeders such as Robert Erskine in Alberta and Stanley Zubrowski in Saskatchewan devoted their lives to developing new, hardier, and stronger varieties of plants for the prairie climate.

New varieties were grown and evaluated, often over a period of twenty years or longer before they were named and introduced to the public. These plants were not bred with the intention of making a lot of money—they were developed with the intent of making life in this world better. Creating hardy fruits, stronger trees and shrubs, and longer-flowering or more disease-resistant plants to benefit the home gardener in this harsh, Canadian climate was their goal.

Now, that has shifted. Today, the goal is usually to make money. Because gardening is such big business, a lot of corporations with a lot of money are breeding and introducing new plant varieties. These plants are being bred primarily for garden *centres*, not garden *performance*. They are meant to look fabulous when you go to the garden centre in May, and if they peter out by the beginning of July, that's perfect. These companies *want* you to replace that $10 plant in your container two months after planting it. They want you to then replace that summer bloomer in late summer or autumn with something else. This way, they ensure that you are spending $60 a year instead of $15!

There's nothing wrong with changing out a spring planter (say, tulips and primulas) with something summery and then putting in a chrysanthemums in fall. In fact, I enjoy doing that. However, many home gardeners are deeply resentful of the fact that they purchase something they expect to bloom all summer and then it fails to perform. They take this as a reflection of their gardening skills, and it is not.

When the Ohio-based Ball Seed Company introduced the award-winning 'Purple Wave' petunia in 1995, it completely revolutionized how people put together planters and containers, dramatically changing how hanging basket plants were perceived. Prior to the 'Purple Wave,' the ability to grow huge baskets of flowers with very little effort was out of reach of most people. 'Purple Wave' eliminated the need for deadheading (new to petunia growing), grew three times

It's important to hug your plants, even if they are genetically modified petunias.

as fast as any other variety on the market, flowered more profusely and for longer than any other variety on the market, and became the new standard by which hanging basket plants are measured.

Research in Japan, Israel, and Australia immediately followed, each company trying to outdo the other. It is no longer required to grow, test, and evaluate a variety before naming and releasing it. This is why a variety that is available this year may disappear from the market and never be seen again by the next. It has either been replaced by something "superior" or they have pulled it because it is disease-prone and they are trying to improve it. The rigour that used to be applied to ensure that only the best selections went to market is long gone.

Marketing is everything.

The garden industry is like any other industry—it's about making money. Gardening is the second most popular leisure activity in the world (golf, appallingly, is more popular), and an estimated $9 billion is spent on gardening annually in North America alone. Whether you are talking about the sports industry, the music industry, the clothing industry, whatever, everything is about how it is *marketed*. Unfortunately, gardening is not immune to this trend.

New is always better, right?

Many of these companies begin by pouring huge money into advertising. They broadcast commercials on the home/garden channel and take out full-page ads and publish advertorials in big-name gardening magazines and online publications, all to create huge demand for plants well before they arrive on the market. They are very often advertising all through the fall and winter for the "big spring release" of this shrub or that one. Very often, these shrubs and perennials are ill-suited to the Canadian prairies, but demand for them is extremely high due to the increased visibility of their products.

"Do you have that new lilac I've just read about?" they ask. No one wants to hear, "Well, that lilac you've just read about is about $45 more expensive than a lilac that is far better suited to your zone, but sure, we have it. Oh, and this new lilac you're buying? It's disease-prone and the flowers are small and only lightly scented."

The facts go out the window because we've been conditioned to believe that whatever is new and being promoted is somehow "best," even when it is far from being the case! Garden centres are in the unenviable position of having to supply what the customer wants, but what the customer wants is often based on inaccurate information, which brings us to our second problem.

Low population = low market representation

Due to the relatively low population of the Canadian prairies, we don't constitute a huge percentage of the sales that these big plant companies are looking to make. This creates several problems for us. If you recall from Chapter 1, companies can't actually put a zone or sunshine recommendation on a plant tag unless they can prove that plant has been officially trialled in that zone. We're not a lucrative-enough market for a lot of companies to put in that extra effort.

The same holds true for their marketing. Frankly, it's cheaper for companies to market to the entire continent in the same fashion than it is to tailor ads regionally. With a few notable exceptions, the gardening magazines are not generally written for Alberta, which makes the information in their articles, and especially the photos, very misleading. Shrubs that are being pushed in Vancouver or Phoenix are also being pushed in Calgary, with the idea that each somehow looks exactly as lovely in all three climates. Reality? I think not.

Buying plants

Now it's time to do some window-shopping. Once you start wandering around the garden centre, choices can become overwhelming. The question becomes, at some point or another, "How am I going to know what plant to buy, what not to buy, or even *how* to buy it?" Should you buy seeds? Should you buy started plants? Should you buy a ticket to Hawaii and just forget this whole, stupid gardening idea in the first place?

Truth is, you probably don't have unlimited amounts of money to spend on your garden. If you already have children or pets (both

GENETIC MODIFICATION

There is a great deal of well-warranted concern about genetically modified organisms (GMOs), but much of the discussion has been focused on plants that we will be eating. What many gardeners don't realize is genetic modification is happening in your newer ornamentals too. Many hanging basket plants are sterile. Not only do they not produce *viable* seed, but they actually don't produce *any seeds at all!* The genes that are responsible for seed production have been "turned off." The plant, not needing to devote any nutrients to seed production, can flower significantly more, thereby making them showier and longer flowering. Plants have evolved over millions of years to produce seeds and recreate themselves. The fact that plants are being wired *not* to do this makes me quite anxious!

expensive distractions from gardening!), it may be too late for you already; you might not be able to finance the garden of your dreams.

> Whoever coined the phrase *dirt cheap* never had a truckload of loam delivered!

That plant is *how* much?

I find that people who are new to gardening are always astounded at what plants cost. Let's say you're at a garden centre looking at a potted rose and the price tag reads $34.95. You're probably wondering, *How in the world could this little rose possibly be worth $35?* Here's how it works.

Someone has to grow that rose. They have to take cuttings from another rose and grow it to a saleable size. That takes time. In that period, those rose cuttings will need to be kept moist, protected from insects and fungus, and then potted, kept alive to grow for likely several years, and then shipped to wherever this garden centre is. Garden centres have to pay for staff, heat, water, shipping, pest control, and, if the plant is imported from a U.S. grower, phytosanitary inspections. On top of that, many companies that are introducing new plants are also patenting their new varieties, and nobody is allowed to propagate (and therefore profit) from the sale of those plants without a propagation licence. This is why container plants are often exorbitantly priced: the high cost of running a garden centre coupled with the fact that garden centres have to pay royalties on these high-demand varieties.

Running a garden centre is a very expensive operation, especially in our climate, and there is only a small window of time in which to make back the considerable amount of money they have put into it. Owners gamble a lot, hoping we don't get stuck with a horribly long winter eating away at their profits. Nine out of ten garden centres that open will be out of business within a few years, so it turns out that $35 for a rose is actually very reasonable.

Shop around

Now, I hear what you're saying: "Why should I pay $35 for a rose at a garden centre when I could go to a big-box department store and buy a rose there for $17?" Well, sometimes that works, but it can still be a gamble unless you know what to look for. A good garden centre should be able to offer you advice about your garden, your climate, and any other questions you may have, and every plant in there has been chosen for your region by a professional. Purchasers at big-box stores usually buy for entire regions, so it's not at all unusual to find stores in your area selling plants that will never survive a winter here. A big-box store can tell you what the barcode on the pot means, what it claims on the package, and very little else. This is fine for experienced gardeners, but new gardeners may need more advice to really succeed with that plant, assuming it's even possible.

If you do find the same cultivar at each store, you still need to take a good look at each plant before deciding what to bring home. Some stores offer their plants far better care than others do, so you need to be vigilant, especially if you're going to stick to that pesky budget. It's no longer a deal if that little drought-stressed plant you got for $5 quickly becomes diseased or dies from transplant shock because it wasn't strong enough to fight for its life any more. The simplest choice is to buy a healthy plant from a reputable grower, and you will save yourself a lot of grief.

That new plant just might be cheaper next year.

Plant prices can also vary considerably year to year, which usually has to do with growth rate and availability. For example, a reliable lily variety that multiplies quickly and has been around twenty years will cost you a few dollars. A brand-new lily variety that has just hit the market and whose demand far exceeds supply might cost you up to $50. A few years after its introduction, the very same plant might cost you $35 or $40, and it will likely continue to go down as the years go by.

This isn't always the case, though—some plants multiply extremely slowly. Not everything can be grown from seed, and some plants are propagated chiefly by division. Fern-leaf peonies are a good example. These gorgeous perennials have been grown for centuries. They hate disturbance, and they multiply very slowly. Average price for a fern-leaf peony is $50 to $75 because it takes a long time to obtain a new one. A poppy that produces a billion seeds every year that all can be easily grown will cost you much less.

Division is when established plants are split into several pieces and then those pieces are grown into new plants.

Tissue culture lowers prices.

Tissue culture has revolutionized plant propagation. This is where thousands of identical plants are grown in a lab via cloning. Cloning sounds rather futuristic, but it really isn't unusual for plants to clone themselves in the wild. People have found many ways to use a plant's natural tendency to clone itself, some of which we've been practising for thousands of years. With tissue culture, cells are extracted from the newest growing tips of a plant and coerced to grow in test tubes until they have gotten big enough to plant into pots. The yellow peony 'Bartzella' was introduced in 1990 and at that time it was selling for about US$3,000 per root—that's about $5,500 in 2014 dollars thanks to inflation. You can now buy a 'Bartzella' peony for about $65 or $70 thanks to tissue culture. Miraculous, isn't it?

Plant warranties raise prices.

I think the one-year warranty was one of the worst things that ever happened to the plant industry. Many nurseries and garden centres will sell you a tree or a shrub and tell you that if it dies within the next year, they will replace it for free. What this has done is encourage people to treat plants like they are products when they are *not*. A tree or a shrub is a living thing. It was not made to spec in a factory and put together by assembly-line workers. This plant is a life form, and buying it is like buying a dog or a cat. If your cat dies because you didn't feed it, do you go back to the SPCA or pet store and demand another cat for free?

The mentality that "the customer is always right even when they obviously aren't" is rampant in our industry, and I can't tell you how many people have wantonly abused this warranty. A few summers ago, I was walking through a new neighbourhood and saw an immense balled and burlapped paper birch tree baking in a driveway, clearly dying of dehydration and neglect. When I spoke to the homeowner, she flagrantly admitted to purposely killing the tree because her husband bought it, she didn't want it, and the nursery will refund them anyhow. She didn't care that this was fraud, she didn't care that this entitlement attitude destroys people's businesses; she simply cared that it was more convenient for her to blame the nursery than tell her husband she didn't like his choice in trees. Unfortunately she isn't the only person with this entitlement attitude.

Sometimes people make mistakes. One year while I worked at a nursery, a woman came back to me with three "dead" Korean lilacs. The problem? It was the beginning of May and the lilacs were dormant. They were perfectly healthy—they just simply hadn't leafed out yet—but she demanded replacements. To my disgust, the nursery conceded that she had made a mistake and replaced them anyhow, just to keep her happy. Is it any wonder that small, family-owned nurseries regularly go out of business and that rose is $35? Someone has to pay for these trees.

Thankfully, most gardeners aren't like that. If your tree dies and you don't know why, by all means speak to your garden centre. They will make every effort to determine *why* it died in the first place. A tree or shrub does die sometimes for no apparent reason, and any reputable garden centre will bend over backward to keep good customers happy. If that means replacing a sick tree, they will happily replace the tree with a healthy one because they want you to succeed. They know how addictive garden success is, and that a successful customer will come back happy.

The B word: Budget

So now that you know why this is going to be costly, how are you going to establish a budget? Before you wander despondently through the perennial aisle grieving for the garden that existed only in your imagination, realize that you do have options here. The first thing you need to do is make a priority list. Say your old-fashioned garden must include the following: roses, tiger lilies, peonies, iris, and poppy. Do the same thing for plants as you would for furniture or a vehicle—ask advice from the people who already have some and look at all your options.

Some things to consider:

- Talk to other gardeners. Ask them where they shop; I'm sure you'll get an earful. Ask them about your plant choices. Knowing what worked for them is always good, and there's always a chance they'll say, "You don't need to buy those lilies! I've got some orange tigers at home that need dividing and if you come over for coffee tomorrow I'll send you home with some."

- Is there a local horticultural society where you live? Do they have plant sales? You might be able to get seeds for next to nothing. This is also a good place to trade that overgrown iris you inherited when you bought the house for the lilies you want.

- Have you checked your local online classifieds? Most communities these days have a free Facebook buy-and-sell group or a local Kijiji section where you can find perennials for considerably less money than retail if you know you want tiger lilies or roses but you're willing to be flexible on the specific cultivar. As an added bonus, if the plants are old enough for the seller to be dividing them, you're pretty much guaranteed that they are winter hardy in your yard too.

- Rather than buying large, established plants, is it possible that you could grow your own from seed? It might take longer for it to flower, but you would also have the thrill of growing it yourself. This option won't likely work if you have your heart set on a specific cultivar, since they don't reproduce predictably through seed, but it can save you a ton of money if you're willing to expand your horizons.

- What about buying a sapling instead of a tree? You might not be able to afford $200 for a tree that is already 2 metres tall, but a seedling for $40 might work—just realize that $160 probably buys you three to five years of growing time.

- Sometimes buying plants bare-root is much cheaper than buying a potted plant. For example, you can buy dahlias as bare-root tubers in the spring for just a few dollars. You can also buy them as big, established plants for considerably more. If you're willing to start small, you can save yourself a lot of money.

- Do you have a friend who is a skilled gardener? You can say to that person, "I'd really like a lilac, but I don't have an extra $25 right now. Can you help me take a cutting?" You could root your own lilac for free. The tradeoff here is it might mean you wait four years for blossoms instead of one.

- A rose garden will cost you more than a herb garden. Why? A yard where you have to devote a lot of your funds to compost and amending the soil is going to cut into your plant budget.

- Leverage your benefits. I have known some new gardeners to apply for part-time jobs at garden centres in the spring just for the benefit of learning as much as they can (which is a great idea) and the discounts they can get on perennials and trees!

- Another alternative for your limited budget is to find someone who works in the oil and gas industry (since this is southern Alberta, after all) and become embroiled in a romantic relationship with them, thereby financing all of your gardening dreams. As the author of this book, I feel I get some say in this and I vote for this option.

Wish I'd known that sooner ...

I find that the more I learn about plants, the less I actually know since answers inevitably lead to more questions! I'm grateful for my garden, but there are a few things that I wish I had known before I really got into it, and these are things that no one ever mentions to you.

Lost in translation

Earlier, we talked about the importance of marketing in the horticultural industry. The following common gardening translations may be helpful to you.

When they say …	They probably mean …
Hardy to zone 4	Your zone 3 market is too small for us to bother testing this outside of Ottawa so we can put zone 3 on the label.
Plant in full sun only	Plant it where it gets at least eight hours of direct, scorching, blistering sun per day or don't bother, especially if there is fruit involved. Ten hours of partially shady is not going to cut it.
Partial sun	Our company tested this in partial sun, but we didn't do enough trials with full sun or full shade to legally say what it will perform best in because we really wanted to get this to market. OR The plant does best with a mixture of sun and shade but still wants mostly sun.
Performs well in shade	Will survive in shade, likely prefers at least partial sun
Establishes quickly or vigorous grower	You will have this plant in your garden for the rest of your life, whether you want to or not.
Carefree growth habit	Self-seeds everywhere and becomes weedy
Excellent filler	It's likely plotting to creep across your yard while your back is turned, so put a barrier around it.
Plant where roots will not be disturbed	Suckers like crazy
Mulch well	Dies at the first sign of drought
Blue flowers	Purple or mauve flowers
Red flowers	Dark pink flowers
Double-flowering	Provides little nectar for bees
Grows 2 metres tall	Will grow 2 metres tall in Ontario, will grow 1 metre tall here
Flowers are best appreciated up close	The flowers are so small you will probably never even notice them.
Richly scented	Stinks horribly
Delicately scented	No detectable fragrance
Smells like (lemon, chocolate, etc.)	I think you will buy this plant if you think it will smell good. No one can stop us from inventing marketable descriptions, and few are likely to question the legitimacy of "the tag."
Slow to establish	Will look like crap for three years before it actually decides to do anything
Provide good air circulation	Very prone to mildew
Provide a sheltered location	Looks like salad after a hail storm

Expensive doesn't automatically mean quality.

A plant that is very expensive means that it is either very new to the market, so that demand far exceeds supply, or that it is very slow to propagate, as in the case with certain waterlilies. You can spend a lot of money on a particular plant, but that doesn't guarantee you are purchasing something fabulous. For example, the variegated form of lily of the valley is highly costly because, unlike its green counterpart, it spreads very slowly. I paid $25 for a tiny specimen in a 10-centimetre pot. If you do not keep the closest eye on it, the variegated leaves you paid so dearly for voluntarily revert to solid green. (If you see the solid leaves, remove them immediately to prevent the whole plant from turning solid green.) Unfortunately, it still neither clumps nor spreads, which was one of the most useful traits of the original inexpensive green one.

> Having variegated leaves means that the plant's leaves have at least two different colours, likely green and a lighter green or white. Variegated plants are less frequent in nature because they have less chlorophyll in the leaves so they tend to be less strong than the fully green plants they compete with.

The flip side is that there are some plants to be had very cheaply that are excellent in the garden but are often disregarded simply because they're cheap. Far too often, we equate price with value. Cheap does not mean common or unattractive, much in the same way that expensive does not always ensure quality. Do keep in mind, though, that when visiting local plant sales, it is worth asking yourself *why* they have so much of that particular plant to spare.

A packet of seeds is another good example of how a great deal of beauty and pleasure can be had for next to nothing. You can buy morning glory or sunflower seeds for $2 and they will bloom all summer, providing endless joy. That hosta you just paid $45 for might not be able to make the same promise.

"Excellent for shade" is usually a lie.

We now live in a world where we are building two houses in the space where we used to put one. It was once a given that you would have a sunny spot for your garden. I am constantly asked for vegetables, flowers, and vines that will do well in a shady spot. The truth is, 90 per cent of plants want sun. Full sun is almost a necessity for anything to be edible—plants simply need sun to make enough sugar for anything to be worth eating.

There are many plants that, if put in a dark corner, will be the same size in three years as they were when you planted them. *Surviving* in

Best plants for shade: ferns and hosta.

shade and *flourishing* in shade are two very different things, and very, very few plants flourish in the shade. Remember, any plant that is merely surviving is quite stressed and much more prone to insect or disease issues; if you're looking for low maintenance, you want your plants to be thriving. Maybe your shady spot is a better place for a relaxation area with a bench, birdbath, or bit of sculpture or art than it is for plants.

Also remember that not all shade is created equal. Dappled or filtered light from a tree is often quite different from darkness provided by a wall or fence. Spaces that are in deep shade in the height of summer may be in full sun in the spring before the trees leaf out. The type of shade and the permanence of that shade in that spot is something you need to consider before you buy into the notion that a plant will do well there automatically, and remember that these patterns will shift over time as trees grow.

You will always see your own garden worse than it actually is.
When people invest time and money into something like a garden, they often feel things have fallen terribly short of expectations. When the neighbour compliments their lovely yard, they may smile and say thank you but inside are thinking, *Oh, they have no idea how bad I am at this—I killed three hostas, still haven't planted those bulbs, and my dogwoods are begging to be pruned.* But that's just it—their neighbour has no idea what went wrong, they just see what went right. Does your

yard look even slightly better than it did last year? Did you learn something? Do either of those and you have succeeded. Even slow progress is still success, and you can expect your garden to get better every year as plants mature and you get a few more planted in the right spots.

One of the things people say to me quite often is "Oh, I'd be embarrassed to have you in my garden" or "Please don't look at my office plants, I am sure they are not nearly the standard they should be." Their shame and self-depreciation always bothers me. I am a professional gardener. I do this for a living. Of *course* I have more skill with plants than you do—*I do this for a living.* If you go over to the home of someone who owns a gym, would you stand in the doorway apologizing to them first that you don't look like a bodybuilder? Or if you have a friend over who happens to be a professional chef, would you not want to have them over for dinner because you can't cook like they do? Of course not—it's one thing to respect their skills, but it's quite another to measure your success against them.

∽ *9* ∽

Look like a garden
genius with bulbs

Wouldn't it be nice if there were a lot of easy answers in life? Human beings are terribly funny creatures. No one would buy an honest book about health that is full of simple workout routines, that encourages you to stop sitting on your couch shoving your face full of bonbons while watching *The Walking Dead*, which, by the way, is a really excellent TV program. We can't imagine wasting all that effort just to have a physique like the average-looking guy or girl on the cover! Oh no. We buy the exercise book with the people on it who look like they could bench-press a tractor. *That* book promises us that in just ten minutes a day with this magical workout routine and complicated

Opposite: Tulip bulbs.
This page: Asiatic lilies add bold colour!

diet, you too will look like Hank and Hanna Hardbody in only seven weeks! We buy the lie. If you want that body, you have to make it a priority and pursue it with great passion, and if you ever get it, it will be just as much work to actually *maintain* that look as it was to get there in the first place.

The truth about gardening is much the same. Want an astounding yard? I hope you love gardening because you're going to have to spend time in that garden and make it your whole life. Now, *wait just one minute . . .* before you throw this book across the room or, worse yet, return it to the place where you purchased it (please don't do that), I am about to reveal a secret of such astronomical proportions that I risk being shunned from the entire horticultural community! Do you see the sacrifice I am making for you here? What I am about to reveal to you can make you look exactly like you are some sort of criminally insane, powerhouse gardener who knows exactly what he or she is doing . . .

And that secret, dear garden book reader, is *bulbs.* Fall bulbs are the easiest, cheapest, most bulletproof way to introduce amazing riots of colour to your garden with practically no effort. Here is what's magical about planting bulbs in the fall—*everything they need to flower is already stored inside the bulb!* That means you can plant them almost anywhere and they will come up and flower beautifully.

Asiatic lily 'Brushmarks'.

Bulbs are glorious things. If you simply must have twenty-five new liatris to fill in that space in your yard, buying them at $10 to $15 per plant in the perennial section adds up quickly. You might just find over in the bulb section that a package of twenty-five bulbs is under $10. The trade-off is time; it might be three seasons before you see blooms. Buying plants "bare root" as bulbs is often a good way to stretch your gardening budget. It can also be a good way to get some plants into your garden that you haven't previously grown.

A bulb by any other name ...

Before I can really get into what bulbs are, I need to clarify a few terms for you. Bulbs, tubers, corms, and rhizomes are all entirely different things, though they are all often sold and packaged as "spring bulbs" or "fall bulbs." Given how ridiculously interesting all these things are, it is really quite unfair to label them all "bulbs," though I understand it's just easier to sell them that way.

Bulbs

When you buy onions or garlic, you are buying bulbs. Despite the fact that they (usually) grow underground, bulbs are not roots. They are actually modified stems that function as food-storage organs. Bulbs can be solid, such as an onion; they can be divided into scales, as lilies are; or they can be split into cloves, as is the case with garlic. The purpose of storing food in these devices is to get a plant through adverse conditions, such as winter dormancy or times of drought. A plant storing food in the bulb is not unlike bears getting fat before winter. True bulbs include alliums, amaryllis, daffodils, fritillaries, lilies, tulips, and certain irises.

Tubers

Tubers are similar to bulbs in some ways but also quite different. The most familiar tuber to most people is the potato. If you examine a potato closely, you will see small scar-like marks (called "eyes") from which new stems will grow. Tubers are produced underground and store a lot of starch and sugars for the plant. Tubers are an excellent means of asexual propagation and serve the same function for a plant as a bulb does. Some of the best-known garden plants that grow from tubers are dahlias, cyclamens, yams, and begonias.

> Does any of this matter if you're not a botanist? Possibly not, but when someone mentions buying begonia bulbs, you'll smirk and say, "I think you mean *begonia tubers*." Don't say I didn't teach you anything.

Rhizomes

Rhizomes are even more fascinating underground stems, and sometimes they are not even entirely buried, as is the case with bearded irises. When you buy ginger at the grocery store, you are not actually buying the root; you are buying the rhizome. Rhizomes are also referred to as creeping rootstalks, and they can be very aggressive in some plants, which is either great or problematic depending on the location. Well-known garden plants that grow from rhizomes include bamboo, lily of the valley, and showy milkweed. Quack grass is a nasty prairie weed that is "rhizomatous" because it sends out creeping rootstalks that can be very troublesome. Creeping bellflower is equally problematic.

> Some plants send out shoots similar to rhizomes that creep above ground instead of below, rooting where they touch. Strawberries and mint are good examples of this. These shoots are called stolons, and these type of plants are called stoloniferous.

I'm a sucker for a good rhizome.
In many cases, trees can produce rhizomes, which are referred to as "suckers." Suckers are shoots that grow from the base of the tree or sometimes a considerable distance from the parent plant. In the wild, this helps the plant form thickets and is essentially a means of cloning itself. Disturbing the roots of suckering plants often causes a proliferation of suckers to appear. Chokecherries, French lilacs, poplars, salt bush, saskatoon berries, and sea buckthorn are all suckering, though there may be cultivars available that sucker less vigorously. Sometimes suckering is a problem and sometimes it isn't, depending on the purpose you had in mind when you planted that tree in that location. Saskatoon berries purchased at greenhouses are often grafted onto cotoneaster rootstalk to prevent this from being a problem.

Corms

Finally, we have corms, the weirdest of the specialized plant-storage stems. Corms are usually covered in a paper-like sheath, and the old corm develops a new corm on top of itself. Thus, you can put gladioli corms in the ground in spring and when you pull them out in fall, the corms you planted will be shrivelled and desiccated and new, current-season corms will be attached to them. In addition to gladioli (often just called "glads"), other common garden plants that grow from corms include snow crocus, crocosmia, freesias (which suck in our climate, so don't even bother planting them), and some of the autumn crocus (*Colchicum* spp.), which are also far from totally hardy here.

Spring, summer, and fall bulbs

What is the difference between spring, summer, and fall bulbs? Perspective. Really. It depends on who is selling them to you. *Summer bulbs* is a broad term largely applied to bulbs that flower in summer. This includes lilies, gladioli, dahlias, and so on. However, if you are buying the bulbs in spring, they may be sold as "spring bulbs." This is confusing for obvious reasons. *Spring bulbs* are usually plants such as hyacinth, crocus, tulips, and so on that flower in the spring, but if you are buying the bulbs in fall, they may be sold as "fall bulbs." Try not to get too preoccupied with this. Just look at it in terms of seasonality. If you buy bulbs in fall, they probably flower in the spring. If you buy bulbs in spring, they probably flower in summer.

Best bets for bulbs

Allium spp. (ornamental onion)
Alliums come in many shapes, sizes, and colours, but pinks, whites, and purples predominate. They are a true species of onion and have an onion-like smell when bruised or crushed. This also means that they are largely pest-proof, and deer and rabbits will rarely touch them. The flowers are held in ball-shaped clusters and attract flurries of bees and butterflies. They also make nice cut flowers and bloom over a long period. If this isn't enough, the flowers give way to attractive seed heads that look great sticking out of the snow. Alliums will also multiply where they are happy, and some are extraordinarily large and interesting. Plant them in sizable groups and your neighbours will be knocking on your door asking what they are. I like alliums with roses because they flower at the same time (late spring or early summer), the contrast in shapes is a lot of fun, and some people believe that alliums will help to repel insects that eat roses.

Camassia spp. (blue camas)
A gorgeous plant from the lily family, camas are medium to tall plants with stunning, sapphire-coloured flowers on elegant spikes. They were once a tremendously important food source for First Nations people both on the West Coast and in southern Alberta, where the nutritious bulbs were dug up and cooked. Not

Allium giganticum.

Tropicana canna.

altogether common but they are worth having in the garden. Sun to partial shade is fine, but they prefer a moist location.

Canna spp. (cannas) All of the same rules for dahlias (see below) apply to cannas, sometimes erroneously called canna lilies. Cannas are very "in" these days because they have huge, beautiful, very tropical-looking leaves and they are being used more and more often in large containers. The flowers are also very attractive and are enjoyed by humming-birds. You can even store dahlias and cannas together for the winter. Easy to do, and worth doing. Both will get better year after year.

Crocus spp. (crocus) What about cro-cus? Well, let's define "crocus" first. The prairie crocus (Manitoba's provincial flower) is not a true crocus. It belongs in the genus *Pulsatilla*, and it's in the same family as clematis, delphiniums, and anemones. Some truly fabulous garden hybrids of this plant are available (largely out of Germany) in brighter colours, with larger flowers, and longer-lasting bloom than the native species. You can buy these great plants at any garden centre.

For true crocus, the majority of cultivars available to us are hybrids derived from several species, usually including *Crocus vernus* and *Crocus flavus*. Hybrid crocus

often have fanciful and beautiful cultivar names such as 'Snow Bunting,' 'Violet Beauty,' and 'Blue Light.' I've grown all of these, and more accurate names would be 'Snow Nothing,' 'Violet Mediocrity,' and 'Cloak of Invisibility.'

Crocus flavus, often called Dutch crocus or snow crocus, sometimes does well on the prairies and sometimes does not. A chinook that removes their snow cover can make them flower up to two months prematurely (they have been known to occasionally flower as early as March), but a chinook can just as easily kill them while they are in full flower.

I'm not sure what the big deal with crocus is. Yes, they bloom early. My experience with them is that they bloom *too* early. They only flower for a short time, and some years I have actually missed it. Not only can they complete blooming within days of popping out of the ground, but also the flowers are so tiny that I often find they are hardly noticeable, and what is the point of that? No, my friends, I would say leave the crocus at the store and plant squills instead.

Dahlia spp. (dahlias) Once upon a time, dahlias could be found in every garden. They grow from large tubers and produce very bright, showy flowers in just about every colour except blue. "Dinnerplate" dahlias can have blossoms up to 35 centimetres in diameter, but 15 to 20 centimetres is much more com-mon. If you're looking for these in your garden catalogue, look for the little girl completely dwarfed by immense blos-soms, which are often far larger than her head. Don't be fooled, that little girl is actually a pixie. Blooms can be single or double, and they are often spectacularly beautiful.

Dahlias are native to Mexico, and as such they want significant warmth and are sensitive to frost. They also want excellent soil with abundant water and good drainage. Due to their large tubers, dahlias are hard to grow in pots, so most

'Alberta Velvet' dahlia.

nurseries offer them as bulbs, though they can also be grown from seed.

Once upon a time, if you grew a dahlia, it was too precious a thing to waste, so you made sure you brought it indoors in the fall. Now we have a new problem. A new gardener goes to a garden centre and comes home with a $3 package of dahlia bulbs. By the end of the year, it produces one measly flower, and she says, "Well, there is no point in saving *this* useless plant!" so she consigns it to the compost. Or worse, she buys it after it has been on the shelf for seven weeks and is entirely dead from drying out. It either won't grow or it produces no flowers. Here's why that is terribly wrong—dahlias, like wine, get better with age. They won't flower really well until they are at least three years old, and they are heavy feeders, meaning they need lots of fertilizer or compost. If you

CARING FOR DAHLIA TUBERS

Your dahlia needs a winter rest, but it can't handle prairie levels of cold. Let it freeze in the fall. Your dahlia's aboveground parts will turn black at the first frost and become mushy. Leave the tubers in the ground for a good ten days following their decimation by cold, which is usually around early October. This tells the tubers their growing season is over so they go dormant. Then carefully dig out the tubers and cut off the old foliage. Bring tubers inside and wash them thoroughly in the sink to prevent any insects, bacteria, fungus, and so on from coming indoors with them.

Once they've dried off a bit, store them in an open pot or a container, buried in some sort of medium. You can use dry peat moss, sand, or even styrofoam peanuts, but the bottom line is, whatever medium you use, it needs to bury the tubers. You will need to put them somewhere that they remain cold but won't freeze. Between about 5°C and 10°C is perfect, so your garage is probably too cold, but a cold storage room or a root cellar is ideal. If it is too cold, the tubers will be damaged. If it is too warm, they can start to grow prematurely.

Check on them once a month. They should be just slightly moist to the touch and should not be sitting in water. If the tubers are shrivelling, give them a little water. I usually bring the tubers out in mid-March, pot them in large containers, and begin watering and fertilizing them. They will grow very quickly, and are so spectacular that it's well worth the work!

Fritillary.

There are few flowers that have the impact glads do.

like to baby and pamper a plant, a dahlia is a good candidate because they respond so well to love.

A mature dahlia in full flower is as beautiful as any rose or rhododendron, but if you really want them here, you're going to have to work for it. My great-grandmother grew huge dahlias in the fertile soil of Hague, Saskatchewan, long before I was born. My grandma has great black-and-white pictures of her mother's dahlias and they are some-thing to be seen. Imagine—in the 1940s she had better dahlias in her yard than most people do now! Those dahlias were grown in a warm, sheltered spot, got plenty of well-rotted manure and rainwater, and were lifted every year.

***Fritillaria* spp. (fritillary)** Smallish plants in the lily family, fritillaries have nodding, bell-like flowers and often a strong, skunky odour when broken or crushed. They are not bothered by pests or disease, flowering in spring. They will multiply where they are happy, and there is no shortage of varieties to try. They are usually listed as being hardy to zone 4 or 5, but most are native to cold, temperate regions so will do quite well here. I'd recommend getting acquainted with *Fritillaria meleagris* first, commonly called the checker lily. This beautiful, low-growing plant has white, purple, or pink flowers marked in a distinct check-ered pattern. It does marvellously under

deciduous trees and makes an excellent companion for hostas. Buy the bulbs in fall as soon as they are available and plant them immediately. They desiccate and die quickly otherwise. Get them into the ground as soon as possible.

***Gladiolus* spp. (glads)** This brings us to gladioli, which are not only one of my favourite flowers but also one of the favourites of Dame Edna Everage, one of my favourite famous people. The word *gladioli* comes from the Latin word *gladius,* meaning "sword," and refers to the shape of the leaves. (Hence the word *gladiator*.) Glads come in a huge assortment of colours, and they are easy to grow. Buy them in spring, and plant them in a sunny spot when it is good and warm out. You will need a sheltered loca-tion if you are growing the tall varieties because they can be easily smashed by wind and/or hail. They make incredible cut flowers, blooming for weeks. They are excellent "fillers" in beds, borders, and containers and can be sensationally showy. Buy the largest possible bulbs you can find (yes, ladies and gentlemen, size does matter!) because these will give you the best show of flowers. Sure, you can lift and store your glads for winter if you want, but why bother? Like tulips, glads are cheap, and finding a place to store them for the winter is a nuisance for me—so I just buy new ones every year. If I buy a big bag of glads for $15 and they give me armloads of flowers and

Hyacinth.

great pleasure all summer, I feel I have gotten my money's worth. (Spend that on a movie ticket and it lasts one evening and might not even be a good show, whereas $15 worth of glads is usually a pretty good show and lasts for weeks and weeks!)

Hyacinthus spp. (hyacinth) The last bulbs for fall planting that I will mention are the hyacinths. Hyacinths are fabulously fragrant and come in lots of colours. They are also only borderline hardy in the chinook zone. Sometimes they make it, sometimes they don't, so be prepared to treat them like an annual or simply play with them like I suggested for tulips (see below). Experimenting in the garden is wonderful, but keep in mind they are comparatively expensive so you could be better off spending your money on tulips or daffodils. Hyacinths are great for "forcing" (flowering indoors), but forcing bulbs is a subject for the next book. Grape hyacinths

If I were told that I must pick out a half-dozen lilies right now that I could not live without, I would recommend the following:

Aladdin's Sun' (yellow), 'Cancun' (orange/gold bicolour), 'La Toya' (deep fuchsia), 'Lollypop' (pink/white bicolour), 'Monte Negro' (brilliant red), 'Nepal' (snowy white), and 'Rose Queen' (deep pink).

(*Muscari* spp.) are perfectly hardy and have dark purple-blue flowers bunched together like clusters of tiny grapes; hence the name. In my experience, they aren't especially exciting garden plants. Stick with squills, okay?

Lilium spp. (Lily) Lilies have been grown in gardens for centuries. Not every plant name with the word *lily* in it is actually a lily, however. Lily of the valley, calla lily, voodoo lily, and lily of the Nile are all entirely unrelated plants and have nothing to do with true lilies. This is why Latin names are useful—all true lilies belong in the genus *Lilium*. There are about a million different varieties for you to choose from, and they come in all shapes, sizes, and colours. You don't have to become a lily expert, but you should know a few basics.

Asiatic lilies are the ones most commonly on offer. They are of complex parentage and almost always flower in mid-summer, meaning they're usually in full bloom in July. I am hesitant to recommend individual cultivars of Asiatic lilies for a variety of reasons. First, there are multitudes of them and how does one choose? Second, a variety that is available today may not be available next year as it may be replaced with a different variety or it might fall from popularity altogether. It is hard to find a bad variety of Asiatic lily. You should shop with confidence and not be concerned that one lily is better than another.

Trumpet lilies have long, tubular flowers. Easter lilies are good examples of trumpet lilies. Some of them are hardy, some of them are not, but they are very fragrant and worth experimenting with. 'Snow Queen' and 'Casa Rosa' are the hardiest ones I have grown.

Oriental lilies have enormous flowers and bloom in mid- to late summer, usually August. 'Stargazer' is the best known, and these are the hot pink lilies with the strong fragrance that florists often use. Orientals are also of varying degrees of hardiness, but most are fairly

'La Toya' is one of my favourite lilies.

reliable. I personally love 'Casablanca,' with 20-centimetre pure white blossoms and an incredible aroma.

Species lilies are also available. These are lilies that have not been hybridized or altered but are just as you would see them in nature. The western red lily (*Lilium philadelphicum*), which is Saskatchewan's provincial flower, is a species lily. The two that are most commonly offered for sale to gardeners here are the tiger lily (*L. tigrinum*) and the martagon lily (*L. martagon*).

Tiger lilies are old-fashioned, quite tall, and have recurving orange petals heavily marked with black spots. They bloom in August and look best when grown in large clumps. Get the pronunciation correct; it makes me twitchy when people call them "tagger lilies." Also, it is incorrect to refer to just any random lily with orange flowers as tiger lilies.

Martagon lilies are the only lilies with a preference for partial shade, and they have beautiful whorled leaves and masses and masses of small, down-facing flowers. They are slow to establish and often expensive, but they are well worth it.

Whatever lily you choose, you'll find these plants require little maintenance, multiply over time, and look gorgeous for a long period. Grow them all in a sunny site with good soil. You can buy them as plants at your favourite garden centre or as bulbs to plant in spring or fall through mail-order nurseries. Deer will annihilate lilies, and the recently introduced Japanese lily beetle is also starting to be a problem. Botrytis and a few other fungal diseases can sometimes cause problems as well. That said, lilies are largely inexpensive, and it's easy to get carried away and fill your garden with them.

Narcissus spp. (daffodils) You will grow better daffodils in Calgary than you will anywhere else on the Canadian prairies! They seem to like our high elevation and cold nights. Certain neighbourhoods in Calgary become like Belgian marketplaces with drifts of yellow daffodils every spring. Daffs do awesome here, and require little. Plant them.

Daffodils are also mildly poisonous, which means that they are usually left alone by deer and squirrels. Unlike tulips, daffodils will actually get better every year and will multiply in good locations. In the wild, daffodils often grow near creeks and streams, so a good location for them is a sunny spot with good soil and decent moisture. Unlike tulips, where just about every variety is perfectly hardy, not all daffodils are created equal. A lot of the doubles and very large varieties are hit and miss here. Very short, dwarf forms of daffodils are almost always quite hardy and are good plants for beginners to start with.

Daffodils are available in oranges, golds, lemons, canaries, saffrons, and butter colours—or, in a word, yellow! Don't buy into any of this nonsense that there are "pink" daffodils—it's a lie. The so-called "pink" daffodils are coral, peach, or soft orange. While nice, they are certainly not pink in real life,

A good general rule (and this is very general) is that the shorter the daffodil, the hardier it is likely to be.

Daffodil.

and absolutely not the Pepto-Bismol pink the Photoshopped picture the bulb catalogue would lead you to believe. There are also some excellent and very fine white daffodils. We definitely do not use enough white in our gardens, so you might want to look for some of these too because they are worth planting.

Squills If you aren't growing squills, you need to be. These are fabulous little plants in the lily family that require virtually nothing and offer so much as to be considered extraordinary. They come up very early in the spring and often flower when there is still snow on the ground. The striped squill (*Puschkinia libanotica*) grows only about 5 centimetres or so tall and does this neat little magic trick wherein up close, the flowers are white with blue veining but from a distance appear as a sort of pale glacier blue. The blooms are fragrant and make charming, tiny bouquets. Plant them in mass to best enjoy them; they will come up every year and multiply.

The Siberian squill (*Scilla siberica*) is slightly taller and has beautiful blue flowers quite early. There are also white- and pink-flowered forms, but they are inferior so forget them. Blue Siberian squill will flower for several weeks in early spring and will multiply.

Squills are great things to plant under deciduous trees such as birch or ash because they flower before these trees leaf out, taking advantage of early spring sunshine. When they are done blooming, they quickly and quietly go to sleep.

They are also *very* inexpensive: you can buy several dozen of them for next to nothing, yet they provide so much. Just plant them in a sunny area with good drainage and off they go.

Tulipa **spp. (tulips)** Tulips are fabulous. They come in all different heights, sizes, colours, and so on, and they can be early, mid-season, or late blooming, though all flower at some point in spring. Try to plant a mix of them to extend your tulip season. It is very important to buy bulbs as soon as they are available, which usually means late August or the beginning of September. Bulbs dry out and desiccate (die) on store shelves. The best place for them to be is in the ground, getting their roots growing before winter comes. If possible, plant them the day you buy them.

The packages always have nonsensical instructions like "plant bulbs six inches deep." Ignore that. Use the size of the bulb as your gauge. If the bulb stands 3 centimetres tall, plant it 3 to 5 centimetres deep. If the bulb stands 6 centimetres tall, plant it 6 to 10 centimetres deep. After planting, water them in well. Keep them well watered, in fact, until the ground freezes. I also recommend mulching them. Squirrels are notorious for digging up bulbs and eating them, so keep a close eye out for these vermin.

As soon as they are planted, the bulbs will begin to root. In spring, they will magically soar out of the ground, flower magnificently, and if you have planted en masse, your neighbours will be tremendously thrilled with your suddenly acquired gardening talent. Tulips are seriously idiot-proof, with no experience or skills required. Most people don't know that, but it's true.

Tulips *are* perennial, if you want to be very technical. They can last for years. But don't try to keep them as perennials. Do you know that every year, the tulips that flower for Ottawa's tulip festival are ripped out of the ground the instant they are finished and new ones are planted in fall? It's true. Want to know why? Because tulips get progressively poorer as time marches on—the blossoms get smaller and their vigour begins to fail. Much like all of us, really. Tulips are also *cheap*. You can buy a decent number of bulbs for the same price as a bouquet from a florist and guess which one will bring you infinitely more joy? Buy bulbs. Plant them. Watch them flower in spring. It's fabulous! This is also an excellent activity in which to involve children.

Once upon a time, people planted tulips. After the tulips were done blooming, there was this lengthy period in which one had to wait for the foliage to "die down" and the bulbs to go dormant. Back then you really couldn't do anything with this space because there were tulip bulbs there. Forget that! When your tulips are done blooming, rip them out. You've gotten your money's worth out of them, and maybe next year you simply don't want red and white tulips—maybe you want purple and pink instead. Planting new tulips every year lets you totally play with the colour scheme, and also with where you put them in the garden. Since they are merely using up the nutrients in the bulb anyway, you can plant tulips in shady spots, they'll flower madly, and you'll look like a genius. When they're done, you can put begonias or impatiens or ferns there instead! Handy, no?

Tulips offer some of the first blooms in spring.

'Havran' tulips are a gorgeous purple that adds depth to your beds, especially if planted with a pale yellow or lime green.

❧ *I O* ❧

The perennial question

Annuals are often referred to as bedding plants because they are excellent in seasonal flowerbeds. Annuals complete their life cycle in a single season; hence, they last only a year. The Calgary Stampede is an *annual* event; we have it once a year. In a similar fashion, you plant annuals *once a year*.

Perennials are plants that return year after year. They are *herbaceous*, which means that all of their green tissue dies and is replaced seasonally. All perennials have a life span; they do not live forever and ever, as many people mistakenly believe. A perennial is not a diamond. You will not always have it with you. Blue flax, for example, is a short-lived perennial. It will last two or three seasons and then it is gone. Most perennials, on average, last between four and six years before they either die or begin to look shabby and need replacing. Some

Rogersia is a handsome, little used perennial with a long lifespan that does well in a moist location.

Opposite: Aster

perennials, such as peonies, are extraordinarily long-lived, lasting any-where from 80 to 100 years.

Biennial: These plants form a rosette of foliage in the first year, then flower, shed seed, and die in their second year of life. Mullein (*Verbascum* spp.) is a good example of a biennial, and so are some kinds of foxglove.

Ephemerals: These plants go dormant (vanish and appear to have died) once they are finished blooming. Most ephemerals are spring bloomers. Shooting stars and some of the fritillaries are good examples of ephemerals.

Monocarps: These plants are often referred to as being *monocarpic*, which means they are genetically programmed to die after they have flowered and produced seeds, and there isn't a blessed thing you can do about it. Many of the famed blue poppies (*Meconopsis* spp.) are monocarps.

Many new gardeners fall into a trap here. Many people, upon de-veloping an interest in gardening, soon realize that it is quite expensive to plant annuals every year. So they say to themselves, "I am only going to plant perennials. Then the garden is done, and I don't need to worry about replacing things every year."

Remember, though, perennials do indeed have an expiry date and they do take a while to establish. There are also a large number of extremely fabulous plants that happen to be annuals. An annual looks good shortly after it's transplanted, and since the incentive is pretty high to make as many seeds as possible, they often flower like crazy. By saying no to annuals, you cheat yourself out of a good many incredible and wonderful plants. The fact is if you want to grow heliotrope or evening scented stocks or nigella or certain poppies, you are going to have to plant them every year. These are absolutely sensational plants, and why should you be denied the pleasure of growing them? Annuals are also just the thing for filling in quickly or providing a show while you are waiting for your perennials and shrubs to take root, and you can change them up every year.

Because annuals don't need to survive our winter, you can pretty much plant anything that tickles your fancy. You may have to trans-plant seedlings to get them big enough to be able to flower during our growing season, but without the limit of climate you have a lot of options available in annuals. This isn't the case with perennials. Some simply will never grow here, and some may survive but not flourish. In this section, I'll give you the scoop on the different perennials you're likely to encounter in the local garden centres.

Yarrow.

Monkshood.

***Achillea* spp. (yarrow)** Yarrow has beautiful, finely divided foliage and large, flat heads of flowers that can be white, red, orange, gold, pink, cerise, or yellow. They bloom all summer and are highly attractive to butterflies. Yarrow is easy to grow and rewarding—I often recommend it for beginners. Keep in mind, however, that if you put yarrow in rich soil, not only will it become floppy and flower poorly, but it will also send out runners and become very invasive. Grow yarrow in lean, well-drained soil, and don't give it your compost or your love. Varieties I like include 'Cerise Queen,' 'Coronation Gold,' 'Paprika,' 'Pink Grapefruit,' 'Pomegranate,' and 'Terracotta.'

***Aconitum* spp. (monkshood)** An old-fashioned perennial often recommended for shade but better in sun. Flowers range from blue through purple mostly, but the pale yellow flowered form is also nice. The pink-flowered varieties are dirty, muddy pinks and ugly. Monkshood grows quite tall, and there are both early and late-blooming species. Most are more than hardy and easily divided. Rich, fertile soil and good moisture is best. They make great cut flowers. 'Spark'

and 'Stainless Steel' are my two favourite varieties, but I also like 'Bicolour,' which is a purple/white blend. Monkshood is extremely poisonous if eaten (so don't eat it), and it is said to have sprung up from the slobber of Cerberus, the three-headed dog in Greek mythology that guarded the gates of the underworld.

***Aegopodium* spp. (goutweed, snow on the mountain)** A member of the carrot family, goutweed was so named because it was once used medicinally to treat gout and rheumatism. It gets white flowers that are neither showy nor interesting, but insects love them. This plant is extremely aggressive and rapidly sends out runners in every direction. It grows equally well in sun or shade and will grow in nearly any soil, as well as being drought-resistant once established. It is an attractive plant with pale green and cream-coloured leaves that are extremely useful for brightening up dark, shady spaces where nothing else is willing to grow. However, be aware that once you have it, you will always have it, so use it with caution.

***Ajuga* spp. (carpet bugle)** Ajuga is a pretty little plant with small,

'Mahogany' ajuga.

Alchemilla.

spoon-shaped leaves and smallish blue or blue-purple flowers. It is primarily grown as a groundcover but can also be a good plant to use as "filler" in your containers. It is happy in sun or shade, but it has shallow roots and requires moisture. The general rule is that the green leaf forms are hardier and more reliable. For these I like 'Bronze Beauty,' and 'Catlin's Giant,' and 'Metallica.' There are some fancier forms, such as the very beautiful, multicoloured 'Rainbow' or the stunning violet-and-cream-splashed 'Harlequin.' These grow much more slowly and do not always survive the winter here, though they are inexpensive and worth trying. Ajuga will spread and eventually form a nice little carpet, but it does so slowly and politely.

Alchemilla spp. (lady's mantle) Oh goodness yes! First of all, you have these gorgeous, soft leaves that are shaped like a lady's shawl. They are delicately furred, and whenever it rains, they catch and hold beads of water like quicksilver. It is astonishing. So astonishing, in fact, that the Latin name refers to *alchemy* because this effect is so striking! Then there are the flowers, which are a brilliant acid-green to chartreuse yellow and billow and froth like a witch's cauldron. It is the perfect plant to use with heucheras, ferns, and primulas. Lady's mantle grows perfectly well in sun or shade and it sometimes self-seeds. It likes fertile soil and moisture but will make do with much less. It also makes great filler for bouquets and establishes quickly. Lady's mantle grows about 60 centimetres wide and about 30 centimetres tall, making it a nice groundcover. You want this plant and you want it badly.

Althaea spp. (hollyhock) There are two types of people in this world—those for whom hollyhocks are weeds, and those who cannot get a hollyhock to grow for love nor money. Depending on their parentage, hollyhocks can be annual, perennial, or biennial, and it is impossible to tell by looking at them which one you've got. These plants are always hugely popular and quickly sell out, but you'll pay $5 or $6 a piece for one, which is ridiculous given the quantity of seeds they produce. My advice? Don't even bother. These plants dislike disturbance, they generally don't transplant well, but they are *really* easy from seed. Grow hollyhocks in lean soil and preferably somewhere sheltered, such as along a wall or a fence because they are tall plants and can easily be taken down by strong winds or hail. They will also self-sow all over the place, and the offspring may or may not resemble the parent plants. Hollyhock rust is a common fungal disease that causes them to develop ugly, blotchy leaves that fall off and leave the plants with bare stems.

There is no cure for it, but you should remove the dropped foliage and double-bag or burn them so that the spores aren't spreading through your garden and neighbourhood.

Anemone spp. (windflower) There are lots of anemones for you to choose from. Many colours and shapes exist, with some extremely tiny, some tallish, and some somewhere in between. There are about 150 species, though certainly not all of them are hardy. Though they can be purchased as bulbs, I kept anemone out of the bulb section since you don't want the kinds available as a bulb in our climate. The poppy anemones (*Anemone coronaria*) are sometimes sold as annuals and sometimes sold as bulbs in the fall. They are definitely not hardy here, so don't be taken in by them. The Greek anemones (*Anemone blanda*) are tiny little plants with blue-mauve to violet flowers and are so tiny as to be ridiculous. In a sheltered spot, they do sometimes overwinter here, but no one is going to notice them. Snowdrop anemone (*Anemone sylvestris*) is a gorgeous plant with large, showy white flowers over a long period in late spring or early summer. It is absolutely beautiful when in bloom, and then you have to spend the rest of the summer looking at its boring foliage. It is an aggressive and fast-spreading plant, so I don't recommend it unless you have a *lot* of space. The Canada anemone (*Anemone canadensis*) is native here and sometimes available to gardeners. It does better in shade than sun and looks very similar to *A. sylvestris* but the flowers are smaller. It is equally aggressive and best used for filling in large spaces. Finally, there are the Japanese anemones (*A. hupehensis* var. *japonica*). These are much loved in milder climates, and in recent years they have been showing up in Alberta garden centres more often. They form tidy, non-invasive clumps and flower exuberantly in late summer through autumn. The flowers are also large and showy. 'Honorine Jobert' (white) and 'September Charm' (pink) are two of the most popular varieties. Here's the

Anemone sylvestris.

problem … while they are usually pretty hardy and usually survive here, that's about all they do. It seems that our season is too short for them. They take a long time to come out of the ground in spring and take a long time to get going. I have found that usually by the time they are setting buds, the frosts have already cut them down. I pulled mine out after three years of not flowering. Having said that, they have done well in the Reader Rock Garden in downtown Calgary, and there are a few gardeners here who have had high praise for them. I say … try a Japanese anemone at least once and see how it does for you. You might get lucky.

Aquilegia spp. (columbine) These old-fashioned perennials come in a huge array of shapes, sizes, and colours but usually bear starry flowers with long spurs. Magnets for butterflies, bees, and hummingbirds, they are fast-growing and easy. Grow columbines in moist, fertile soil in a dappled or filtered light for best results. Full sun is fine if they have

Columbine.

moisture, but they tend to suffer in deep shade. After they are finished blooming, columbine will self-seed very freely if allowed to. They also hybridize, and you can get some very interesting results. Individual plants are short-lived, but they are inexpensive and easily replaced. Columbine worms can defoliate these plants overnight, but healthy plants will regrow so it's nothing to worry about.

Artemesia spp. (artemesia) Often incorrectly referred to as sage, artemesias were named for the Greek goddess Artemis. Most are quite large plants growing about 1 metre tall, and like many other extremely drought-resistant plants, they are almost always silver or grey-green. Pests and disease almost never trouble them, and as they are strongly scented when broken or crushed, deer and rabbits usually leave them alone too. Almost all of them are hardy, but be careful as a few of them are also invasive, especially in rich soil. Grow artemesias in lean, poor soil for best results. 'Valerie Finnis' and 'Powis Castle' are two excellent varieties, and the plant commonly known as silvermound is also a favourite of mine. 'Oriental Limelight' has golden-and-green-splashed foliage and is quite attractive but also aggressive and will revert back to solid green if you don't stay on top of removing the solid green leaves.

Asclepias spp. (milkweed) Milkweeds are some of my most favourite plants of all time! They are the only host plants for the monarch butterfly, so they are absolutely worth adding to your garden. They have gorgeous, starry, nectar-rich blooms that attract a wide range of foraging creatures, and they can be visually stunning in the garden. Although there are many kinds, they are still fairly uncommon in garden centres. Butterfly weed (*A. tuberosa*) is highly resentful of disturbance and usually sulks for several years after being planted. It is also very reluctant to break dormancy and is usually the last perennial in my garden to come out of the ground. Flowers are brilliant pumpkin orange (or occasionally yellow) and

it will do best in lean soil in a sunny, fairly dry area. They bloom for most of the summer. The swamp milkweed (*A. incarnata*) is tall and willowy and prefers a damp location. The flowers can be white or pink and are sweetly scented, appearing in mid- to late summer. It is a gorgeous and highly desirable plant. The showy milkweed (*A. speciosa*) is native to western Canada; you may have seen it growing in the ditches around Lethbridge or Brooks. As the common name suggests, the blooms are indeed showy, and they are sweetly scented as well. The large, pale green leaves are quite distinctive. It is easy from seed and one of my very favourite garden plants. Unlike the other two I mentioned (which are not weedy at all), this species can become very aggressive under garden conditions, but it is not difficult to control if it gets out of hand.

Aster spp. (asters) From the Latin word meaning star, asters do indeed have starry flowers. There are bazillions of choices when it comes to asters, and they come in a huge array of shapes, sizes, and colours. Butterflies and bees adore them. There are spring-blooming asters such as the alpine aster, and there are tonnes of native species available from wildflower specialists that are worth having. The fall-blooming asters are my very favourite, and they begin blooming in late summer, often blooming well into October. Mine have still been in bloom at Thanksgiving! Plant as many asters as you can get your paws on and see which ones you like best. The only caveat to keep in mind is that several cultivars can be prone to powdery mildew.

Astilbe spp. (astilbe) I have sad news for you. Your astilbes are never going to look as good as they do on the labels or in the gardening magazines. They just won't. I have never seen a real-life astilbe look as good as the ones in the books and catalogues. I don't know why, it's just the truth. Astilbe is one of the very first plants that will be recommended to you if you go into a garden centre

Astilbe.

Astrantia.

and ask for plants that will do well in shade. They are long-lived and have very handsome foliage and showy flowers, but you need to know a few basics. First, while they will certainly grow in deep shade, they will flower far better with a few hours of sun. Second, they are very late to break dormancy in the spring, and given that the shade garden takes the longest to thaw out, sometimes we are well into June before you see any signs of life from these plants. Third, they have no tolerance for wind or hail. Or drought. A moist, very rich soil in a sheltered spot is what they want. If you fail to accommodate them, they will either die or they will limp along like a wounded animal on a highway. Guess how many astilbes I have in my garden—*None!* I don't have time for any plant to be a diva or a princess. Oh, you want more compost? Oh, you can't bounce back after a thunderstorm? Well, let me tell you something, "Your Majesty … " ain't nobody got time for that! I sometimes buy large astilbe plants in full bloom to use in containers, but I don't have them anywhere else.

***Astrantia* spp. (masterwort)** Loved by the British for years, these plants are only just starting to gain a following in North America. They are very hardy and bloom for a long period. Flowers

> The best astilbes I have seen are at the Calgary Zoo, where they are using hippopotamus manure for fertilizer. Got a hippo in your garden? Be my guest.

can be white, reddish, pink, or purple. Although they are (again!) recommended for shade, a dappled or filtered shade is much better than deep shade. In very deep shade, they survive but they don't flower properly. The thing you need to know to be successful with them is moisture. That's pretty much it. They aren't terribly fussy about soil and partial shade is usually fine, but they don't deal well with drought. If you've got a moist spot, they are worth planting. They also look best in large clumps rather than as single specimens. They will attract butterflies and florists.

***Baptisia* spp. (wild indigo)** A fabulous plant in the pea and bean family, wild indigo is slow to establish but long-lived and gorgeous. It becomes a large plant with beautiful spikes of blue or blue-purple flowers in early summer, followed by interesting and decorative seed heads. It wants full sun, average soil, and to

The pink stems of bergenia flower heads are especially attractive.

Bellflower.

be left undisturbed. It's very drought-resistant once it's mature and is loved by bees.

***Bergenia* spp. (bergenia)** From Siberia comes this evergreen perennial with large, paddle-like leaves. The flowers appear in early spring and can be almost any shade of pink. Occasionally, the leaves will take on red or pink colouring in the fall. Bergenia either looks fabulous or like crap. There seems to be no in-between. It will grow absolutely anywhere (sun or shade doesn't seem to matter) and can eventually form large clumps. Where it's happy, it's valuable and attractive. In open, unprotected sites such as the chinook zone, it can get fried in the winter. Try it and see how it does for you.

***Brunnera* spp. (brunnera)** Sort of a sophisticated forget-me-not, brunnera has very large, heart-shaped leaves that are quite attractive. In some varieties, such as 'Jack Frost' or 'Looking Glass,' these leaves are heavily marked in silver, making them even *more* attractive! Flowers appear in early summer and are brilliant turquoise blue. Brunnera will do best in partial to moderate shade with good soil and moisture.

Cactus *Cactus* is definitely not the scientific name; don't be fooled. Perfectly hardy, native cacti *are* available to southern Alberta gardeners. You will see native cacti growing around Drumheller, Medicine Hat, and Lethbridge. They have spectacular flowers, and the

formidable spines make them excellent barrier plants. If you want to grow native cactus, you have to grow them in a site with flawless drainage (otherwise, they are prone to root rot) and where you will not slip and fall on them or step on them. Full sun is essential. You can find them in your favourite native plant catalogue; don't take them from the wild. Native cacti are a unique addition to your garden, and one of the few that will prefer to be completely neglected.

***Caltha* spp. (marsh marigold)** You're most likely to find this in the greenhouse with the water plants, being sold as a "pond marginal." It is a fabulous perennial that does not have to be grown in shallow water—a moist location where its roots won't dry out will do just fine. It has very handsome foliage and erupts into flower usually in May. The flowers are golden yellow, cheery, and gorgeous. I love this plant, and I think more gardeners need to know about it. It's native throughout North America and is apparently a favourite food of moose, so perhaps avoid planting it if moose are an issue in your yard.

***Campanula* spp. (bellflower)** There are multitudes of bellflowers for you to choose from, and they range from tiny little alpines suitable for the rock garden all the way up to giants that grow several metres tall. Almost all are worth having. The flowers are showy and appear over a long season, and they are usually quick to establish. The only one I would avoid

Bugbane.

Clematis 'Blue Ravine.'

is the creeping bellflower (*Campanula rapunculoides*), which is so horrifically weedy I am amazed Hollywood hasn't made a film about it yet.

Chrysanthemum spp. (mums) I am madly in love with fall chrysanthemums! It is actually botanically incorrect to call them chrysanthemums anymore since they have been renamed *Dendranthema*, but whatever you call them, you want them in your garden. These are clumping plants for a sunny location, most growing a little over a half-metre tall. Colours include ivory, scarlet, orange, gold, yellow, and pink. They begin to flower in late summer or early fall and bloom basically until the snow claims them. Don't bother with any mum not in the Morden series, which was developed in Manitoba. All the others aren't terribly hardy here, so don't be swayed by what the tags claim.

Cimicifuga spp. (bugbane) Due to similarities in their mitochondrial DNA (I'm not kidding), *Cimicifuga* has now been reclassified as *Actaea*. This causes me no small amount of irritation because it causes needless confusion. Bugbane is an absolutely gorgeous, slow-growing perennial that will live for decades. It has very handsome dark green foliage and bottlebrush-like flowers in white or pale pink in late summer. It is happiest in moist, fertile soil in a sheltered spot. Often recommended for shade, it actually needs a few hours of direct sun to perform its best. Many cultivars exist, but 'Brunette' (with heavily

purple-stained new growth) and 'Black Negligee' (burgundy leaves) are my favourites.

Clematis spp. (clematis) Getting into clematis can be overwhelming since there is so much choice. We have large-flowered hybrids such as 'Jackmannii' and 'Nelly Moser' and hardy 15-metre climbing giants such as 'Prairie Traveller's Joy' (*C. vitalba*). Want a superb, easy-care big vine? Try *C. macropetala* or *C. alpina*. Numerous non-climbing forms or sprawling forms are available, such as *C. heracleifolia*, *C. recta*, and *C. integrifolia*. We also have gorgeous native species such as *C. verticellaris* and some that are sometimes weedy, such as the yellow-flowered *C. tangutica*. Some clematis are nicer than others, but I recommend growing as many different ones as you can get. They generally like rich, moist soil in a sunny site. Most would prefer some shelter from the wind. Some bloom early, some bloom late. Much fuss has been made of pruning clematis and what "category" it falls into. For now, don't worry about pruning it; just get it to grow first. After you've got one that's blooming and well established, then start thinking about pruning.

Convallaria spp. (lily of the valley) Although in the lily family, this is not a true species of lily. Many gardeners will say terrible things about this plant, such as how invasive and relentless it is, but this plant is only a problem in a bad location. It does indeed spread

Delphinium.

prolifically, but it is low-growing and can flourish in places that few other things can. From full sun to deepest shade and everything in between, lily of the valley is highly adaptable. It forms a lush, weed-smothering carpet of deep green leaves and it flowers very early, usually May. The flowers are white and quite small, but they are so powerfully fragrant that a couple tiny bouquets will perfume a room. The scent is hard to describe, but it is unique and heavenly. Occasionally, showy reddish-orange berries will follow the blooms. A pink-flowered form is also available, but it is ugly with little scent. Lily of the valley is very poisonous, so don't eat it, though this means that deer and rabbits won't eat it either.

***Corydalis* spp. (corydalis)** This large genus of very delicate-looking plants has lacy, attractive foliage and spur-shaped flowers. Depending on the species, flowers can be ivory, scarlet, yellow, purple, pink, or blue. Some are hardy, some are less hardy, but all are worth experimenting with. They tend to be short-lived but will often self-sow. The yellow-flowered species are the hardiest and generally the ones I recommend for new gardeners. The blue-flowered Tibetan species *Corydalis flexuosa* has stunning sky-blue flowers in small clusters that I love because they resemble schools of fish swimming over the leaves! 'Blue Panda' is a particularly vigorous cultivar. Grow corydalis in compost-enriched, well-drained soil. They like moisture, but they can't handle standing in it, so many of them die

in prolonged spring seasons where the garden stays cold and wet. These plants should not be in full sun (or they will burn) or full shade (or they will die), so find a balance between the two. Underneath a birch tree in a nice, filtered light suits them perfectly.

***Cypripedium* spp. (lady's slipper orchid)** About fifty species of lady's slipper are known throughout the world, with three or four of them being native to Alberta. They are exquisite, fragrant, and usually very expensive. The yellow lady's slipper is the one normally on offer here. These plants are critically endangered in the wild, so when purchasing these from a nursery, please inquire as to whether they are from cultivated stock. If they have been dug from the wild, you need to stop shopping at that nursery and then report it to Fish and Wildlife because Canadian law protects all native species of orchid. Grow lady's slippers in partial or dappled shade, with humusy, moist soil. They flower in early summer and are one of the most fabulous things you can grow. They are also among the hardiest orchids in the world, and why shouldn't you have an orchid in your garden? Several hybrid lady's slippers are vigorous and stunning, though sometimes difficult to obtain. 'Giselle' is a particularly outstanding one.

***Delphinium* spp. (delphiniums)** Always say yes to delphiniums! These generally very tall plants (anywhere from 1 to 2.5 metres) come in shades of white, blue, purple, mauve, lavender, and pink, with the blue forms offering some of the best blues in the garden. They flower in early summer and are loved by bees and hummingbirds. Delphiniums are easy to grow, wanting only a sunny spot and good soil. Though they can be short-lived, they will self-sow, and sometimes you get interesting offspring. Delphinium worm can be a problem (see the chapter on pests), but they are mostly trouble-free. They have hollow stems so they may need to be staked or tied up, but I would recommend planting them in a sheltered spot in a large group so that the stems support one another. The Chinese delphiniums are very small, usually around half a metre tall, and have spectacular cobalt blue flowers. They won't break in the wind and add a shocking element of blue to the garden.

Dianthus **spp. (dianthus)** Dianthus are sometimes called "pinks" not so much because the flowers are pink (though they often are) but because in many kinds the petals are jagged like they've been cut with pinking shears. This is the genus to which carnations belong, as well as a whole host of other fabulous plants. Different kinds of dianthus include cheery little cheddar pinks, tiny alpine varieties that bloom early, as well as old favourites such as sweet williams and clove pinks. There is also a delightful little groundcover called maiden pink (*Dianthus deltoides)*, of which 'Flashing Lights' is my favourite and probably the most insanely hot cherry-pink flower you will ever see in your life. There is also the strange-looking yellow-flowered species *Dianthus knappii* and a host of beautiful hybrids, including the award-winning 'Firewitch,' with fragrant pink blooms all summer. Since they need only a sunny spot, average soil, and little else, dianthus can be grown by absolutely anyone. Both butterflies and gardeners enjoy the sweetly scented, long-blooming flowers. Dianthus can be short-lived and not all of them are hardy, but pick up a package of seeds and experiment with these plants because it's easy to fall in love with them.

The heart-shaped flowers of bleeding heart are quite unique.

Dicentra **spp. (bleeding heart)** The best-known type of bleeding heart is *Dicentra spectabilis*, often called old-fashioned bleeding heart. This large plant usually grows just under a metre tall and has beautiful pink and white heart-shaped flowers in late spring or early summer. Few things are hardier or more dependable than a bleeding heart. They like partial (not deep) shade and may go dormant or become shabby-looking by midsummer if they are not in a cool, moist location. The stunning white-flowered form, although not as vigorous, is worth having. Fern-leaf bleeding hearts are much smaller and have finely cut, somewhat fern-like foliage and pink, reddish pink, or ivory flowers, depending on the cultivar. All bloom profusely, are quite pretty, and will do best in a rich, moist soil with moderate shade. A filtered or dappled light suits them especially well. Many will go dormant after flowering, so be sure not to disturb them if they suddenly disappear.

Digitalis **spp. (foxglove)** Dear prairie gardeners, please stop trying to grow *Digitalis purpurea*. This is the foxglove you see naturalized all along the West Coast and in England. It is a tall plant with very showy tubular flowers in shades of purple, pink, or magenta. Every year garden centres sell them, every year they are much in demand, and every year all of them except the yellow ones die without ever flowering. The only exception to this is the award-winning dwarf strain called 'Foxy,' which will flower in its first year if started early enough but won't live any longer than that in our climate. Foxgloves typically form a rosette of leaves the first year and flower the second. Many garden centres sell it already in bloom, but please realize that once it's done blooming, you will never see it again. Regardless of what the tag claims, they winter poorly here, if at all, so don't bother with them unless they are already in bud when you buy them and you don't mind spending that much money on an annual plant. The two yellow-flowered species that are exceptions to this are *Digitalis lutea* and *Digitalis grandiflora*. Both are beautiful but not

Shooting star.

See, I told you the yellow foxglove are beautiful!

as showy as the purple-flowered species. They are 100 per cent hardy, I absolutely love them, and they are fantastic in our climate. They bloom all summer and are prized by bees. Grow foxglove in a sunny spot with average soil and good moisture. Also keep in mind that they are very poisonous, so don't eat them.

***Disporum* spp. (fairy bells)** Not often grown, fairy bells are slowly but surely working their way into the nursery trade. There are both Asian and North American species, but if you are looking for flash and dazzle, this is not the plant you want. They are elegant, sophisticated, and subtle. Small, lily-like white or yellow flowers appear usually singly or in pairs in early summer. The flowers are exquisite but not showy and are often followed by attractive berries. Partial shade and good moisture suits them best.

***Dodecatheon* spp. (shooting star)** These fabulous little plants with pink, mauve, magenta, white, or lavender flowers resemble cyclamens, and the blossoms are also scented. They bloom

in early summer and are among our most glorious native plants. In the wild, shooting stars grow along creeks, streams, riverbanks, and in moist meadows. They are usually found in places that are damp in spring and often quite dry or even hot in the summer. After flowering, they go dormant. The best place for them is a moist, sunny location. They are also good under deciduous trees, as they flower just as the trees are leafing out. They are worth searching for. Most native plant specialists offer them, as do more than a few garden centres.

***Echinacea* spp. (purple coneflower)** There aren't many perennials I would label as being "essential," but these are one of them. Purple coneflowers (which are usually more pink than purple) are tidy, non-aggressive plants that form compact, attractive clumps and begin to flower in late summer when many other perennials are well past their prime. They provide a huge banquet for bees and butterflies and will often bloom well into October. The seed heads are much loved by songbirds, especially finches. They are heat- and drought-resistant, they want average soil, and they don't really have any pest or disease issues. (Although deer, rabbits, and grasshoppers will demolish them if they get the chance.) Here's the problem with purple coneflowers ... some are hardy and some are not. New "fancy" echinaceas are hitting the market in record

SHOPPING WITH LYNDON

Globe thistle.

Echinacea.

Do not plant any echinacea variety that has been on the market for less than twenty-five years. If you're not sure, ask. Also, look at the price tag. Any echinacea that costs more than $10 is probably pretty new.

numbers—with outrageous colours and bizarre and peculiar double- and triple-flowered forms. You stay away from those crazy, wild hybrids, do you hear me? They are exorbitantly expensive, and they have more or less failed right across the board in prairie trials.

'Magnus' has huge flowers and was perennial of the year for 1998. It is entirely reliable. 'White Swan' is a gorgeous and desperately underused variety with white flowers and just a hint of green in the cones. It is a favourite of mine, and looks absolutely stunning with ornamental grasses. 'Kim's Knee High' and 'Prairie Splendor' are also perfectly reliable.

Echinops spp. (globe thistle) This is a big perennial, reaching 1.5 to 1.75 metres tall and about 1 metre wide. The flowers are perfectly globe-shaped and blue to blue-purple in colour. Bees are absolutely crazy about them, but they also make good cut flowers and have excellent winter interest. Although not weedy, globe thistles will self-sow if you let them. These are easily removed if unwanted, provided that you do it when they are quite young. The sharp, prickly leaves

make it a great barrier plant, and it is best in average to poor soil in full sun. Globe thistle makes a stunning background plant and is fantastic for a "hedge." I love it. Do not be sucked in by the white-flowered forms—they are a dirty white and not pretty.

Epimedium spp. (barrenwort, bishop's hat) Ten years ago, these perennials were still fairly obscure but are now becoming increasingly common. Barrenwort are extremely reliable and extremely valuable. Most are native to cold parts of Asia, and they can be either herbaceous or evergreen. The herbaceous ones are usually fine here, and the evergreen ones might be okay in a sheltered spot with some extra winter protection. Both are compact, tidy plants that do not spread. Barrenworts have gorgeous foliage that reminds me of Roman shields. Depending on the species and variety, some of them colour up brilliantly in the fall. The flowers, small and spidery, come in a multitude of colours and are pretty although not flashy. They have a preference for shade

Sea holly.

Joepye weed.

and moist soil, although once established they can tolerate a surprising degree of dryness, abuse, and neglect. You should grow these!

***Erigeron* spp. (fleabane)** These plants are not used that often, I suspect, because of the unattractive common name, coined because they were once used to make a flea and tick repellant. They are in the aster family and produce very showy, daisy-like flowers over a long period in early to mid-summer. They are great for cutting and easy in the garden. Fleabane matures quickly and is low maintenance. Lots of varieties exist, but my favourite is 'Pink Jewel,' with its large, clear pink blossoms. Grow them in full sun and average, well-drained soil.

***Eryngium* spp. (sea holly)** Sea hollies want full sun and average to poor soil with good drainage and will draw flurries of bees. They are usually blue, gorgeous, and offer great winter interest. They also hate disturbance, so buy them when they are as small as possible. 'Blue Glitter' is a particularly stunning cultivar. Always say yes to sea hollies!

***Eupatorium* spp. (joepye weed)** This is another misleading common name

because joepye weed isn't weedy at all! The Latin name has recently been changed to *Eutrochium*, which doesn't impress me, again because I think such renaming causes confusion for amateurs and professionals alike. Joepye needs a moist location because it's a very big plant. About 2 metres tall and almost as wide is average, although the cultivar 'Little Joe' grows about half that size. Flowering in late summer, joepye produces a huge and impressive clump of violet to light purple fluffy clusters of flowers that look a bit like cotton candy. Bees and butterflies love them, and if you are looking to create some drama in the garden, this is the plant to do it with. Set it up as a background plant or use it in place of a shrub. Joepye will not thank you for shade, and it is very late to break dormancy in the spring, which is a real benefit for us in the chinook region. Don't be discouraged if it's not out of the ground until sometime in June.

***Euphorbia* spp. (spurge)** Every year in June, dozens of people contact me to ask, "What is this fabulous little cushion-like, mounding plant with the chrome yellow flowers?" That, my dear friends, is the cushion spurge, *Euphorbia polychroma*. It forms a perfect dome-like mound of brilliant blossoms in early summer, and in a good year, the foliage will become flaming red in fall. It wants full sun and average to poor soil and has no pest or disease issues. You really want this plant. Cushion spurge is always tidy, stays where you put it, and only very occasionally self-seeds. The cypress spurge (*Euphorbia cyparissias*) is quite the opposite, spreading like a bad rash, though this is actually not a bad thing in some areas. The cypress spurge has fine, feathery foliage like a little cypress tree and makes a charming, rapid-spreading groundcover for a sunny site with poor soil. It has dusty yellow blooms in early summer and once established requires nothing in the way of love or attention. There are many, *many* kinds of spurge in the world, and most of them are not hardy where we live. These two, however, are 100 per cent reliable. These two plants should not be confused with leafy spurge (*Euphorbia esula*), which has become a serious weed in some parts of Saskatchewan and Alberta.

Ferns Like *cactus*, *ferns* is not a scientific name, but there are so many, it's just easiest to put them all together. First, this might be my favourite group of plants— I passionately *love* ferns. Ferns will grow best in rich, humusy soil with generous amounts of compost and well-rotted manure. They like shelter from the wind, moisture, and dappled or filtered light. They can even handle deep shade with little to no trouble, as long as it isn't too dry. In the wild, ferns like to grow along the coast or near waterfalls and streams, all places where both the ground and the air are quite moist. Try to recreate this in your garden for your best success, such as planting near shady ponds or fountains. Don't feed your ferns with commercial fertilizers. You can actually hurt ferns this way since most fertilizers are formulated for flowering plants, which ferns are not. Ostrich ferns (*Matteucia struthiopteris*) grow throughout the continent

If you're looking at adding lush greenery to a shady spot, few plants can match a fern!

and grow almost a metre tall. They are easy to grow and they multiply where they are happy. The royal fern (*Osmunda regalis*) and the cinnamon fern (*Osmunda cinnamomea*) are also excellent choices. Try any of the wood ferns (*Dryopteris*) because a goodly number of them do fine here. The northern maidenhair fern (*Adiantum pedatum*) is a favourite of mine. I absolutely love the Japanese painted fern (*Athyrium nipponicum*) but would like to discourage you from buying it. This fern is really, really beautiful and really, really slow-growing. Although it survives just fine here, it takes a long time to wake up in the spring and by the time it starts to look like anything, it's basically winter. It just wants a longer season than we can offer it, so I say buy a big one and use it in a container as an annual, and don't bother with it in the garden. A hybrid form of it called 'Ghost' is more reliable. You should also try the lady fern (*Athyrium filix-femina*), with long, smooth leaves and an elegance that is hard to match.

Gaillardia spp. (blanket flower)
Possibly the best plant for someone new to gardening, and loved by butterflies, gaillardias flower all summer if they are deadheaded. The blossoms are daisy-like and usually yellow with a circular red band, though there are also yellow, orange, and "burgundy" (actually dark red) flowered forms available too. They want full sun, good drainage, and average to poor soil. Blanket flowers are quick to establish and require very little. Most

Nothing is quite so spectacularly blue as gentians.

of them grow about a half-metre tall, but there is also a widely available very compact dwarf called 'Goblin' that I find charming.

Galium spp. (sweet woodruff) This is a groundcover plant for partly shady to shady areas with beautiful whorled leaves and charming, pure white flowers in early summer. It likes moisture and forms lush carpets without becoming weedy. Since it's so highly adaptable and easy to grow, it makes great filler beneath trees.

Gentiana spp. (gentians) Buy every kind of gentian you can get your hands on, okay? Gentians are so famous for their blue flowers that the term *gentian blue* has come to mean rich, true blue colouring. Few plants in the garden, if any, can make the claim to blue flowers that these plants can. Not all gentians are blue—there are white-flowered forms and some with yellow blossoms, but they range from easy to grow to extremely challenging. The stemless gentian (*Gentiana acaulis*) is a low-growing plant with trumpet-shaped blossoms that are huge in comparison with the size of the plant. It flowers in early spring and it's easy, if a bit slow-growing. Stemless gentians are so striking that when in flower, strangers will knock on your door to ask you about it. The willow gentian is often listed as zone 4 or 5, but it does well here with a bit of winter protection. As the name implies, it is willowy and graceful. The summer gentian, *Gentiana septemfida*, blooms mid- to late summer and

the blossoms are pretty but not showy. The Chinese gentian, *Gentiana sinoornata*, is a spectacular autumn bloomer that doesn't always make it through the winter, but nonetheless it is worth trying. There are more than four hundred species and many hybrids and cultivars, so see what's on offer at your local garden centre and experiment madly. To perform the best, all need full sun and moist soil.

Geranium spp. (cranesbill) The perennial geraniums are not to be confused with the annual plants called geraniums, as they are quite different. Cranesbill are carefree, robust perennials that bloom all summer in a variety of shapes, sizes, and colours. Most are quite compact and easy to grow. Give them full sun and average, well-drained soil for best results. Several hybrids are available, including 'Johnson's Blue,' which, despite its name, is actually purple and can be quite weedy if not deadheaded. *Geranium sanguineum* does well in hot spots in the garden with poor soil and has showy white or magenta flowers for weeks. *Geranium macrorhizum* has softly furred leaves that often colour red in the fall and pink to reddish-purple blooms. Cranesbill makes a nice, slow-moving groundcover that is pest- and disease-resistant. There are many, many to choose from. They are worth acquiring and growing.

Grasses So many ornamental grasses are now available that they are being given their own section in many garden centres. Some grasses are very aggressive and can take over, but this does not mean they are to be avoided. Ribbon grass and blue lyme grass both send out runners and fill in considerable space but can also be gorgeous if planted in a site where this is an asset and not a problem. The feather-reed grasses such as 'Karl Foerster' are tidy, well behaved, and increasingly popular for winter interest. Panic grass (*Panicum* spp.), moor grass (*Molinia* spp.), and hair grass (*Deschampsia* spp.) are all favourites of mine, but there are certainly others. There are some spectacular millets and sorghums that are annual but

How can you not fall in love with the dark beauty of purple millet?

Every garden needs grasses since they create a sense of movement and texture and often add invaluable winter interest. They also look best planted in clumps, so don't buy a single kind of grass—buy several of them and really make an impact!

self-seed enough that you can consider them perennial. Blue fescue, blue oat grass, and big bluestem are others that you may wish to try. When purchasing grass, ask whether that particular variety is aggressive and choose its location accordingly. They come in all shapes and sizes, and virtually no grasses want shade. Grow them in full sun and keep them well watered until they are established. Many grasses are drought-resistant once they are mature, but not all. The moor grasses, for instance, want moisture.

Gypsophilia spp. (baby's breath)

Gypsophilia is a pretty mixed bag, as far as plants are concerned. There are a few good things here, and some not so much. In the first place, if you want baby's breath for use in bouquets, grow one of the annual forms like 'Covent Garden.' The old-fashioned baby's breath (*Gypsophilia paniculata*) has become a serious weed in many parts of the prairies and should be absolutely avoided.

Further to this, it is ugly and undesirable. Creeping baby's breath, *G. repens*, is very low and cute and available in white or pink. It's a desirable rock garden plant and only wants sun and good drainage. Better still is the obscure *G. cerastoides*, a tiny alpine species with surprisingly large flowers.

Helleborus spp. (hellebore, lenten rose, winter rose)

I know it's beautiful, but you're going to have to put that back on the shelf. I know the tag says great for shade. I know you really want to give it a try. However, it's $21, and not only is it going to die this winter, but it's also not going to flower this summer. Save yourself the heartbreak. Hellebores are mostly evergreen perennials with handsome foliage and absolutely gorgeous flowers that appear anywhere from December through February. This is fantastic if you live on the West Coast but less fantastic if you live here. A few (and I mean a very few) gardeners on the prairies have been successful by mulching the living bejeesus out of hellebore and growing them in extremely protected locations. There are several clumps of them in the Reader Rock Garden in downtown Calgary, and they bloom in May and appear to be flourishing. Please know that this is the *exception*, not the rule. These are expensive plants to fool around with, and they are selling out at garden centres all across the prairies. I can't be bothered to spend $20 on a plant that won't produce a single bloom all summer and has an 85 per cent chance of dying at the first sign of an actual, legitimate winter. There *are* herbaceous species of hellebore that look promising, and these are very, very slowly working their way into the nursery trade. If by some miracle you find these on offer somewhere, you should absolutely buy them! Otherwise, put that hellebore down and spend money on something else.

Hemerocallis spp. (daylily)

How would I describe daylilies? Old-fashioned and fabulous. These are long-blooming, low-maintenance plants that form large clumps of attractive, grassy foliage

Daylilies have been hailed by some as the perfect perennial, and it's no wonder why!

Coralbells.

and lily-like flowers over a very long period—usually all summer. Each individual blossom only lasts twenty-four hours, but they are replaced daily. Some kinds spread rapidly, others slowly. They come in almost every imaginable colour except blue and will live for many years. Daylilies run the gamut from very inexpensive to exorbitant, depending on how new the variety is. A few of them are fragrant. You should have some of these. Grow them in full sun in fertile to average soil and expect no pest or disease issues. They like good moisture, but most are fairly drought-resistant once established.

***Hepatica* spp. (hepatica)** This will easily be the first plant to flower in your garden in the spring. They have flowered for me the second week of April, and given that I live in Alberta, this is quite something. Under 10 centimetres tall, hepaticas can be mauve, white, blue, purple, pink, or any shade in between. The tiny, jewel-like flowers are showy and exquisite and are usually here while there is still snow on the ground. Sun to part shade is fine, and they are great beneath deciduous trees. Try to get some of these for your garden; they are marvels.

***Heuchera* spp. (coralbells)** Heucheras (pronounced *hew-ker-ahs*) are now available in about a hundred zillion different varieties. They are grouped into two categories—those that are grown for their blossoms, and those that are grown for their foliage. A very few combine the best of both. The flowering types often have red or pink blooms, are loved by hummingbirds, and appear in early summer. The fancy leaf types produce scalloped, almost maple-like leaves in a dizzying array of silvers, purples, plums, greys, blacks, reds, oranges, yellows, and golds. Some of these are hardy, some are not. They are very quick to establish and make excellent substitutes for geraniums in containers. In the garden, a filtered or broken light suits them best. Deep shade is a very bad setting for them since they will lose their colour and become prone to mildew. They want fertile, moist soil, and they are a favourite of slugs and snails, so do watch out! There are innumerable varieties, but some of my favourites include 'Amber Waves,' 'Amethyst Mist,' 'Chocolate Ruffles,' 'Dolce Blackcurrant,' 'Obsidian,' 'Pewter Veil,' 'Plum Pudding,' 'Purple Petticoats,' and 'Silver Scrolls.'

***Hosta* spp. (hosta)** If you walk into a garden centre and ask for perennials that do well in shade, I bet hostas will be the first thing recommended to you. Hostas are really gorgeous plants, but you have to know a few things about them first. First, always cut the size in half. If a tag tells you this hosta is 1.75-metres wide at maturity, remember that's under ideal growing conditions. Here, it will be amazing if it reaches 1 metre wide.

Hostas.

Second, hostas are useless when it comes to drought-resistance. If you're not prepared to keep them in rich, moist soil, don't bother planting them at all since they don't respond or recover well from drought. Third, not all hostas are created equal. Some establish quickly, and others are painfully slow-growing. Hostas with blue foliage are the best ones for deep shade; the ones with green, golden, or variegated foliage are better with a few hours of sun. There are more than 25,000 registered cultivars of hostas, and not only do they have beautiful, luxurious leaves, but they also produce tall wands of lily-like flowers that are pretty (if subtle) and some of them are quite pleasantly fragrant. Hostas range in price from a few dollars to nearly a hundred bucks, depending on the variety.

If you are looking for hostas that are easy, no fuss, and totally reliable, I recommend 'August Moon,' 'Aureovariegata,' 'Frances Williams,' 'Gold Standard,' 'Krossa Regal,' and 'Royal Standard.' Of the other varieties, try any that appeal to you, knowing some will succeed, some will not. This is the fun of gardening!

Iris **spp. (iris)** Iris are among my favourite perennials. Named after Iris, the Greek goddess of the rainbow, iris have absolutely spectacular flowers in a wide array of colours. We first mentioned iris in the bulb section, but I've listed them with the perennials. Why?

Siberian irises are never sold as bulbs, and bearded irises do not do well with a fall or spring bulb planting here; they are best propagated in summer via division. The bulbous irises, the ones that are hardy, are fine but too small to be of any real interest. (Except *Iris danfordiae*. Dreamy sigh.)

Iris usually have bold, sword-like leaves, which makes them valuable plants for creating foliage contrast when the flowers are gone. Most are extremely low maintenance. Bearded irises like a sunny, well-drained location and range from tiny dwarves to immense giants. The general rule with bearded irises is that the taller they are, the less hardy they are. This is not to say that they are weaklings, only that a bit of extra protection will be appreciated. The Siberian irises have thin, almost reed-like foliage and delicate-looking flowers that last several weeks. They mostly come in shades of blue and purple, but there are some sensational white-flowered forms too. Siberian irises prefer more moisture than bearded irises. Some iris are aquatic and make good plants for the edges of ponds, though there are some very tiny species that are good in the rock garden. Iris are usually inexpensive and will bloom well from a young age.

Bearded iris.

Lamium spp. (lamium) If one more person recommends lamium as a groundcover for shade, I am going to scream. Lamium does *not* want shade, it wants sun! The fact that it *survives* in shade does not mean that is where it will be most healthy. Given that there are so many nice groundcovers for a shady spot, why do we keep sticking lamium in there to suffer through and cling to life? Lamium might grow around half a metre wide in a shady spot. It will create a spectacular blanket well over a metre in diameter in sun and be far healthier to boot. Which would you prefer? Low-growing and ill-scented when crushed or handled, lamium produces snapdragon-like flowers for months and often has attractive foliage. 'White Nancy,' 'Pink Pewter,' and 'Chequers' are all excellent varieties. They are drought-resistant but will look better if kept well watered. They are not the least bit fussy about soil and grow rapidly.

Lavendula spp. (lavender) I hate this plant. In my last two seasons working in a Calgary garden centre, hardy lavender was our number-one selling perennial. People would come in, go straight for it, and immediately begin stroking it and exclaiming about the "rich, beautiful fragrance." I think it smells disgusting. A few things you should know about

lavender. Spanish lavender, which I do like, is pretty in containers but isn't hardy here. French lavender, whose oil is used in soaps and perfumes, is also not hardy here and is the most sweetly scented of all the lavenders. English lavender is the hardiest, and the only one that will survive the winter here. It has a harsh, bitter scent and purple flowers that are practically invisible. It's also not a particularly impressive bloomer in the garden, and is easily overwatered and therefore killed. Further, not *all* kinds of English lavender survive here. 'Munstead' is the hardiest one, available at most garden centres. Grow it in full sun in average to poor soil with flawless drainage. Lavenders want to be evergreen, so give them good snowcover to prevent them from burning. 'Hidcote' is also hardy enough to survive here. There are lots of other things you can grow instead. Just saying.

Leucanthemum **spp. (shasta daisy)** Many of us remember shasta daisies growing in our parents' or grandparents' gardens. These are your traditional, classic, pure white daisies. The problem with the old-fashioned kind is that it can be extremely weedy, and they have naturalized and made a problem of themselves in many places, including Banff National Park. They also don't flower very long, and plants can be floppy and untidy. Many varieties and cultivars of shasta daisy have been introduced over the last few years, but there is only one, maybe two, that you want. The first is 'Becky.' This was the 2003 perennial of the year and was originally bred for the cut-flower trade. It is an outstanding garden plant with huge, very clean white blooms all summer long. It is vigorous and compact and has no pest or disease issues. The other you might like to try is 'Broadway Lights,' which should not be hardy here but has done well in many prairie gardens, including mine. It is the palest shade of moonlight yellow and looks fabulous with purple foliage beside or behind it. Grow shasta daisies in full sun with average soil.

Lamium.

Ligularia spp. (ligularia) These beautiful, often large perennials have gorgeous foliage and incongruent, sometimes ridiculous-looking flowers. Usually well over 1 metre tall, they require a fair bit of moisture or they will look like crap. There are different species and different varieties, but all of them want the same care. These are yet another perennial often recommended for shade but actually do not do well there. A dappled or filtered light is fine, but it isn't sun they dislike so much as high temperatures. When it's hot, the leaves go very limp and look dreadful. A moist site with morning sun and some shade from the hottest part of the afternoon can be a good location for them, but mostly they just want to be cool and moist. 'Othello' is a favourite variety, with beautiful rounded leaves stained in reddish-purple. It has yellow, daisy-like flowers that are so at odds with the foliage that I actually remove them. 'The Rocket' has been popular for many years and has gorgeous, triangular leaves and tiny yellow flowers held in long spikes that are well worth keeping on the plant.

Linum spp. (flax) There are many kinds of flax in the world, but the blue flax is the one you want. I also mentioned this plant in the section on drought-resistance. It's a feathery, short-lived, graceful plant with brilliant blue flowers all summer. It will self-seed and prefers sunny areas with good drainage and average to poor soil. It is flawless.

Lupinus spp. (lupines) Lupines are beloved garden plants with handsome foliage and tall spires of beautiful flowers that can be white, reddish pink, yellow, blue, purple, rose, or any combination of these. There are both annual and perennial lupines, and they are inexpensive to buy and easy to grow, either as plants from a nursery or from seed. The 'Russell' hybrids are the most popular, but 'Band of Nobles' is a bit more compact with better mildew-resistance. Lupines bloom in early summer, and when they are finished, I rip them out and replace them. They will look wretched all summer after blooming has concluded, and they are the only garden plant I know that can actually be killed by aphids. There are lupines native to Alberta, such as the gorgeous silvery lupine (_Lupinus argentea_), and these are sometimes available from native plant specialists. These are much better garden choices, but they

Ligularia.

Lupine.

are definitely not as posh as the hybrids. I grow both. (The species lupines, by the way, do not need to be pulled out post-flowering. It's just their inbred relatives that you will want to get rid of.) Lupines are nitrogen fixers and enrich the soil around them, and they are easy to grow in any sunny spot. A bit of shelter is helpful as they can be seriously flattened in a summer thunderstorm. Some of the dwarf lupines, such as the 'Gallery' series, can make good subjects for containers.

Meconopsis spp. (blue poppy)

Although not true species of poppies, these are in the poppy family and closely resemble them. Not all of the *Meconopsis* are blue either. There are whites, creams, reds, yellows, oranges, and violets. As a rule, they all form a rosette of foliage in their first year of life and flower the second. Most of them die after flowering, and there is nothing you can do about this since it's what they are genetically programmed to do. These plants mostly come from high up in the mountains of Tibet, China, Pakistan, and through the Himalayas. They like sunny to partially shady locations and cool temperatures. Ironically, our winters are not too cold for them, but our summers are usually too hot! Welsh poppies, *Meconopsis cambrica*, are native to western Europe, including the British Isles. The blossoms are orange to yellow or gold, they self-sow freely, and they are probably the easiest species to cultivate. *M. grandis* and *M. betonicifolia* are probably the best known, but several hybrids and cultivars have been developed through these two species, notably the outstanding *M.* x *sheldonii*, which is one of the most spectacular plants I have ever grown. All the *Meconopsis* want rich, moist soil with sharp drainage. They dislike a windy location, and a filtered or broken light suits them better than total shade. Although they have a reputation for being finicky, if you have a good location for them, they really are not that difficult. The immense, silky blossoms of

The nodding electric blue flowers of *Meconopsis grandis* are easy to grow if you have the right spot.

electric blue that appear in early summer are so beautiful as to border on unreality; every gardener will try them eventually. Just because blue is the usual colouring doesn't mean you should neglect the white or the violet forms—they are equally exquisite. *Meconopsis* are good companions for ferns, primula, and hostas.

Mertensia spp. (mertensia) There are about forty species of *Mertensia*, and they aren't common in gardens, which is really unfortunate because they are lovely and interesting. Anyone who has hiked in southern Alberta in early summer has probably seen northern bluebells, *M. paniculata*, growing along the edges of moist woodlands and near rivers and creeks. It has pendant blue to mauve flowers that sometimes show elements of pink. It likes moist soil in partial shade and can often be obtained from native plant specialists. It spreads slowly and sometimes goes dormant if conditions become too hot and dry. *M. maritima* is a sprawly, flopping plant with intensely dusty blue leaves and small blue to blue-purple flowers. It is an interesting addition to a sunny rock garden, and gardeners either love it or hate it. *Mertensia virginica* is usually called Virginia bluebells, and although it does not succeed in every garden, it is

worth experimenting with. Pendant blue flowers arrive in spring on elegant, compact plants. It looks absolutely smashing planted with yellow daffodils, and will flower at the same time. After blooming has concluded, Virginia bluebells go dormant.

Monarda spp. (bee balm, bergamot, Oswego tea)

I love these plants, and frankly, I wouldn't want to garden without them! Unlike most things in the mint family, monardas are not invasive, although they do slowly spread to form large clumps. They range from compact little dwarves to 1-metre-plus-tall giants with tubular flowers arranged to make them look just like fireworks. The flowers are rich in nectar and draw hummingbirds, bees, and butterflies. They flower for weeks at a time, make great cut flowers, and are entirely untroubled by deer, rabbits, or other pests. Powdery mildew is an issue for some varieties, and they can't tolerate dry soil, but other than that, they are trouble-free. The entire plant has a strong, oregano-like fragrance when bruised or touched, and the button-like seed heads provide food for foraging songbirds and also offer some winter interest. This is a perennial that you must consider! Monardas come in lots of colours, including white, scarlet, purple, pink, and rose. The white forms are rarely grown, and I have no idea why. The cultivar 'Snow White' is a profuse bloomer and fabulous. 'Gardenview Scarlet' has shocking, brilliant red flowers but unfortunately is prone to mildew. 'Prairie Night' (purple) and 'Croftway Pink' (pale pink) are both magnets for mildew, so don't bother with them. 'Violet Queen' (purple) is an excellent choice, as is 'Blue Stocking' (which is definitely not blue). 'Marshal's Delight' is a light pink, Canadian introduction that blooms all summer and has fantastic disease-resistance. 'Coral Reef' (hot pink) is not very hardy although heavily marketed. The very dwarf forms such as 'Petite Wonder' and 'Petite Delight' have also done poorly, though I do like them in containers.

Monarda.

Narcissus spp. (daffodil)

You definitely want to be growing these, so check out the bulbs section for my favourites!

Nepeta spp. (catmint)

Okay, let's be clear about something here … catmint is not the same thing as catnip. Yes, they are closely related, but catnip grows quite tall, has white flowers, and isn't all that attractive. It also attracts cats. Catmint is a hardy perennial, usually with blue-purple flowers, and will not attract cats unless the foliage is heavily bruised or crushed. If you have a cat, it is not going to devour or destroy these plants, so don't have any fear about planting them. 'Walker's Low' was the 2007 perennial of the year. It has masses of blue-purple flowers over a long period and is much loved by bees. 'Dropmore Blue' is similar, but the flowers are darker. 'Six Hills Giant' grows quite tall and has very large, purple-blue blossoms. 'Dawn to Dusk' is a soft pink, but I don't find it especially showy or attractive. All the catmints have a lovely fragrance when you brush up against them, and they establish very quickly and can be good for filling in large areas. They draw flurries of bees and are excellent "filler"

It's not unusual for peony flowers to be bigger than your hand.

plants. They are also drought-resistant and can deal with almost any soil type. In Calgary, they have been planted along Memorial Drive and they look marvellous; many people have mistaken them for lavender for some reason.

Oenethera spp. (evening primrose)
These should not be confused with true primroses. Evening primroses, as the name implies, usually open their blossoms in the evening. Many of them are fragrant, and most of them flower in white, yellow, orange, cream, or pink. Some of them are extravagantly beautiful. Grow them in full sun with lean, poor, well-drained soil. Many of them will self-sow, and they will flower all summer long. They dislike disturbance, so take care when transplanting. Most of them are easily grown from seed and they make worthy additions to the garden.

Paeonia spp. (peony) You should have a peony. Actually, you should have half a dozen peonies, but most of them take up a fair bit of room so you might only have space for one. Peonies are generally quite large plants that more closely resemble shrubs than perennials. They can have single or double flowers, and they come in white, red, yellow, pink, purple, rose, magenta, peach, coral, and even pale green! They are sturdy and dependable plants, very drought-resistant once established, and absolutely stunning while they are in bloom. Some of them will also develop attractive fall colouring. Grow peonies in full sun and don't disturb them since they are highly resentful of this! Moisture and fertility is appreciated, but peonies are highly adaptable. They are long-lived and range from just a few dollars to several hundred dollars in price. Pest and disease issues are few and far between. There is a prevailing idea that ants in some way assist the peony, but there is no truth to this. They enjoy eating the sticky syrup exuded by the buds, but they neither help nor harm the plant. If you don't want ants sneaking into your house, don't plant peonies by your door.

Papaver spp. (poppy) Both annual and perennial forms of poppy exist, but the best-known perennial kinds are the Iceland poppy, *Papaver nudicaule*, and the Oriental poppy, *Papaver orientale*. Iceland poppies bloom in early summer, and though they are usually orange or yellow, they can also be white or pink. They are carefree plants that self-seed profusely, so don't bother purchasing them in the nursery. Buy a packet of seeds instead; you'll get much better

Oriental poppies have enormous blossoms. They are great for gardeners who want something dramatic and undemanding.

results. Oriental poppies have enormous, showy flowers that are usually red with large black blotches inside. They can also be white, pink, or purple. Oriental poppies have bristly, almost prickly, foliage, and they should be planted in a site where they will not be disturbed. A population of poppies can live for decades in any sunny spot with good drainage and reasonably fertile soil. Though they don't flower for long, that's no reason to shun them.

Penstemon spp. (penstemon) We need to be growing a lot more of these plants! They are showy, diverse, highly attractive to hummingbirds, and very easy in the garden. Not all species are winter-hardy, but who cares? Plant every kind of penstemon you can get your hands on; just expect some to act like annuals and some to be perennial here. They have long, tubular flowers in every colour except orange, which they hold over a very long period. I have grown literally dozens of penstemons over the years. My current favourite is a hybrid called 'Dark Towers,' with purple-stained foliage and white to very pale pink blooms. Grow them in full sun with sharp drainage and enjoy!

Perovskia spp. (Russian sage) Russian sage is not really a sage, but it does smell a bit like one when you brush up against the leaves. Woody and shrub-like in milder climates, Russian sage behaves mostly as a perennial around here. It usually grows about 1 metre tall and begins producing masses of blue-violet flowers in August that are loved by bees. It prefers full sun and average to poor soil with really, really good drainage. Even though this was the 1995 perennial of the year, expect to kill it several times before succeeding. Russian sage is a great plant for hot, dry areas where few other things are happy.

Persicaria spp. (fleeceflower, knotweed) I'm not sure how these plants got so popular. Persicarias are a diverse, multifaceted group of plants that range from tiny to tall, but all with bottlebrush-like flowers mostly in shades of

Russian sage.

white, pink, and red. Some are very drought-resistant, and some require even moisture. Some are hardy, and some are not. Some are extremely invasive, and some are extremely well behaved. They want a sunny spot with average soil and have no pest or disease issues. They also flower over a long period. My problem is that I don't find them particularly attractive. When you find these at the garden centre, I would recommend reading the label carefully and asking the staff some pointed questions. Moist or dry? Is it invasive? How hardy is it? These are the three most critical things to find out. If they appeal to you, by all means try them.

Phlox spp. (phlox) An ancient plant, phlox dates back to biblical times when the shepherds watched over their phlox by night. (Ha ha ha. That was a little joke.) Phlox can be either perennial or annual, and there are dozens of varieties for you to choose from. For the most part, they are lovely plants. The creeping or Arctic phlox, *Phlox subulata*, forms a low, creeping mat of evergreen foliage and they flower exuberantly in the spring. Colours include white, mauve, light pink, and dark pink. Tall phlox, sometimes called summer phlox, forms a clump usually just under 1 metre tall

Phlox.

with large, full heads of often sweetly scented flowers in mid- to late summer. They come in a vast array of colours and are loved by butterflies. 'David' is my favourite one, with huge ball-shaped clusters of very fragrant white flowers and excellent disease-resistance. It was the 2002 perennial of the year. Many of the tall phlox varieties are prone to blackspot and mildew, and not all of them are especially hardy. 'Starfire' (electric pink) and 'Blue Boy' (mauve) are nice. There are also some interesting variegated forms. Wood phloxes prefer partial shade and are sometimes available. They are worth trying. Grow phlox in a sunny spot with moisture and good drainage.

Polemonium spp. (Jacob's ladder)

Jacob's ladders are beautiful, tidy plants that form attractive clumps of finely divided foliage and are said to resemble the ladder climbed on by angels in Jacob's dream in the bible. They have blue, purple, or white flowers often for a long season and are low maintenance in the garden. They want full sun and good drainage, and they aren't especially fussy. *Polemonium caeruleum* is the most commonly grown, and it's quite nice. *P. acutiflorum* has blue flowers and is native to Alberta; it establishes quickly and is surprisingly beautiful, but its rhizomes and seeds can be aggressive.

P. pulcherrimum is also native to Alberta and makes a superb garden plant. It is low-growing and rather sprawly, with large blue flowers that have a prominent yellow eye. It self-sows vigorously, but unwanted seedlings are easily removed. It can also tolerate more shade than other kinds. *P. yezoense* is an Asian species with large, purple flowers that are strongly scented of grape. Several other selections, mostly hybrids, should be mentioned. 'Purple Rain' has gloriously burgundy foliage when it first emerges from the ground in spring that slowly ages to green. 'Brise de Anjou' has intensely cream variegated leaves and is quite nice. 'Snow and Sapphires' is also variegated, though it is a poor performer best left at the garden store. However, it is not as yucky as 'Stairway to Heaven,' which is a mildew-prone, sprawly thing that flowers poorly and generally looks miserable. Jacob's ladders will bloom all summer if deadheaded.

Primula spp. (primrose)

Primroses can be short or tall, rangy or compact, and come in a wide assortment of colours. Most of them have fragrant blooms fairly early, and are great plants for moist, partly shaded areas. They combine well with ferns and hostas. Though they are steadfast little plants, I find them quite bland. It's not a good idea to upset the primula lovers out there, but the truth is I actually can't recommend a single variety to you because I haven't liked any enough to keep a single one in my garden. When they are finished flowering, they kind of look like lettuce. Lame.

Pulmonaria spp. (lungwort)

Pulmonaria are great plants, but since they were once used to treat respiratory problems they have been cursed with an unattractive common name. They have bristly, often spotted, or silver-marked leaves and glorious blue, purple, white, or pink flowers in early spring. Pulmonaria multiply fairly quickly and grow very

Pulmonaria.

well in sun or shade. They are not the least bit fussy, and once they are finished blooming, they are attractive foliage plants. 'Mrs. Moon' is an especially vigorous cultivar that I highly recommend, but I also like 'Smokey,' 'Dora Bieleveld,' and 'Sissinghurst White.' Others, including the stunning silver-leaved beauty 'Excalibur,' are also worth finding a spot for, so try any that catch your eye.

Pulsatilla spp. (pasque flower, prairie crocus) The provincial flower of Manitoba, the garden forms of pasque flower have larger blooms in showier colours for longer periods than the wild forms. Lilac to light purple is normal, but there are also varieties with deep red, white, or pink blooms. They are one of the most low-maintenance, showy, dependable plants you can have in your garden. Plant them in full sun in average soil and they will bring you pleasure for years and years. After they are finished flowering, they develop curious-looking woolly seed heads. Some people love these, but I am not a fan so I remove them. It's up to you, but either way, you should buy some of these. If at all possible, plant a large group of them.

Rodgersia spp. (rodgersia) Rodgersia is uncommon but perfectly hardy and, in the right spot, quite fabulous. Rodgersia favours a moist, sheltered site and produces huge leaves reminiscent of a horse chestnut or a buckeye. Its fragrant creamy or pink flowers are nice but not the main attraction. This plant is quite tropical-looking and deserves a wider fan base.

Rudbeckia spp. (brown-eyed Susan) Perennials in other climates, most of the brown-eyed Susans are not fully hardy here regardless of what the tag says. They do make spectacular annuals though, and even if they don't survive, it's not really a big deal. A good example of this is the award-winning variety 'Indian Summer,' which is showy beyond words, essential in every garden, but it rarely overwinters here. The hardiest (and one of the nicest) brown-eyed Susans I can recommend to you is the cultivar 'Goldstorm,' which was the 1999 perennial of the year. It grows about 1 metre tall and produces an explosion of chocolate-centred, brilliant yellow flowers from late summer through fall. It is best in full sun with excellent drainage, and looks especially good with echinaceas and grasses.

Salvia spp. (sage) This genus contains all the true sages, including the cooking sage. It was once so widely used medicinally that it garnered its own proverb: "Why should a man die while sage grows in his garden?" Salvia and the word *salvation* are actually derived from the same source. Most of the true sages are not hardy here, but a few hybrids and cultivars are. *Salvia* x *sylvestris* is usually called meadowsage. 'May Night' is fabulous, forming a large clump about three-quarters of a metre tall smothered in deep purple-blue flowers for weeks and weeks. 'East Friesland' is similar. 'Blue Hill' is also nice. Pink- and white-flowered varieties are also worth exploring. Grow meadowsage in full sun with average, well-drained soil. It is tolerant of heat and drought and has no pest or disease issues. Bees love it, and it will self-sow all over the place if not deadheaded.

Saxifrage spp. (saxifrage) These charming little plants are low-growing and well suited to alpine gardens and rockeries. There are dozens of varieties, most of which have flowers that are extraordinarily large in comparison with the size of the plant! Some are slow-growing, some are quicker, and most bloom in spring or early summer. They

Sedums.

Scabiosa.

are inexpensive and worth planting. Grow them in a sunny site with good drainage.

Scabiosa spp. (pincushion flower)
Annual and perennial forms of scabiosa exist, and it is my opinion that the annual varieties are much prettier than the perennials. 'Butterfly Blue' (the 2000 perennial of the year) is a compact, mounding variety with blue-purple flowers all summer if it is deadheaded regularly. It's a nice-enough plant, but nothing that makes me want to get terribly fired up.

Sedum spp. (sedum)
Sedums are perennial succulents that come in a wild assortment of shapes, sizes, and colours. They are prized for their foliage as much as their pretty, starry blooms, and they can be upright and clumping or low and creeping or anywhere in between. Some of them border on invasive, and some of them are extremely well behaved. All perform best in full sun with sharp drainage and average to poor soil. They are ideal for hot, dry locations, and they draw flurries of bees and butterflies. While I could write pages about sedums and all the varieties I love, my favourite

one is 'Autumn Joy.' It begins to flower in late summer and continues until the snow buries it. They have no pest or disease issues and they aren't expensive. Put some sedums in your garden, and quickly!

Sempervivum spp. (hens and chicks)
These fascinating low succulents thrive in hot, dry places in the garden with good drainage. They produce a central rosette (the "hen"), usually with a myriad of baby rosettes peeping out from beneath it (the "chicks"). Many varieties are available, some with red, grey, or green colouring, some marbled or spotted, all interesting! They are also excellent in containers, and they will sometimes produce curious, star-shaped flowers in pink or yellow. They die after flowering, but usually their little chicks take their place. They are excellent groundcovers and highly addictive. They are happiest with compassionate neglect. The tropical succulents called *Echeveria* resemble them in shape and sometimes colour, but they are larger and definitely not prairie-hardy.

Solidago spp. (goldenrod)
Desperately underutilized, goldenrods are invaluable for late summer colour and for attracting butterflies! The blooms range from yellow through gold, and they also make excellent cut flowers.

'Crown of Rays' is a compact, disease-resistant beauty that flowers explosively and is probably my favourite variety. 'Golden Baby' is another good choice.

> Goldenrods are often blamed for allergies and hay fever, but this is ridiculous since goldenrod pollen is heavy and not carried by the wind. More often than not the culprit causing issues is the sweet clover (ragweed) growing along every ditch and roadside throughout the continent.

Thyme.

Grow goldenrods with echinaceas and grasses in full sun and sharp drainage.

Stachys spp. (lamb's ears) Children are very fond of growing this plant. Lamb's ears is a clumper with luxuriously soft grey foliage that both looks and feels like a lamb's ear. Spikes of purple flowers appear in the second year. If the flowers are not deadheaded, it will self-seed. Grow lamb's ears in full sun with good drainage and don't worry if it's short-lived since this is quite normal. It is an excellent contrast plant. The flowers are highly attractive to bees.

Thymus spp. (thyme) We usually think of thyme when we are cooking, and not as a garden plant. However, most of them are quite hardy, they make excellent little carpets for sunny spaces, and many have tiny, attractive blooms that will draw bees. Some, such as the lemon thyme, are deliciously scented. Experiment with them and try as many as you can. They tend to be short-lived, but they are wonderful and make good subjects for growing in confined spaces. The woolly thyme rarely flowers and produces minuscule, grey-green leaves that form large carpets. It is often encouraged to grow between paving stones, as it can handle some light foot traffic. It sells out very fast because nobody ever buys just one—they buy an entire flat! So if you want some, go early.

Tradescantia spp. (spiderwort) Spiderworts are attractive and pretty (though not flashy) plants with interesting, three-petalled flowers in a variety of colours. They have grassy foliage and spread slowly but surely to form large clumps. They bloom all summer and want only sun and moisture. Some of them are also excellent container plants. You should try some of these. Not every cultivar is hardy, so you may have to try a couple of them before you succeed.

Trollius spp. (globeflower) Globeflowers are so named because the unopened buds are round (globular), but this is a pretty vague description. Globeflowers want a moist to wet location in sun or partial shade. They flower in early summer, and the blossoms are unapologetically orange, though there are also some good yellow varieties. I recommend these.

Tulipa spp. (tulips) I wrote about these in the section on bulbs, but the answer is yes, you definitely want these!

Valeriana spp. (valerian) The most commonly grown species is *Valeriana officinalis*, once widely acclaimed for its medicinal

Veronica.

properties. This is a tall perennial that grows anywhere from 1.5 to 2 metres and produces white or pale pink flowers that are quite strongly scented. Butterflies love them. Valerian is a fabulous plant in a moist, sunny site and does well beside a pond. The plant itself is quite tidy, but if allowed to, it will self-seed and become weedy. I like the way the valerian blossoms wave and dance in the wind.

Veronica spp. (speedwell) There are multitudes of speedwells: some are spreading, carpet-like plants; some are clumpers; and some grow quite tall. They come in a wide range of colours, although blues and purples predominate. All veronica are loved by bees, butter-flies, and hummingbirds. 'Sunny Border Blue' and 'Royal Candles' are two of my favourite varieties, but I also madly love the carpeting species *Veronica whittleyi*. 'Crater Lake' is a gorgeous hybrid with spectacularly blue flowers, and 'Red Fox,' though prone to mildew, is a lovely pink and great for cutting. Speedwells are very easy to grow since sun and good drainage are really all they need. Most are quite drought-resistant, although they look better when watered regularly.

Vinca spp. (periwinkle) One of the very few hardy members of the oleander family, *Vinca minor* is a marvellous ever-green groundcover that grows well in sun or shade and is highly adaptable to all kinds of growing conditions, including dry, poor soil. Though they will survive rather happily in poor soils, moist, rich soil will help it spread much faster. The leaves are small and dark green. The star-shaped flowers resemble oleander and are usually a very distinct shade of blue-purple, but there are also white-flowered and variegated forms available. 'Illumination' is a stunning golden form but very slow-growing. I use it in con-tainers rather than the garden so that it can be better appreciated.

Viola spp. (violet) Violas are often referred to as "perennial pansies." They resemble these much-loved annuals but usually have much smaller flowers without the distinctive "faces" pansies are known for. There are tonnes of varieties available, with most being short-lived. They are extremely cold-tolerant and often bloom through several frosts or while there is still snow on the ground. By all means, go crazy with hybrid violas! They prefer moist soil in a cool, sunny spot, so please stop planting them in shade. Two native species of violets that are very much worth acquiring are the Canada violet (*Viola canadensis*) and the early blue violet (*V. adunca*). The Canada violet has gorgeous, heart-shaped leaves and small white or pink flowers in great profusion. It can spread rampantly and may need to be controlled, but it will grow even in the darkest of corners and can tolerate much neglect, including mild abuse. The early blue violet is highly adaptable and grows well in sun or shade as long as it has moisture. It has bright blue flowers in early spring and self-seeds freely, although unwanted specimens are easily removed.

Yucca spp. (yucca) Yucca is an evergreen perennial with sharp, stiff leaves and resembles a sea urchin. Since they are evergreen, they don't always do well in the chinook zone without a bit of care. They generally want to be somewhere with excellent snowcover, and need sharply drained, poor soil in full sun. Heat and drought are exactly what they need to be happy, and as such they are often planted with cacti. Yuccas produce tall spikes of

Violet.

ivory or creamy-coloured flowers that are fragrant at night and absolutely bewitching. Only two species are hardy here. *Yucca glauca* has narrow, blue-green leaves and white flowers. It is the most northerly ranging species and is common in northern Montana and parts of southern Alberta. *Yucca filamentosa* has wider, green leaves that have a variety of thread-like filaments around them. The flowers are more ivory or cream. Both take some time getting established. Yuccas usually don't flower until they are three or four years old, but occasionally they take as long as ten years to flower. After they bloom, they die. This is poetic and beautiful, and usually little offsets called pups appear around the base of the parent plant to replace them when they go. Structurally and architecturally interesting, yuccas do not suit every garden, but you absolutely have to try them if you can. A well-placed yucca can literally stop traffic, but you cannot imagine how much work it is to get someone to buy a plant that will die after it flowers, even knowing it will be uniquely beautiful for many years and graciously leave a litter of pups behind. Yuccas can also be grown from seed fairly easily, but seed to bloom is usually about seven to nine years.

❧ *II* ❧

Trees and shrubs

The difference between shrubs and perennials is that shrubs form woody tissue. This can be confusing because there are some *woody perennials,* such as Russian sage and certain artemesias. Don't let this worry you; I mention this just so you know that it can sometimes be a bit of a grey area, even for experts.

The difference between trees and shrubs is primarily size: some people describe lilacs as large shrubs; others as small trees. A shrub is *generally* less than 4.5 metres, and anything taller is usually referred to as a tree. Other important terms that you should know include the following:

Deciduous trees shed their leaves seasonally and are bare in the winter.

Evergreen plants keep green leaves year-round. Most people think this means *conifers,* and it is true that nearly all conifers are evergreen. However, there are also a large number of broadleaf evergreens, and

Opposite: 'Ivory Halo' dogwood takes centre stage in this low-maintenance planting scheme. This page: 'Dart's Gold' ninebark is an excellent shrub that is both attractive and low maintenance.

these can be shrubs or perennials and not just trees. Holly and rhododendron are two broadleaf evergreen shrubs, and yucca and bergenia are examples of evergreen perennials.

Now we're going to get into trees and shrubs, and this is going to be interesting. To most people, trees and shrubs are just a green background, if they notice them at all. Let me assure you, the secret life of

> Never cut evergreen perennials back or you will either kill them or injure them severely.

trees is worth investigating. Buying a tree or shrub is something to be taken seriously, because this is something more or less permanent in your landscape. No one wants to put a tree or a shrub in a bad place, and I hope the following information will make your life way easier when you're out there on the tree lot.

Abies spp. (fir)

Firs are absolutely gorgeous trees, and they aren't grown all that often. The term *fir* is frequently used interchangeably with *spruce* and *pine*, which is incorrect. Firs are distinctive trees with flat, soft needles (you can hug a fir) and some of the prettiest cones that trees are known to produce. Cones are always held in an up-facing fashion. They range from small shrubs to very large trees, are low maintenance, and are often very fragrant.

Sub-alpine fir often looks better in cultivation than it does in the wild.

Abies balsamea (balsam fir) The balsam fir grows throughout Canada and is occasionally cultivated as an ornamental, but it's not often on offer from local garden centres unless it's December and it's being sold as a Christmas tree. The dwarf balsam fir, *Abies balsamea* 'Nana,' shows up from time to time, and it is a cute, charming, slow-growing little shrub that will grow nicely in a sunny, well-drained spot. It will also tolerate partial shade but won't look as nice.

Abies concolor (silver fir, white fir) The silver fir is rarely planted here, but it is hardy enough to be worth experimenting with. It's a beautiful, large tree with handsome, soft needles and attractive cones. I planted one in spring 2008 in my southeast Calgary garden, it did fine all summer, and then in autumn the deer wandered through and promptly ate it.

Abies lasiocarpa (sub-alpine fir) The best fir choice for the landscape here is probably the sub-alpine fir, with lush, dark green needles, gorgeous cones, and gently ascending branch tips. This large tree looks especially smashing when planted in small groves, and it can tolerate substantially adverse conditions, including wind, drought, poor soil, and so on. Anyone who has hiked in the Rockies will have seen this tree, and it's a lot nicer in cultivation than it is high up in the mountains.

Abies siberica (Siberian fir) The Siberian fir is another large tree that is rarely offered, but it's 100 per cent hardy and quite stunning. It deserves to be more widely grown and recognized.

Acer spp. (maple)

There are so many kinds of maples and they are all so different! Most maples do not have a high tolerance for alkaline soils, instead preferring rich, moist soils with high organic matter and good drainage. They are, however, quite adaptable and able to survive in conditions that are less than ideal for them.

Acer ginnala (amur maple) The amur maple comes from northern China and is a visually appealing, fine-textured small tree that grows anywhere from 3.5 to 4.5 metres tall. Its leaves turn flaming red in the fall, and small clusters of showy seeds called keys appear in late summer. It has no pest or disease issues, grows reasonably fast, and is extremely hardy and drought-resistant. The only issue you might find with it is that in some prairie soils it develops chlorosis, with characteristic pale and "veiny" leaves.

Acer tatarica (tatarian maple) The tatarian maple is so similar to the amur maple that for many years these two were considered variations of each other. DNA testing has proven that they are actually distinct species. The tatarian maple has a slightly different leaf shape and the fall colour is usually more of an orangey red than scarlet. Both are fabulous trees for small spaces.

Acer glabrum (Rocky Mountain maple) The Rocky Mountain maple is common in the Rockies and grows about 4.5 to 6 metres tall. One of the most shade-tolerant of all maples, it has a lovely shape and a fall colour that can range from red to orange to yellow. New growth twigs are also bright red and attractive. It is occasionally offered for sale but does not always adapt to gardens due to its preference for high elevations and cooler temperatures.

Acer negundo (Manitoba maple) The Manitoba maple is also called the box elder, and at one time it was one

Normal growth of Manitoba maple tree trunk.

of the most planted trees on the prairies. Found throughout the continent, Manitoba maple is very heat- and drought-resistant, extremely hardy, and very fast-growing. It grows to 18 metres, making it ideal for shelterbelts and windbreaks. While a great farm tree, it isn't so hot for growing in town. Not only does it usually get too big, but female trees also produce copious amounts of seeds, so it can become quite weedy. It also attracts the box elder beetle, a handsome black and red beetle that appears in great numbers in the fall and often alarms people. I do not recommend Manitoba maple unless you have an acreage, in which case, have at 'er.

The exception to this is the variety called 'Sensation.' First, it is much more compact, maxing out at around 9 metres. Second, it is a male selection, so there are no seeds. Third, it was selected for its unusual bright orange-red fall colour—usually Manitoba maples turn yellow. It is a fine tree and perfectly fabulous.

Acer palmatum (Japanese maple)
"What about a Japanese maple?" I hear you asking. Sadly, the answer is no, you cannot have a Japanese maple. If you want one, you will have to move to Japan, or at the very least Nanaimo. Spectacularly beautiful Japanese maples are the darlings of coastal gardens. They are small, umbrella-shaped trees with a dizzying array of colours and leaf forms, and *none*

of them want to grow here! This has not stopped prairie garden centres from bringing them in and they tend to be a sell-out, so I expect that garden centers here will continue to offer them. They even seem to be gaining in popularity.

Can you grow a Japanese maple in a large container? Well, yes, sort of. There are people who do that. But how are you going to bring that container inside in the fall? How are you going to keep that maple dormant? Some prairie people go to great lengths to grow a Japanese maple and mulch the stuffing out of it or bury it in a trench in the vegetable garden a metre deep and they have actually been successful at making it survive … and if you want to go to that kind of trouble and effort, don't let me stop you.

Getting it through the winter is just half your battle. We also have a hot, dry, windy climate. Japanese maples are seaside trees. They are rarely found more than 10 or 15 kilometres inland. They want ocean breezes, humidity, and calm. They want mild winters and long summers. The reality is, they simply don't suit our climate, and they aren't cheap either! Want one? Be my guest! Don't say I didn't warn you.

Acer pseudosieboldianum (Korean maple)
If you are absolutely *insistent* on having a Japanese maple, might I recommend a substitute? The Korean maple is a small tree growing to about 4.5 metres that is at the northernmost limit of its hardiness on the prairies. In fact, it rarely becomes a tree in this climate but tends to be low and shrubby. It has handsome, exotic leaves that often become orange in the fall, and if you can give it a sunny, very sheltered site, you will probably do well with it.

Acer platanoides (Norway maple)
The Norway maple is a common street and boulevard tree in British Columbia and Ontario but not seen on the prairies very often. It is a large tree, and it does sometimes adapt to conditions that are not normal for it. There are mature Norway maples in Winnipeg, Edmonton, Saskatoon, Calgary, Medicine Hat, and Lethbridge, but they are very

Few trees can match the fall colour of a scarlet maple. This stunning specimen is in Bowness Park in Calgary.

and rare in the prairies. Some hardy cultivars *are* coming out of Minnesota and Manitoba, and although they are hardy, they are still not entirely suited to our climate: our summers tend to be too short and dry for them and they don't usually like our soils. Having said that, there are probably a dozen or more of them in Calgary. If you have a hankering to try one, you should.

Acer saccharinum **(silver maple)** The silver maple is a large tree that I madly love, so much so that it actually appears on my business card. Silver maples have large, light green leaves that are paler beneath, presenting a flash of silver when the wind blows. They become a luminous shade of soft yellow (never gold!) in the fall, and the smooth, silvery grey bark is enigmatic and alluring. These trees do best in non-alkaline soils with abundant moisture and fertililty. They grow quite fast, and will reach a mature height of at least 24 metres. They are too large for most yards, but they are truly magnificent if you have the space for them. Sadly, they do not do well in the chinook zone, so you need to choose something else.

Acer saccharum **(sugar maple)** The sugar maple—which adorns our national flag—is in much the same boat as the scarlet maple, and a few hardy cultivars have been introduced. The problem is that our season is just too short for them, and they don't do well with air pollution or compacted soils.

uncommon. A purple-leaf form called 'Prairie Splendor' was actually developed in southern Alberta and is worth trying.

Acer rubrum **(scarlet maple)** I also get asked fairly often about the scarlet maple, which is common in Ontario

Aesculus spp.

Although most species in this genus are not hardy on the prairies, there are at least two that are worth having. I am fond of both of them.

Aesculus glabra **(Ohio buckeye)** The Ohio buckeye is a slow-growing tree with unique hand-shaped leaves that sometimes become golden or orange in the fall. Its white flowers are pretty though not showy, and it produces

large, reddish brown nuts encased in a spiny husk. (The nuts are definitely not edible.) It has a deep taproot and is highly resentful of disturbance, so if you buy one from a nursery, buy it as small as possible. They are prone to transplant shock. In milder climates, Ohio buckeye can be an absolutely huge tree; here, due to our short growing season, it is more medium-sized. There

SHOPPING WITH LYNDON

is a particularly fine specimen on 20th Avenue northwest in Calgary that was planted in the 1920s. It is around 12 to 15 metres tall and it is extremely beautiful. Grow buckeyes in soil as moist and rich as possible and protect them from the wind for the first few years of their life.

Aesculus hippocastanum (**horse chestnut**) The horse chestnut is another large tree, and it is well known by anyone who has ever walked around in Stanley Park in Vancouver. It is, in fact, a common tree all over the world. Horse chestnuts, if babied and pampered when they are small, sometimes adapt to prairie growing conditions. Mature specimens exist

Ohio buckeye.

in Edmonton, Camrose, and Calgary. They are worth trying, particularly from seed.

Alnus spp. (alder)

Alders should not be confused with elders, which are a different plant entirely. Alders are closely related to birch and are worth considering. They have a preference for moist or even wet soil. Since they generally don't transplant easily, they are not all that common here. Depending on the species, alders range from shrubs to medium-sized trees. They have lovely smooth bark and often have an attractive fall colour, usually yellow.

Amelanchier spp.

These beautiful large shrubs from the rose family are not planted nearly often enough. I like plants with historical importance, and these certainly qualify. A misunderstanding between Europeans and First Nations people gave the city of Saskatoon its name. First Nations people settled along the banks of the Saskatchewan River, where this fruit grew abundantly. When the Europeans attempted to learn the name of their campsite, the First Nations people thought they were being asked about this fruit. They enthusiastically said, "Saskatoon!"—their word for this important plant. And so the city of Saskatoon was named.

Amelanchier alnifolia (**saskatoon berry**) The best-known representative of the *Amelanchier* genus is the saskatoon berry. When I recommend this, sometimes people say, "Oh no, I don't want a fruit tree. I want an ornamental." Well, this is both. Saskatoon berries are

ornamental in the extreme. They are native here, making them well suited to our climate, and were very important to First Nations people, who used them for food and dye. Planting saskatoons makes me feel a little more connected to the history of the land I live in. 'Martin' is by far my favourite variety, but 'Thiessen,' 'Smoky,' and 'Northline' are also good choices. In the wild, saskatoons are thicket-forming and will sucker. In cultivation, they are often grafted onto cotoneaster rootstalk to prevent this from happening.

Ideally, saskatoons want a sunny spot with abundant moisture. There is a reason they often grow along riverbanks, but they are highly adaptable. Most will become medium to large shrubs. The white flowers in the spring are showy and beautiful, the fruits are both decorative and delicious, and they have stunning fall colour ranging from yellows through oranges and red. The smooth,

Saskatoon berries.

grey bark is another nice feature and offers some winter interest. Even if you don't want the fruit, the birds will thank you for planting these!

***Amelanchier* sp. (serviceberry)** The serviceberry is a related species from eastern North America, and a hybrid form called 'Autumn Brilliance' is often offered for sale here. It is a small tree with showy white flowers and stunning red and orange fall colour. It has been known to survive in the chinook zone, but that's really all that it does. Since it tends to get a lot of tip kill and dieback, I think you have better choices available.

Andromeda spp. (bog rosemary)

There is only one species in this genus, and the Latin name for it is derived from the Greek myth in which Andromeda, a princess, was to be sacrificed to a sea monster. She was rescued by, and later married to, Perseus. In the same way that Andromeda was chained to the rocks with the sea lapping at her feet, so it is with the plant named for her. *Andromeda polifolia* is a circumpolar species that has never been common, likely due to its preference for acidic, peaty soils, low temperatures, and perpetual moisture. To further complicate things, it will not tolerate standing in water.

It is a small evergreen shrub with narrow blue-green leaves that resemble the cooking herb rosemary, although they are completely unrelated. It will grow in sun or partial shade but requires deep snowcover in the winter and dislikes both wind and heat. This makes it difficult to grow, but where it is happy, it will colonize. Charming, bright pink flowers appear in the spring and last a long time.

Bog rosemary has become the darling of growers. Because it is so showy and

unusual-looking, it is almost always a bestseller. Pots of bog rosemary in full bloom show up in garden centres across Canada in May, and people can't buy them fast enough! Famed Alberta gardener Lois Hole recommended bog rosemary as a "good shrub for a damp location." She failed to mention how easy it is to kill and how piling too much snow on top of it can easily break the plant in half.

Bog rosemary certainly does not suit every garden, and in fact, it may not even do well in a bog!

If you really need to grow this plant, I would recommend doing so in a specially prepared bed along with blueberries and other acid lovers. Bog rosemary also does well in a container and can be wintered in a cold storage room. 'Blue Ice' is the cultivar most often offered, as it is more compact, flowers more heavily, and its foliage is intensely blue-green. 'Alba' is occasionally offered, with white instead of pink blooms.

Bamboo

Wait a minute. Am I *really* talking about bamboo in a book about gardening in southern Alberta? Yep, I really am; so thank you very much, climate change!

Botanically speaking, bamboo is actually a grass, but what separates bamboo from other grasses is that bamboo forms woody tissue while other grasses do not.

There are many genera and species of bamboo, and all of them come from cold regions in Asia. Since they are a primary food source for pandas, do not plant bamboo if you have a panda problem in your garden!

Bamboo is heavily cultivated in China, Japan, on the West Coast, parts of Europe, southern Australia, New Zealand, and so on. For years, those of us who live in the central parts of North America were denied the ability to grow it. While California gardeners complained about how invasive some species were, we couldn't grow *any* of them! That has changed ... somewhat. For years the theory has been that since there are many bamboos that grow at high altitudes in places with long, cold winters and short, hot summers, there surely must be at least a few that would be hardy here. The best candidates, it seemed, were the bamboos in the genus *Fargesia*. These are small to medium, clumping (as opposed to "running") bamboos that grow at high elevations from China to Vietnam and throughout the Himalayas.

There are about 90 known species at the minute, but give the botanists some time with this and I'm sure they'll have everything restructured again by the time this book is printed. I have experimented with two that have shown promise, but there could be others.

Fargesia dracocephala This is a species about which I know practically nothing, except that it has a solid little cultivar called 'Rufa,' which has now been changed to 'Sunset Glow' to make it more marketable. It is slow-growing and under ideal growing conditions will

> If you want to try growing a bamboo, find out where it is native to. If it's from the regions around Hong Kong, it's probably pretty tender, but if it's from the area where China meets Mongolia, it is likely worth trying.

reach about 2.5 metres high and wide. On the prairie, cut that in half or better. It's an attractive, light green bamboo that rustles beautifully in the wind and turns a brilliant, warm yellow in the fall; hence, the new name. It has done well in a number of southern Alberta gardens when grown in a sheltered spot and protected from chinooks. Mine lived through three winters before it was eaten by deer. A friend of mine in Calgary has had hers for five years and it's lovely! Feedback from other gardeners in the area has been good, but you have to really want one because they are *expensive*. I paid $50 for a small plant in a 4-litre pot.

Fargesia nitida The other bamboo to consider is *Fargesia nitida*, a native to northcentral China and Tibet. Its dark canes with fine, bright green leaves are very pretty. It is clump-forming and non-invasive but needs considerable moisture to do well. It is also a large bamboo, but who knows how big it might get here? The cultivar 'Great Wall' is compact and tidy and has been slowly working its way into prairie garden centres. Both of these are officially zone 4, but you might have just the right microclimate and location where they can thrive.

Berberis spp. (barberry)

Barberries are getting a lot of attention in our landscapes these days. For years, we were denied the right to grow them because of wheat stem rust, a devastating fungal disease that could have a considerable impact in a part of the world that grows a lot of wheat. Wheat stem rust requires an alternate host to complete its

life cycle, one of which is a certain species of barberry. Instead of differentiating between one species of barberry and another, the Canadian government simply banned the growing of all of them. From the 1960s on, it was illegal to grow, sell, or possess any species of barberry. Gardener outcry finally reached a point

Barberry.

or rapidly (depending on the variety). They are excellent barrier plants. Grow barberry in full sun with good drainage. They aren't fussy about soil and are drought-resistant once established, but they will do best with regular watering. Some are very small and some grow quite large. They are primarily cultivated for their foliage, which can be green, variegated, purple, or streaked with pink. Many of the green-leaf forms are stunning in the fall when they colour up red or scarlet. The flowers are yellow and largely go unnoticed, and these give way to tiny berries, also usually unnoticed. Barberries do not typically have pest or disease issues, but jackrabbits will chew them to the ground, especially young plants you've just purchased.

where it could not be ignored anymore, and in 2002, it was legal to grow and sell barberries here again.

These great little shrubs, armed with sharp, stout spines, will grow slowly

Betula spp. (birch)

Birch are fabulous and beautiful trees. The paper birch is Saskatchewan's provincial tree, and there are many kinds to choose from. The weeping birch from Europe, the North American and Asian forms of paper birch, and, of course, the native river birch are all lovely trees. Depending on the variety, birch range from medium to very large. They are some of the hardiest trees on Earth, with stunning golden fall colour and equally beautiful white bark in the winter. They are fine-textured and cast a beautiful, dappled shade. Birch like moist but well-drained soil and grow at a moderate rate. Although much has been made of the bronze birch borer, a beetle that preys on birch, it wants elderly, drought-stressed trees, and many of the newer cultivars have *some* resistance to it. Don't be afraid to plant birch if you have the space for one! They are stunning and long-lived and offer beauty in all four seasons.

Birch fall colour.

Caragana spp.

Can the caragana please get a little respect? Even though there are some good cultivars available, caragana is widely hated by people on the prairies. Familiarity breeds contempt, one might say. Caraganas have been much planted,

terribly abused, neglected, ignored, maligned, cursed, and just generally treated badly. However, this is unfair! We owe the caragana an enormous debt of gratitude. Most of us would not be here without these shrubs. They created

Caragana flowers.

shelters and windbreaks so that our ancestors could farm and make a living here. They helped to divide property lines. They have created habitat for birds and shelter for wildlife. They have made barriers and enriched our soils with their nitrogen-fixing—yes, that's right, they literally pull nitrogen out of the air and improve our soil with it. They have helped prevent soil erosion. They have kept snow from drifting across the roads in days when people still travelled by horse and buggy. In short, they are pioneers and survivors. It is time we began treating them with a little dignity and appreciation.

The word *caragana* comes from the Tartar word *Karaghan*, which is what the ancient Mongols and Tartars called this shrub. When we think of caragana, we are usually thinking of *Caragana arborescens*. Introduced to the Canadian prairies in the 1880s, these hardworking shrubs were a fixture of prairie landscapes by the 1920s. Native to Russia, Siberia, and northern China, they are basically indestructible. From semi-arid and almost desert conditions, the caragana can endure intense heat, intense cold, and requires no care once established. Aphids and powdery mildew are afflictions that caragana suffers here that are not issues in its homeland. It can endure crowding, extremely poor soil, browsing animals, and probably nuclear fallout. The yellow pea-like flowers are actually showy (if brief), and bees use them as a nectar source. For a plant that is not native here, it has certainly done well for itself!

***Caragana arborescens* (caragana, Siberian pea shrub)** This is your typical caragana, which grows 3 to 4.5 metres tall and 1.75 to 2.5 metres wide. It makes an excellent hedge and barrier plant. I am not suggesting that you go out and plant one of these in your garden, but I would like us to start being a little more grateful. Caraganas still have a place here (despite their tendency to self-sow and become a nuisance). Conquest, Saskatchewan, proudly proclaims itself to be the caragana capital of the world.

When we do see this species used in landscaping, unfortunately it is usually one of several particularly hideous forms. The first is 'Pendula,' which is sold as "weeping caragana." The branches are indeed pendulous. It closely resembles a large green dishrag. 'Walker' is not much better, also top-grafted and also weeping but with extremely fine, almost threadlike foliage. Both of these shrubs could be attractive in the right setting, but typically they are just plunked down in the most inappropriate of settings.

Two forms that I do like are 'Sutherland' and the Lorbergii caragana. The Lorbergii caragana is also called fern-leaf caragana, as it has fine-textured leaves and an open, airy habit. It grows about 3.5 metres tall and 1.75 to 2.5 metres wide and is extremely beautiful. 'Sutherland' was developed in Saskatoon and introduced in 1944. This is a columnar caragana that grows about 4.5 metres tall and only about 1 to 1.5 metres wide. It is also sterile, meaning that self-seeding is not an issue.

***Caragana frutex* 'Globosa'** It is important to note that *Caragana arborescens* and its cultivars are not the only species available! *C. frutex* 'Globosa' is also called globe caragana or, simply, pea-shrub. It was introduced by Frank Skinner in the 1930s and can be found in many prairie gardens. This is a compact slow-grower that makes an excellent hedge. It neither flowers nor produces seedpods, though it will occasionally produce suckers if its roots are disturbed. It grows just under 1 metre tall and around 30 centimetres wide.

Caragana microphylla This little-known, handsome species just might be on the shelf at a nursery near you. Native to cold parts of northern Asia, this slender species has fine silvery-green leaves and large yellow flowers followed by dark red seedpods. It is quite spiny and is sometimes planted as a windbreak in parts of Siberia. Growing about 2.5 metres tall and under 1.5 metres wide, this very drought-resistant shrub is well suited to xeriscaping. In 2007, 'Silver Spires,' a cultivar selected from a windswept Mongolian steppe was introduced. It is a bit more narrow and refined than the species and is hardy to at least zone 2.

Caragana pygmaea (pygmy caragana) The pygmy caragana is a stunning, small, spiny shrub that grows just under a metre tall and about 2 metres wide. The golden-yellow flowers in the spring are produced in great profusion and are extremely showy. It is native to Siberia and northern China. Few shrubs are more heat- and cold-tolerant.

Celtis spp. (hackberry)

Related to elms, hackberries are medium to large trees that aren't grown very often due to their dislike of disturbance, making transplanting difficult. But they are beautiful, have stunning yellow fall colour and a textured, light grey bark, and they absolutely deserve to be more widely used in our landscapes. The cultivar 'Delta' is the hardiest. The tiny edible fruits appear in September, and they taste a bit like raisins. Do be careful though, as they contain a hard stone that can easily chip a tooth; hence the name.

Cornus spp. (dogwood)

Dogwoods are almost indispensible in our landscape, and we seriously need to stop planting them in shady places! Although dogwoods are okay with partial shade, they suffer in deep shade and become magnets for aphids. Many of them will also develop curly, yucky leaves in response to an aphid infestation. Grow dogwoods in full sun for best results. They like moisture, but they are very drought-resistant once established, whereupon they will grow fast and become handsome and bulletproof.

The red osier dogwood is native to North America and is very similar to the Siberian dogwood. Both can become quite large, maxing out at 3 metres tall and just as wide, though 2 metres tall and wide is more average. They have white flowers in the spring that are hardly anything to get excited about. Small clusters of white berries, which are eagerly devoured by birds, usually follow. Fall colour on the dogwoods is stunning, usually red to purple, and the twigs of the new growth are brilliant red or yellow, creating fantastic winter interest. Since the best colour is on the new growth, it is a good idea to give dogwoods a good, hard pruning every few seasons to encourage this. Otherwise, they tend to lose this attribute with advanced age. There are also some excellent variegated forms of dogwood; I especially love 'Ivory Halo.' Dogwood are among the first shrubs I would recommend to beginners.

Variegated dogwood.

Craetaegus spp. (hawthorn)

Hawthorns are magnificent small trees or, more usually, large shrubs that offer interest in all four seasons. The bark and the spines provide marvellous winter silhouettes. The white flowers in spring are pretty and much sought-after by bees. In the summer, they are perfect nesting sites for birds, and in the autumn, they have spectacular colouring. Many of them also produce huge crops of fruits that are loved by birds and other wildlife. I recommend any of the species hawthorns, if you can get them. The ones you find most often in garden centres are the varieties 'Toba' and 'Snowbird,' both of which are beautiful in bloom and have great fall colour. They are also small and low maintenance. My problem with them is that they are largely spineless, and they produce no fruit. If I plant a hawthorn, I want thorns! Grow hawthorns in full sun with good moisture.

Hawthorn.

Cytisus spp. and *Genista* spp. (broom)

These two genuses are so closely related that, honestly, I can hardly tell the difference! Not all of them are hardy here. These shrubs in the pea and bean family produce beautiful flowers that are usually yellow, often fragrant, and resemble sweet peas. Although you can find broom in many garden centres, they are highly resentful of disturbance. They should always be planted where they are to stay. You may also remember broom trees from the bible; the prophet Elijah sat under a broom tree while ravens brought him food.

Cytisus purpureus (broom) Unusual in its family, *Cytisus purpureus* is a perfectly hardy, gorgeous little shrub reaching about 45 centimetres and about 1 metre wide. It is slow-growing but produces a profusion of soft lilac flowers in early summer. It will self-seed where it is happy.

Genista lydia (broom) *Genista lydia* is from western Asia and the Balkans. For whatever reason, it is usually listed as a zone 5 or 6 plant, which is utter nonsense! It does perfectly well here provided it has excellent drainage and good snowcover to protect it from chinooks.

The brilliant yellow blooms are stunning, and it is a beautiful low shrub for a hot spot with poor soil.

Genista pilosa.

Genista pilosa (broom) *Genista pilosa* is a well known and hardy species, surviving well even here in zone 3. It comes from central and western Europe, growing about 30 to 45 centimetres tall and just under 1 metre wide. The flowers are brilliant golden yellow. 'Vancouver Gold' is an excellent and vigorous selection. It flowers in early summer, as do most broom.

Daphne spp.

Not all daphnes are hardy on the prairies, but I do like them. They are petite evergreen shrubs that are best given a bit of winter protection, but they are well worth it. *Daphne cneorum*, the rock daphne, is easily the hardiest species and the only one I recommend planting here. The brilliant pink flowers appear very early in the year and will scent the whole garden! Butterflies love them, and they are ideal for rock gardens or near a window that you like to open. Give this plant moist soil in a sheltered spot with sun or partial shade and hope for the best. Daphne tends to be slow to establish, and even once it does, it has been known to suddenly die after flourishing for years. A challenge for sure, but well worth it.

Eleagnus spp.

There are about sixty species of *Eleagnus* and a surprising number of hybrids. All of them are from cold parts of Asia and North America, and a number of them host nitrogen-fixing bacteria in their root systems, a little trick they stole from the pea and bean family. They aren't common in gardens here, but a few of them are good choices if you have the right setting.

Eleagnus angustifolia (Russian olive) Russian olive is a medium to large tree with stunning silver foliage and beautiful dark bark. It is both heat- and drought-resistant and can grow in very poor soil. It has long spines that make it interesting in the winter and tiny, olive-like fruits that the birds will enjoy. In some parts of North America (including Montana), Russian olive has escaped from cultivation and has become something of a weed. This is not something I would get too concerned about. What does concern me is that in recent years, a mysterious fungus is attacking Russian olives across the prairies. It interferes in the tree's ability to take up water, and so what is happening is that old, mature Russian olives are suddenly failing to leaf out in the spring or failing to leaf out on one side, the result being a mis-shapen, half-dead tree. Until we know more about this fungus and its life cycle,

Russian olive.

we can't really do much about it. Having said that, I don't think you should be deterred from planting one of these trees.

Eleagnus commutata (wolfwillow) The wolfwillow will be familiar to anyone who grew up on the Canadian prairies. It is native to hot, sunny hillsides across the continent and performs best in poor soil with good drainage. The foliage is intensely silver, and the tiny, dull yellow flowers have a silver cast to them. These give way to small, silver-coloured berries that are edible but dry and tasteless. It will grow 1.5 to 2.5 metres tall and just as wide, suckering profusely and forming thickets. It lends itself well to hot, dry areas where soil erosion is a problem, but it has limited landscape use. The flowers appear in early summer and are not showy, but they are heavily fragrant. To my nose, it is an intensely sickly-sweet smell, and although I don't mind the scent as it carries across the pasture, up close I find it nauseating. The scent of wolfwillow is the scent of the prairie to many people. There are few shrubs more drought-resistant, and some gardeners will be able to make good use of it, though it's certainly not well suited for every space.

Euonymus spp. (burning bush)

There are dozens of species in this genus. Few of them are hardy here, but you might like to consider the following:

Euonymus alatus (winged burning bush)
The winged burning bush is heavily marketed in garden centres right across the prairie provinces. Elderly specimens have unusual, corky ridges or wings along their twigs that give it the common name. It is cultivated primarily for its stunning, brilliant red fall colour. This shrub is very "hit or miss" here. There are some very large specimens of it in both Calgary and Lethbridge, but for every one that I see that has done well, there are a dozen that have not. We also don't *really* have a long-enough growing season for it. Some years it colours up beautifully; other years it is not so reliable. Winged burning bush normally grows 1.5 to 2.5 metres tall and just as wide, but there are dwarf, more compact forms available, such as the popular 'Fireball.' Grow burning bush in full sun and average soil.

Euonymus fortunei
This beautiful broadleaf evergreen is a very common shrub in British Columbia and often has gold or green variegation. It does survive here sometimes in a sheltered spot with good winter protection, but largely it isn't worth bothering with in the garden. As a container plant or annual, it is fabulous and often available very cheaply from big-box stores in the spring.

Euonymus turkestanica
This shrub comes from cold regions of Asia and is 100 per cent hardy and reliable here. It has small, fine leaves that colour up brilliantly in fall—anywhere from dull red to deep plum purple. The flowers will not be noticed, but they become brilliant hot pink and orange seedpods that resemble expensive earrings. These are very showy and attract a lot of attention. Grow this shrub in sun or partial shade and it will get about 2 metres tall and wide. 'Nana' is a dwarf form of it, growing well under 1 metre tall and about 1 metre wide.

Euonymus alatus.

Forsythia spp.

Medium to large shrubs, forsythias are much loved in many cold parts of the world. They are native to Korea, Japan, and China, and they are easygoing shrubs that ask very little. Most grow anywhere from 1.75 to 3 metres tall and

Forsythia.

just as wide, though in our short growing season they are often smaller. Forsythias flower very early in the spring, before they leaf out. The brilliant yellow flowers appear in great profusion. After they finish flowering, forsythias become a dense, solid green shrub that will occasionally turn purple in the fall. Not every kind of forsythia is hardy here. By far the most dependable one is 'Northern Gold' (really the only one I recommend), but 'Meadowlark' has also proven trustworthy. 'Show-Off' has particularly large flowers and is compact and heavily marketed; it is prone to serious dieback in the chinook zone, and I have yet to meet a single gardener here who has gotten a decent performance out of it. You should also know that while 'Northern Gold' and 'Meadowlark' are fully hardy as shrubs, they are not necessarily bud-hardy. What this means is that while the shrub can survive −40°C, the flower buds are only hardy to about −30°C. This means that if we get a week of −37°C, your flower buds will die. The shrub will be fine, but you won't get any flowers, or only the branches that were below the snow line will flower. Keep this in mind. Grow forsythia in full sun and average, well-drained soil.

Fraxinus spp. (ash)

Ash are beautiful trees, though at 18 to 24 metres, they are often too large for many gardens. They are attractive trees but not flashy, although a number of them can be quite showy in autumn. There are sixty-five species of ash, mostly from temperate regions, and while most are deciduous, there are a few evergreen species. Ash are members of the olive family (*Oleaceae*), and as such they are closely related to olives, of course, but also privet, lilac, mock orange, jasmine, and forsythia.

Ash are so common a tree that most people, gardeners included, entirely disregard them. In many instances they are considered a weed tree or are passed over as ornamentals in favour of smaller or showier trees. Why is it that ash is so common a tree that it has entirely fallen off our radar? Ash are remarkable. They are medium to large in size, usually quite fast-growing, and they are astonishingly tolerant of salt spray, wind, pollution, alkalinity, heavy clay soil, and drought. This has made them popular as both city and farm trees for centuries.

Ash have also become remarkably adept at passing on their genes, and they are often known for producing copious amounts of seeds, which will germinate everywhere. Their strategy has worked well for them, and fossil evidence indicates that the ancient forests of the world (most notably what is now Europe) were heavily populated by ash trees.

Ash are dioecious, meaning that they produce male and female flowers on separate plants. They are wind-pollinated and produce much pollen, but only female trees will produce seeds. Most fast-growing trees are short-lived, and ash are no exception. The average lifespan for an ash is sixty to seventy-five years, and while they are tolerant of a wide variety of harsh growing conditions, ash do best in a sunny spot with fertile, moist soil. They produce extensive, very large, fibrous root systems, and ash should not be planted in places where this will be a problem. They are well suited to acreages and parks but not as well to towns and cities.

As a rule, ash are shapely trees that require little pruning. If you must prune one, be sure to do it when they are in full leaf, as they have a tendency to bleed quite badly when they are cut. Although they are not disease-prone, an entire army of things like to feed on ash. They are highly prone to a large number of pests and insects, although it must be said that most of these insects cause only cosmetic damage and rarely affect the overall health and well-being of the tree. Perhaps the most significant pest that preys on ash is the emerald ash borer (*Agrilus planipennis*). This insect is closely related to our native bronze birch borer and was accidentally introduced to North America in the late 1980s or early 1990s. Since that time, it has quite literally killed tens of millions of ash trees in Ontario and the eastern United States. So far, it has found prairie winters to be too cold to its liking and it has not been found here, but that is likely to change over time. The emerald ash borer is controlled in its homeland by several species of wasp, but it has no predators in North America. Although it favours trees that are elderly and suffering from stress, when populations are high and they are hungry enough, they are quite capable of taking down any mature, healthy tree. They lay eggs beneath the surface of the bark, and their young tunnel downward, interfering in the tree's ability to conduct water. This results in the death of the tree, usually in as little as three years. It is estimated that there are several billion ash trees in North America; it would be a great tragedy if this insect were to wipe them all out.

Other insects that are known to be fond of eating ash include aphids, lygus bugs, canker worms, box elder beetles, caterpillars, leaf rollers, and bud gall wasps. Horses, cattle, goats, and deer will also eat and destroy young ash trees if given the chance.

Fraxinus pennsylvanica (green ash)

The best-known species is the green ash, which ranges throughout the continent and usually grows in areas where moisture conditions are good. This is a very robust, highly adaptable species with bark that is smooth when young and deeply furrowed with age. The pinnate, lance-shaped leaflets are attractive and become brilliant yellow in fall. It is usually the last tree to leaf out in the spring and the first to drop its foliage when autumn arrives.

Green ash was planted extensively across the prairies in the early 1900s and right into the 1940s. Fast-growing, highly adaptable, and untroubled by harsh winters or disease, the green ash soon found itself growing on nearly every farm, in nearly every shelterbelt, and in every small town and city. It was immensely popular, but after a few decades it became increasingly apparent that this tree was much too large for most urban settings and that it self-seeded so prolifically that it made a huge nuisance of itself. The immense, spreading root system is also sometimes a problem, as are the hordes of caterpillars and leaf rollers that the foliage attracts. Eventually, green ash fell from popularity, and many people developed a dislike for these trees.

Eventually, several male selections of it were named and released to the nursery trade. 'Patmore,' selected in Vegreville, Alberta, is one of these, as is the very similar 'Bergeson.' In more recent times, green ash has slowly started to come back to the consciousness of gardeners and city planners. 'Foothills' is a cultivar selected near Calgary for its ability to tolerate chinook winds. It is also a male selection and quite compact. 'Prairie Spire' was introduced by the University of North Dakota and has the most pyramid-shaped growth habit of all the green ash. 'Excel' is yet another male clone that was selected for its much slower growth habit, making it less likely to outgrow a more confined space. For my part, I like green ash a lot. However, I think they are better suited to farms and acreages than they are to city life.

Fraxinus americana (white ash)
The white ash is similar to the well-known green ash but not as hardy. Normally best in zone 4 or 5, there are exceptions

to this. It comes from eastern North America, where it is often used as a street tree, and it is also common in Vancouver. One of the features that sets white ash apart from the green ash is that it generally turns rich shades of brilliant red through deep purple in the fall instead of yellow and it retains its leaves somewhat longer. Although white ash has been little planted on the Canadian prairies, this is slowly but surely beginning to change. Over the last number of years, a variety of new, much hardier cultivars have been released. One of the most noteworthy is 'Calypso,' an introduction from Manitoba that is very upright, fast-growing, and hardy to zone 3 and possibly zone 2. The fall colour is dark purple and it does not produce seeds. 'Northern Blaze' is very similar and equally hardy but with distinctly more red-purple tones in fall than just merely purple. 'Nobility' is a promising new selection from Jeffries Nurseries in Portage La Prairie, Manitoba. It was selected from the very northernmost part of the white ash's range in northern Wisconsin and it has done fabulously well in trials across the prairies. White ash reaches a mature height of around 15 metres.

Fraxinus mandschurica (**Manchurian ash**) The Manchurian ash is an absolutely magnificent tree from cold parts of northern Asia including China, Mongolia, and Siberia. It is a dense, round-headed tree with a thick canopy that casts a heavy, deep shade. Averaging around 18 metres tall and 12 metres wide is typical, but heights of 30 metres have been recorded. The leaves are long and, frankly, gorgeous. They turn a brilliant yellow-gold in the fall and the show is quite long-lasting. First planted on the prairies in the 1930s, this tree has been widely used in Saskatoon, Edmonton, Regina, and Winnipeg, but it has done poorly in Calgary and the rest of southern Alberta due to a serious intolerance for chinook winds. As a result, it remains uncommon and little known here.

Fraxinus nigra (**black ash**) Black ash is another native of North America, and it is one of the slower-growing species. It reaches an average height of 15 metres, though 25 metres is not unheard of. Black ash has beautiful, pinnate foliage that turns a stunning brilliant yellow in autumn. It is very drought-tolerant once established but prefers good moisture and appreciates fertile soil. 'Fall Gold' is a particularly compact, vigorous variety that was selected in Manitoba. It is often used as a street and boulevard tree but can be prone to leaf rollers and caterpillars.

Hybrid ash Two highly attractive hybrid ash trees were introduced by Dr. Wilbert Ronald of the Morden Research Station: 'Northern Treasure' and 'Northern Gem.' He started working on these crosses in the late 1960s and spent decades selecting the strongest and best offspring to be named and introduced. They are both hybrids between the black ash and the Manchurian ash. 'Northern Treasure' used Manchurian ash pollen, with the black ash as the seed parent, and 'Northern Gem' is the reverse. Both are superior, spectacular trees. Both grow faster than either of their parents, and both are vigorous and highly adaptable. 'Northern Treasure' reaches 9 to 12 metres tall and 3 to 6 metres wide. It has elegant foliage similar to the Manchurian ash and turns a gorgeous pale orange or light golden yellow in the fall. 'Northern Gem' has shorter, wider leaves and also becomes yellow in the fall. It also grows a bit wider and taller than its sister. Both are being widely used as boulevard and park trees, although they are as pest-prone as any other species of ash and often succumb to frost cracking and chinook damage in southern Alberta. This has not stopped landscapers and gardeners from trying them. I have seen these trees planted in several places in southern Alberta in the spring, only to be replaced the following year when they leaf out poorly or the tree is 50 per cent dead.

Ginkgo biloba

Ginkgo biloba is the sole surviving species of an entirely extinct genus that was once found throughout the world. It has gorgeous, fan-shaped leaves that colour up golden in the fall. Slow-growing ginkgos are officially hardy to zone 4, but remarkably they have been able to adapt very occasionally to certain places on the prairies. It's perfectly fine with me if a ginkgo chooses to remain a shrub; just the thrill of having one is enough, and I don't need for it to get to tree size. There are a number of gardeners here who are growing it, and while it usually suffers tip kill and dieback, this isn't necessarily a problem.

A beautiful, small specimen grew at the University of Saskatchewan for several years before some scoundrel dug it up and stole it! A large and healthy specimen grew at the Calgary Zoo for more than twenty years before it finally met its doom via the flooding of 2013. In excellent health, it was in a sheltered spot and never had any tip kill or dieback. A ginkgo in Drumheller, Alberta, faces north and receives the worst brunt of the winds from across the river. It is stunted and small, perhaps only about 4.5 metres tall. It was planted in the 1960s and appears to have fully adapted to a situation far less than hospitable.

I say, if you like ginkgo, get a small one (I bought a seedling at the floral department at the local grocery store) and start there. Mine lived for several years before the neighbour's children stepped on it. Grow ginkgo in full sun with well-drained soil.

Ginkgo leaf.

Hippophae rhamnoides (sea buckthorn)

The sea buckthorn is one of my favourite shrubs. No, actually, it's one of my favourite plants. It might actually be one of my favourite things on our planet. (Maybe I should get a sea buckthorn T-shirt, or maybe a sea buckthorn tattoo.) Sea buckthorns are in the same family as Russian olives and buffaloberries, and, like their relatives, they are armed with very stout, sharp spines. Male and female flowers occur on separate plants, and female plants erupt into colour in the fall covered with enormous, very full clusters of brilliant cantaloupe orange fruit.

While it may not be well suited to every garden due to its size (2.5 to 3.5 metres tall and just as wide), if you have the space for one they are wonderful and very low maintenance. They are native to the Atlantic coast of Europe, right across into the cold parts of Asia, and as they are so tolerant of salt spray, they have

> The fruit of the sea buckthorn, while difficult to pick, are high in vitamins C and E and taste a bit like pineapple. The berries are gorgeous on the bare branches in winter, and birds love them.

been able to colonize in places where other shrubs cannot. Colonize they will, I might add! Although they are sometimes difficult to establish, once they do, sea buckthorns will makes themselves at home and promptly send out suckers to form dense thickets. They are fantastic windbreak plants on farms and are also good on boulevards, where their suckering is not a problem and their resistance to salt spray is a blessing. Sea buckthorns

Sea buckthorn is structurally interesting, and the berries are glorious.

do best in well drained, average to poor soil and do not tolerate shade or flooding. The silvery green leaves are handsome and they make an excellent barrier shrub. Few hardy shrubs are as drought-resistant, and I do not know of any pest or disease issues that affect them. Curiously, they are also nitrogen fixers and will enrich the soil around them.

Hydrangea spp. (hydrangea)

Hydrangeas do not suit every garden, and not all of them are hardy. They want a moist, sheltered site and we live in a dry, windy climate. They will look like salad after a hailstorm. They cannot handle wind or drought. I know I mentioned that already, but it's important enough to say it twice. If you have a moist, sheltered site, they can be stunning. 'Annabelle' and 'Peegee' are by far the most reliable, but 'Quickfire' and 'Limelight' are also hardy and beautiful. Contrary to popular belief, hydrangeas should not be planted in the shade. Partial shade is fine, but if you want flowers, a sunny site is much better.

Ilex spp. (holly)

The truth is that I love holly, but I've learned it won't easily grow in my Alberta garden. I'll give you the facts on them just in case you are feeling adventurous.

Ilex aquifolium (Christmas holly)
Um … no. It ain't gonna happen. If you'd like to grow it, by all means move to Kelowna. In southern Alberta, it's not an option, despite what you may have been told. Hollies produce male and female flowers separately, and only female plants produce berries. For several years, a male and female cultivar (usually sold together) called 'Blue Boy' and 'Blue Girl' have been sold in prairie garden centres. In a very protected spot with serious winter protection, they survive sometimes. I know several gardeners who grow these hollies in Calgary and take great pride in them but go to a lot of trouble to get them through the winter.

Ilex verticillata (winterberry) The
winterberry is a deciduous holly, and it

is much loved and well used by florists around the world. It is a medium-sized, suckering shrub from eastern North America. Tiny white flowers appear in spring and are followed by vivid scarlet, extremely showy red berries on female plants. After the foliage has dropped, these berries will persist for many weeks, and they are stunning!

Winterberry is officially hardy to zone 3, but I think this is being a bit optimistic.

Holly is a broadleaf evergreen. I would grow it for the leaves or the berries. If I have to cover it up in winter to save it, I won't be able to see it, so I won't be enjoying it. What's the point? No, my friends, you need to leave holly at the store.

I think zone 4 is closer to the truth. It will grow in most sites from sun to considerable shade but insists on having a humusy, neutral to acidic soil with good moisture. It is also intolerant of drying prairie winds, especially in the winter. Even though winterberry acts like a diva, if you have a sheltered, moist site with the right soil, few things are more stunning. There are never enough colours in winter, and some gardeners really like something challenging. If this is you, winterberry might be just the plant for you.

There are a few gardens in both Calgary and Medicine Hat where they are flourishing. Cultivars including 'Berry Heavy,' 'Berry Nice,' 'Jim Dandy,' and 'Red Sprite' have done very poorly here, but the species itself has not done badly. You might have just the spot for one, but don't feel bad if you don't.

Juglans spp. (walnuts)

I bet you didn't know you could grow walnuts here. Depending on the species, most walnuts are extremely hardy and extremely beautiful. They tend to be quick-growing when young, but the growth rate slows tremendously as they get older. Walnuts are generally very long-lived and fairly easy to cultivate. A cool, humid climate suits them best and they tend not to grow well in open, windy sites. A deep, fertile soil high in organic matter is their preference, and although they can withstand significant drought, walnuts perform best when they are well watered.

All species produce a very significant taproot, and they are resentful of being confined in a container. If buying a walnut tree, it is best to buy them as small as possible, preferably as a seedling. Walnuts often succumb to transplant shock, and their disregard for being in a container can make them difficult for nurseries to handle. Fresh seed sown in fall will generally germinate quite easily the following spring. This is the best way to obtain a walnut tree!

Of the twenty-one species, only three or four can be considered hardy on the prairie. Their large size and penchant for sheltered sites does not make them an immediately obvious choice for most gardeners, but having said that, a mature walnut tree is a thing of great beauty and rarity. Mature, gorgeous specimens exist in Saskatoon, Regina, Calgary, and Medicine Hat and probably elsewhere on the prairies as well.

In addition to their nuts, perhaps the best-known thing about walnuts is that they are allelopathic, which means that the roots secrete a toxin known as both juglose and juglone that inhibits the growth of other plants. Juglone primarily prevents seeds from germinating, but some plants are very sensitive to it. This is especially true of both apple trees and tomatoes—neither wants to grow anywhere near a walnut tree. Walnuts do not want to compete with their own offspring, and therefore they have devised this clever way to prevent their own seeds from germinating beneath themselves.

Juglans regia (English walnut) The walnut of commerce that we know so well from baked goods and ice cream is the English walnut. It is *not* hardy on the prairies since it is probably about a zone 5 or 6, but it's certainly not the only species that is edible.

Juglans nigra (black walnut) The black walnut is native to southeastern Canada and the northeastern United States. It is a highly regarded, much-loved timber tree that can grow as tall as 30 metres and live for several hundred years. The black walnut is slow-growing and slow to break dormancy in the spring. The bark becomes progressively darker with age, giving this tree its name. The large nuts are richly flavoured, but the shells are very tough and somewhat difficult to get into. It is hardy on the prairies but care should be taken to plant it in a suitable site. You need a spot with reasonably

Black walnut.

good soil that is at least somewhat sheltered from the wind.

So-called "Carpathian walnuts" are hybrids between this species and the English walnut. They are reputed to have the flavour and easy shelling of the English walnut and the hardiness and fine-grain wood of the black walnut. They are little known in North America but have gained some popularity as shade trees in Europe.

Juglans cinerea (butternut, white walnut)

Also native to eastern North America is the butternut, sometimes called white walnut. Reaching up to 18 metres in the wild, butternut trees are usually about half that size in cultivation. They grow extremely rapidly when they are young, with growth slowing down with age. They are often multi-trunked and therefore not as widely used for timber as the black walnut. The medium- to large-sized nuts are well flavoured but extremely oily; hence, the common name. In the last ten years, butternuts have been nearly wiped out in the wild due to a strange fungal disease called "butternut canker." The disease is fatal to the tree, and so far no cure has been found. Butternuts are hardy on the prairies and should be treated the same as the black walnut.

Juglans cathayensis (Chinese walnut)

Although I do not know anyone who is or has grown it here, it is my suspicion that the Chinese walnut would do well in our climate even though it is officially listed as a zone 5 plant. It is native to Taiwan and central and western China, which is a climate not dissimilar to our own. It grows 15 to 20 metres tall and produces rather excellent nuts. It is very similar to the Manchurian walnut, *J. mandschurica*, which comes from northern China and Korea. This is an elegant, medium-sized tree with very long, pinnate leaves and good crops of small walnuts. Officially, the Manchurian walnut is listed as zone 4, but two mature specimens proudly exist in the Prehistoric Park of the Calgary Zoo.

Juniper spp.

Among the hardiest conifers in the world, junipers are largely divided into upright forms and creeping. They need to be in full sun with excellent drainage, though they are not fussy about soil. Junipers need to be well watered until they are fully established, and they should be well watered again in the fall until the ground freezes. They are extremely wind- and drought-resistant, and there are many, many varieties.

Every year in the spring, people say to me, "I hate junipers. They are always dead in the spring. They always turn brown." My usual response is that gardening is not for crybabies. Winter browning of evergreens can mean that (A) they were seriously under watered, which is very common, or (B) they were purchased from a big-box store and weren't propagated from especially hardy stock. Sometimes it is a combination of both. If you pay $11 for a juniper and it is dead in the spring, you probably got your $11 out of it. Keep in mind that winter-kill happens in the wild too, and I have seen brown and dead junipers around Drumheller, Canmore, and Medicine Hat after a particularly harsh winter.

Junipers offer some fantastic colours as far as evergreens are concerned and come in many shades of gold, green, and blue-green. Upright varieties that I recommend include 'Grey Gleam,' 'Medorra,' and 'Wichita Blue.' Any of

the savin junipers are great for spreading types, and I highly recommend 'Arcadia,' 'Blue Carpet,' 'Calgary Carpet' (selected for its incredible resistance to winter browning), 'Golden Pfitzer' (which is a far better choice than 'Gold Coast'), 'Mint Julep' (also listed as 'Sea Green'), and the almost flat 'Prince of Wales,' which becomes immensely wide (up to 3 metres) and takes on highly attractive plum and purple tones in the fall and winter. Junipers provide excellent habitat and nesting areas for birds, as well as creating visual appeal in the winter.

Larix spp. (larch)

Larch are unusual trees in that they are deciduous conifers.

***Larix laricina* (North American larch, tamarack)** The North American larch—most commonly known as the tamarack—is one of the hardiest trees in the world. It can handle temperatures as cold as –60°C! It grows anywhere from 9 to 18 metres tall and is highly variable in shape and size. The needles are soft and feathery, becoming a luminous golden yellow in the fall before falling off and being replaced in the spring. It grows in northern parts of Canada right at the tree line and also at high altitudes in the mountains, where "larch viewing" has

become a popular autumn pastime for many hikers and outdoor enthusiasts.

Tamarack is the official tree of the Northwest Territories. It is not often cultivated, in part because it gets very large but also because of its variable growth habit. These trees are intolerant of shade and prefer moist, cool conditions.

***Larix siberica* (Siberian larch)** The Siberian larch is frequently cultivated. Although they somewhat resemble the North American larch, the Siberian species is much fuller and more proportionate. It can also handle drier conditions and lower elevations. The Siberian larch is a large tree, topping out at 18 metres or more, and makes a spectacular windbreak or shelterbelt. There are also a few very dwarf and weeping forms, though these are often expensive.

Larch and tamarack—two names, same tree.

> Larch are low-maintenance, absolutely stunning trees whose soft, delicate foliage is inviting and visually appealing. Their fall colour is luminous, and they have no real pest or disease issues.

Lonicera spp. (honeysuckle, honey-berry, haskap)

Whenever someone tells me that they are interested in planting a honeysuckle,

I ask if they are looking for the shrub or the vine. This is a diverse group of plants, and not every kind of honeysuckle in the world is prairie-hardy. Honeysuckles will grow in just about any soil provided they have good drainage and full sun.

Lonicera tatarica **(Tatarian honeysuckle)** The best-known shrubby species is probably the Tatarian honeysuckle, which grows about 2.5 metres tall and 1 to 1.5 metres wide. It has white or pink flowers in late spring or early summer, followed by red berries that birds enjoy. For many years this was one of the best, easiest, most low-maintenance shrubs one could plant here. That changed with the arrival of the honeysuckle aphid, which causes these shrubs to develop stunted, misshapen foliage and generally ruins their appearance. I rarely see them offered for sale anymore, which is a shame because they are so beautiful. The Queens Park Cemetery in Calgary is lined with pink and white Tatarian honeysuckles. When they flower in early summer, driving down 4th St. NW is delightful.

Tatarian honeysuckle.

Lonicera maackii **(Maack's honeysuckle)** The Maack's honeysuckle is a better choice and seems fairly resistant to the aphid. It grows to about 3.5 metres

and produces a profusion of white flowers in early summer. Unfortunately, it isn't available very often.

Lonicera xylosteum **(European fly honeysuckle)** I think it's called the European fly honeysuckle because the flowers are about the size of a fly. You won't notice the blooms, but it is a rounded, very dense blue-green shrub good for hedging.

Lonicera caerulea **var. *edulis*** This Asian species has no fewer than nine geographical variations. This shrub grows very large and dense and was once used widely across the prairies. It has tiny yellow-green flowers in early spring that are loved by bees, leafs out very early, and has no pest or disease issues. The flowers are followed by small, teardrop-shaped blue fruits eagerly eaten by birds.

In recent years, the University of Saskatchewan has done a lot to develop new and superior fruiting forms of this species. These are being marketed as "haskap." 'Borealis,' 'Indigo Gem' and 'Tundra' are new cultivars that have been released specifically as a fruit crop. I personally am not a fan of how they taste, but I think they are decorative and I like that they attract birds.

Diervilla **spp. (dwarf bush honeysuckle)** *Diervilla* is a genus of closely related shrubs that are sometimes offered for sale. They sucker and have tiny yellow blooms, and little to recommend them beyond drought-tolerance and an attractive bronze colour in the fall.

Climbing honeysuckles The climbing honeysuckles are much loved by both gardeners and hummingbirds, and they are quite different from the shrubby types. The best one for our climate is an old hybrid introduced by Frank Skinner of Manitoba called 'Dropmore Scarlet.' It climbs about 3 metres and flowers profusely in early summer. The long, tubular flowers range from orangey red to almost coral-coloured. It becomes very woody with age and needs something strong to support its

weight. The other excellent climbing form for southern Alberta is 'Mandarin,' an introduction from the University of British Columbia. It is a profuse bloomer and vigorous grower, covered in masses of brilliant tangerine orange flowers in early summer. Both want full sun and good drainage, and both are drought-resistant once established. Although 'Dropmore Scarlet' is often recommended as a good choice for a shady spot, this is untrue. In shade, it will flower poorly and get mildew. Plant it in the sun.

Climbing honeysuckle, like 'Mandarin' shown here, are one of the most beautiful ways to block your view of your neighbour's yard.

Magnolia spp.

Ancient and mysterious and totally garden worthy … if you live in Victoria. No matter what you might have been told, magnolias are not worthy additions to an Alberta garden. The star magnolia, *Magnolia stellata*, occasionally survives here if heavily mulched and babied and pampered and treated like a tea rose, but why bother? If you want to see magnolias, you book a flight to Vancouver and you go visit Van Dusen Gardens in April.

Malus spp. (apples)

Apples are many splendoured things. The number of people who wistfully say, "If only we could grow real apples here like they grow in BC" amazes me. I say, "We *can!*" Multitudes of fabulous apples can be grown here. To grow an apple, you need full sun, reasonably fertile soil, and a decent amount of space. Most of them grow 6 to 8 metres tall and often just as wide. They are fabulous ornamentals and excellent bee forage with their stunning blossoms in the spring, they provide wonderful shade in the summer, and many of them develop yellow fall colour.

We have a wide variety of edible apples available to us.

You have no shortage of wonderful, delicious, fantastic apples to grow here. High on my recommendation list would be 'Battleford,' 'Boughen's Delight,' 'Fall Red,' 'Honeycrisp,' 'Red Sparkle,' and 'September Ruby.' I also like 'Prairie Sensation' and 'Prairie Sun.' For crabapples, 'Dolgo' is particularly productive and excellent for crabapple jelly, as well as being a pretty sensational ornamental. 'Rescue' and 'Renown' are also absolutely worth growing.

In terms of ornamental crabapples (often simply referred to as "flowering crabs"), there are also multitudes of choice. "I don't want anything that drops fruit all over … " is something I hear over and over again. Don't plant ornamental crabapples near decks, sidewalks, driveways, and so on. Problem solved! 'Thunderchild' is by far the most popular, with pink flowers and burgundy foliage. It's stunning and low maintenance. The marble-sized fruits are held tightly on the tree and do not drop and make a mess. 'Royalty' is even darker in colour but prone to disease. It has largely been replaced by 'Fuchsia Girl,' which is a nice choice. 'Strathmore,' 'Big River,' and 'Makamik' are other flowering crabs that are not seen as often but are absolutely hardy and absolutely gorgeous.

Most of the flowering crabs produce blossoms in shades of pink or rose, but 'Spring Snow' is a brilliant pure white. It's stunning and it's virtually sterile, which makes it perfect for people who can't stand a tree that produces fruit. There are also a goodly number of columnar and semi-columnar flowering crabs being introduced, and they make excellent substitutes for the hideous Swedish aspen. 'Dreamweaver' and 'Emerald Spire' have only been on the market a short time, but they are getting rave reviews, and I expect we will see a lot more of them in the future.

Microbiota spp. (Russian cypress, Siberian cypress)

Microbiota decussata is the only species in its genus. At first glance, it looks like a juniper, and you could be forgiven for thinking it was one. However, junipers are quite spiny, whereas the Russian cypress is feathery and soft. It is quite slow-growing but extremely hardy and sometimes takes on bronze colouring in fall and winter. It eventually forms large, dense carpets. It's a great evergreen to use in a rock garden or to cover a slope. Highly resistant to winter browning, it can handle serious drought once established, although it will do best in good soil with abundant moisture.

Philadelphus spp. (mock orange)

The mock orange is so named because the white flowers both resemble and smell like orange blossoms. They burst into flower in early summer like a great white storm. Their perfume can fill an entire garden. After they have concluded blooming, they are a lovely, low-maintenance shrub. Most mock orange varieties get quite large, and the dwarf forms tend to have less scented blooms.

Mock orange.

'Blizzard' is one of the best-known varieties and will grow 1.5 metres tall and just as wide. It is absolutely my favourite variety. 'Waterton' grows about 2 metres tall, and though it is less common than it once was, it is worth seeking out. It was selected in Waterton Lakes National Park in southern Alberta many years ago and does not disappoint as a garden specimen. 'Snowbelle' was an introduction from the Ottawa Experimental Farm and produces very large blossoms with outstanding scent. It is a profuse bloomer.

For something different, you may wish to try 'Primrose,' with palest yellow to ivory blossoms instead of white, or 'Aurea,' which flowers less prolifically but produces gorgeous golden-green foliage. The double-flowered mock oranges such as 'Buckley's Quill' and 'Minnesota Snowflake' are neither as fragrant nor as profuse bloomers as their single-flowered counterparts. Grow mock orange in full sun or light shade with average, well-drained soil. They tend to become very "twiggy" with advanced age, and a hard pruning every few years will help keep them vigorous and flowering well.

Physocarpus spp. (ninebark)

Ninebarks are lovely small to medium shrubs that are low maintenance, attractive, and widely available. In the wild, they are usually little green shrubs with exfoliating bark and rounded clusters of pretty white blooms. For best results, ninebarks should be given a fairly hard pruning every few years to keep them vigorous and at their best. Full sun produces the best colour in their foliage, and they aren't fussy about soil. Ninebarks make excellent informal hedges.

'Diablo' ninebark.

The ones we see in our gardens are generally cultivars: some are good; some are not. 'Diablo' grows 1.8 to 2.5 metres tall and wide and has dark purple foliage. It is vigorous, hardy, and fast-growing. 'Dart's Gold' is a bit more compact but has brilliant golden yellow leaves. They look awesome grown together. Some of the newer cultivars, such as 'Coppertina' and 'Satin Chocolate,' look nice at the nursery but are prone to powdery mildew in the garden.

Picea spp. (spruce)

Spruce are among the most successful plants on Earth. They are by far the dominant tree in the world's northern forests, and they are accustomed to short, hot summers and long, cold winters. They can handle soil that is far less than ideal, have few pest or disease issues, and look wonderful in the winter. Indeed, their branches are designed to shed snow. Spruce range from small, dwarf, and medium shrubs all the way up to immense trees. They have sharp needles, and they come in a variety of shapes, colours, and sizes. If it's a spruce, it's probably worth planting. Just make sure you have *adequate space* for the one that you want. Grow spruce in full sun and well-drained soil.

Picea pungens (Colorado spruce, blue spruce) This is the most commonly cultivated spruce here. This tree can grow 23 metres tall and up to 7.5 metres wide, though usually we see them sadly butchered with their lower limbs removed. How "blue" a blue spruce appears is primarily genetic, and there are dozens of different cultivars. Some are bluer than others; some are more pyramidal or columnar in shape; and some stay shrub-sized. This species has a lot of variability. I love Colorado spruce for its drought-tolerance, winter interest, and ability to create significant shelter. It makes an excellent windbreak and provides a home for a variety of small creatures. The columnar form of blue spruce is an excellent substitute for Swedish aspen. The globe form of blue spruce is a beautiful rock garden shrub.

Picea abies (Norway spruce) The Norway spruce is an immense tree that has huge cones and graceful, sweeping branches like a green curtain. The nest spruce (*Picea abies* 'Nidiformis') is a teeny dwarf form of it that grows just under 1 metre tall and about 1.5 metres wide, developing a sunken, lowish spot in the centre as it ages. It sort of resembles a bird nest once established. It is very resistant to winter browning once it's mature and can make a welcome alternative to a juniper. The brilliant green new growth in spring is incomparable.

Picea omorika (**Serbian spruce**) Found throughout much of Europe, this is a slender tree that grows to about 18 metres tall with very short, two-toned needles that are very handsome. Uncommon in cultivation, when you do find it in the garden centre, it is usually one of several dwarf forms. These are slow-growing, often handsome, and ruggedly hardy. They also tend to be more "full figured" than the species.

Picea glauca (**White spruce**) Found throughout the continent, this is an extremely important timber tree and also the provincial tree of Manitoba. The species itself is rarely used in garden, but the dwarf Alberta spruce (*Picea glauca* 'Conica') is an exception—you can find it for sale just about anywhere. An extremely petite and compact form of this species that was first discovered near Lake Louise in the early 1900s, it has very tiny, bright green needles and an exceptionally dense growth habit. It is also very slow growing. People hear "Alberta" in the name and immediately assume it must be perfectly suited to all parts of the province, but that is definitely not the case. While it is a great choice for large containers or as an annual, it is prone to infestation from spider mites and is also more prone to winterkill and browning than any other evergreen that I've grown. Most garden centres will not warranty a dwarf Alberta spruce for this reason.

Pinus spp. (pine)

Pine trees, like spruce, are absolutely gorgeous trees that provide excellent windbreaks and provide shelter, winter interest, and shade. The sound of wind in the pine trees is beautiful and cannot be matched. You have a lot of choice with pines, but they are less tolerant of heavy clay soils than spruce.

Pinus sylvestris (**Scots pine**) The most common pine tree here is the Scots pine, which grows very large and makes an excellent farm or acreage tree. They are usually too large for growing in town. The exfoliating, coppery orange bark is distinctive, and there is really no other pine like it.

Pinus cembra (**Swiss stone pine**) The Swiss stone pine is perfectly shaped, like a flawless Christmas trees, and reaches 7.5 to 12 metres tall. The needles are very soft, begging to be touched. The tree itself is wickedly hardy and almost never experiences winter browning. No pest or disease issues are noted. So why don't we see it more often? Because it grows slowly, *very* slowly. Frankly, I don't think that should be a reason not to grow it. It is highly adaptable, gorgeous, and becoming more available. It is unlikely to outgrow its allotted space and can be a welcome addition to a small yard or garden if you make allowances for the fact that someday it is going to be quite large. A few large specimens do exist on the prairies, but they are rare and infrequent.

Pinus strobus (**white pine**) The white pine is often used as a Christmas tree and is Ontario's provincial tree. It has long, soft needles and beautiful, slender cones. Although officially it is hardy to zone 4, white pines are known to adapt to the prairies sometimes. There are mature specimens in both Saskatoon and Calgary.

Scots pine bark.

***Pinus contorta* (lodgepole pine)** The lodgepole pine is Alberta's provincial tree and also has soft, luxurious needles. It is occasionally cultivated, but it is so highly variable that it is kind of like bringing home a puppy from the SPCA: you might get a terrier, you might get a St. Bernard!

***Pinus aristata* (bristlecone pine)** The bristlecone pine is a slow-growing, stunning tree that is often wider than it is tall. It has short, soft needles covered in flecks of white resin, and it often grows in peculiar shapes, resembling antlers. The oldest living things on the Earth right at this moment are bristlecone pines growing high in the mountains of California. Planting one of these trees is a surefire way to leave something valuable to all those who come after you. They are spectacularly beautiful trees. While they have done well in both Calgary and Canmore (perhaps due to the high elevation), gardeners in other parts of the prairies have not been nearly so successful with them.

***Pinus ponderosa* (ponderosa pine)** Ponderosa pines are common in British Columbia and have huge, sharp cones and very long, very sharp needles. They are known to adapt here sometimes and might be worth trying.

***Pinus mugo* (mugo pine)** Or maybe you need just a shrub, in which case, say hello to the mugo pine. Mugo pines have considerable genetic variability and can range from just a few centimetres tall to towering over a two-storey house. Mugos can withstand significant abuse, neglect, and poor growing conditions, and so that is often how we see them: neglected and abused! This has led many people to believe they are unattractive. They are not. When well grown, mugos are a thing of great beauty.

Best to buy a named variety though, or what your mugo pine grows into could be anyone's guess. Grow pines in full sun, as they are intolerant of shade and in well-drained, preferably sandy soil.

Mugo pine.

Populus spp. (poplar, aspen, cottonwood)

If you have a farm or an acreage, these are a great choice. Otherwise, why are you planting these? Most people don't realize that poplar, aspen, and cottonwood are all names for the same group of trees. There are twenty-five to thirty-five species in the genus *Populus*, but it is hard to be sure because, like their close relatives the willows, they hybridize freely and it can be difficult to tell what is a true species and what is a hybrid.

The word *poplar* is derived from the Roman word for these trees, which means "the tree of the people." This is also where the word *population* comes from, as poplars were much planted around city squares, along streets and roads, and to mark property boundaries.

Poplars are nearly all northern hemisphere plants, and they are famous for being among the fastest-growing and hardiest of all trees. They are also generally quite large, growing from 15 to 50 metres tall. Most of them turn bright yellow in the fall (or very occasionally scarlet), and they have been valued as timber and shade trees for thousands of years. A number of them have medicinal properties as well.

Poplars are an ancient group of trees; the fossil record places them from 50 to 58 million years ago. Poplar fossils are not uncommon as far as fossilized foliage is concerned, and excellent specimens have been found in North Dakota, Wyoming, Colorado, and Utah. Although a few poplars are drought-tolerant, most prefer moist or even wet conditions. Poplars can grow anywhere from 1.5 to 3 metres in a single growing season. Many can reach their full height in as little as twelve or fifteen years.

These trees have immense, aggressive root systems and sucker and colonize freely. This makes them excellent for farms, shelterbelts, and parks but not ideal for towns or cities. They are not in the least bit fussy about soil, and can

Aspen need love too, just not in the city.

tolerate wind, pollution, poor soil, alkalinity, and salt spray, although one thing they *cannot* abide is flooding. They are preyed upon by vast armies of caterpillars, aphids, and other insects, and many botanists believe that their rapid growth rates evolved as a way to combat these frequent issues. As a general rule, poplars have smooth, often light-coloured bark when they are young, becoming dark and deeply furrowed with age. Leaves range from triangular to rounded or even diamond-shaped, and the foliage moves in even the lightest breeze—another trait they are known for.

In nearly every species, male and female flowers appear on separate plants. They are pollinated almost entirely by the wind, and female trees produce minute seeds surrounded by silky, cotton-like fibres. This can be messy and unpleasant, so usually only male trees are grown. On both genders, the flowers and the scales that cover the developing buds drop quickly, and although these decompose rapidly, they can make a huge mess. You should avoid having a poplar in places where this will be a problem.

Poplars *do* self-sow, but they do not become weedy like Manchurian elms or green ash. Poplars would prefer *not* to grow from seed—they would much rather propagate asexually. Cuttings root extremely easily, and poplars clone themselves by suckering. In the wild, the river often carries broken branches away, and these branches frequently take root and become new trees. Fallen branches are also known to take root, and poplar root systems have remarkable powers of regeneration.

As you might expect from such a fast-growing tree, poplars are not long-lived. Their lifespan is sixty to seventy years, though they can live to be a century or more under ideal growing conditions. As a general rule, when poplars get elderly, their heartwood goes first and they rot on the inside. They appear structurally sound, but then a windstorm comes up and they come crashing down onto houses, cars, and so on. Elderly poplars in cities are carefully monitored. In many prairie towns and municipalities, bylaws now often regulate the planting of poplars, and in many places, planting poplars has been banned. These are important farm and shelterbelt trees, no question, but I would not even dream of planting one within municipal limits.

Potentilla spp.

Once you have been gardening for a while, you'll eventually come to have a sincere disdain for the humble little potentilla. I am here to tell you that potentillas are lovely things, and if you are brand new to gardening, I can offer you nothing finer. I think, for most people, the contempt for potentillas is related to out-of-control overplanting. They are *everywhere*! You can't drive down the street without seeing them planted somewhere, usually outside of gas stations and car dealerships and fast food joints, and often in large numbers. This has led to many gardeners being dismissive of them, but they became that popular for a reason.

As a child, my grandma's garden was a place of wonder and beauty. She had (and still has) a great many of these shrubs. She grew every variety she could find, and they flowered profusely all summer. Through wind and storms and perverse growing conditions, they not only survived, they flourished! I was astounded. The word *potentilla* comes from the Latin word meaning "potent," or powerful. I understood that after seeing them in Grandma's garden, and I still love these shrubs. I remember her saying things like "Just *look* at this potentilla! It has so many blooms you can hardly see leaves! Aren't they something?" I had to admit they really were.

Perennial forms of potentilla grow as groundcovers, and there are also shrubby potentillas. They are members of the rose family, and the single flowers have five petals just like a wild rose. Most commonly, we see the yellow-flowered varieties and most grow just under a metre tall and just as wide. Potentillas want full sun and sharp drainage. That's it. They are untroubled by pests or disease, and they will bloom profusely from May to October. Bees love them, and they are extremely hardy and extremely reliable.

Potentilla fruticosa, from which many of the modern hybrids are derived, is native to southwestern Alberta. I have seen it thriving on Nose Hill Park in Calgary in the middle of bald, windy hillsides, and I have seen it in Waterton Lakes National Park, providing a feast for bees. The variety we most often see is 'Coronation Triumph,' which has relentlessly golden flowers. 'Katherine Dykes' and 'Primrose Queen' have softer, pale lemon yellow blooms that are quite different.

'Abbotswood' has white flowers, and I once interplanted a long row of them with 'Diablo' ninebarks. The white flowers with the purple foliage were quite fabulous together. Red potentillas such as 'Red Ace' and 'Red Robin' are beautiful and barely hardy. Don't bother with them. Orange potentillas such as 'Orange Whisper' are superb and rarely seen, likely because people don't bother to think about potentillas anymore. The pink forms such as 'Pink Beauty' and 'Pink Princess' are not my cup of tea, but many gardeners fall in love with them. The only thing to really remember about potentillas is that they live for about twenty years, and they look good for about ten years. You can sometimes rejuvenate an old specimen with a hard pruning, but after a decade, it's best to pull it out and buy another one.

Prensepia sinensis (prensepia)

Sometimes called cherry prensepia, the prensepia is a fairly uncommon shrub native to China. It is perfectly hardy and I'd like to use it more often, but it takes up a fair bit of room. It grows anywhere from 1.8 to 2.5 metres tall and up to 3 metres wide. It has arching, very spiny branches that have the graceful

Prensepia.

appearance of bamboo and sharp spines that make it an excellent barrier plant. It is extremely early to leaf out, and insignificant yellow blooms become dime-sized cherry-like fruit. These range from pleasantly sweet to outrageously bitter, though they are loved by birds. The fall colour is brilliant yellow, and it is tolerant of heat, drought, and poor soil. This is a great plant for creating habitat for wildlife.

Prunus spp.

This is an absolutely huge genus in the rose family, and includes peaches, nectarines, cherries, almonds, plums, and apricots. It's impossible to write a short entry about this group, but I will try to be brief.

Apricot The apricot of commerce is *Prunus armeniaca*, and it's not hardy in our part of Canada. However, the Manchurian apricot, *Prunus mandschurica*, comes from northern China, Mongolia, Korea, and Siberia and it *is* perfectly hardy here. Some really excellent hybrids between these two have been created, but on its own, it is a beautiful small tree that produces little fruits and has significant cold tolerance. In the wild, it usually flowers in late February or March. Here, it flowers in May. The fruits are just okay for fresh eating, but they are excellent for making apricot jams and jellies and also for canning and preserving. It is likely that even better hybrids will eventually come from these.

Apricots are prone to several fungal diseases, and aphids can be a problem. Since chinooks easily kill the flower buds, trees in Calgary usually produce a crop maybe once or twice every ten years. The buds begin to swell in late winter, and sudden drops or increases in temperature will kill these dormant buds, often preventing them from flowering at all. No flowers mean no fruit. To further complicate issues, apricots bloom very early in the year and the flowers are easily claimed by frost. If temperatures

are too cold for bees to be flying while they are in flower, this will also prevent a crop. Having said that, though, they are lovely trees with attractive leaves and sometimes golden fall colour. Good varieties to try include 'Brookcot,' 'Debbie's Gold,' 'Sub-Zero,' 'Sunrise,' and 'Westcot.'

Cherry What to say about the cherries? There are so many of them! Some are grown for fruit, some for beauty, and some for both.

Prunus cerasus **(sour cherry, Evans cherry)** The 'Evans' cherry is a form of the sour cherry, which is now widely grown on the prairies. Grow it in full sun with rich, moist soil. The white flowers in spring are gorgeous, and it produces huge quantities of delicious, pleasantly sour, quite large fruits. The bark is also especially beautiful. It's a nice small tree for front yards and has few pest or disease issues. The 'Romance' series of cherries introduced by the University of Saskatchewan has 'Evans' cherry in its parentage and is also totally garden-worthy.

Prunus maacki **(Amur cherry)** Once a popular front-yard specimen, the Amur cherry has fallen from common use over the last decade for a variety of reasons. Native to northern China, Siberia, and Korea, this is an extremely rapid-growing tree that can occasionally grow as tall as 15 metres, with around 9 metres as the average. A dwarf cultivar called 'Goldspur' maxes out at around

Evans cherry.

half that. Amur cherry can be single- or multi-trunked, it does not sucker, and it is rarely affected by the black knot disease that infects so many of its relatives. Its off-white blooms are not particularly showy, and they give way to tiny dark purple or black fruits that are loved by birds. These cherries will also drop when they are overripe, staining sidewalks, decks, driveways, and clothing a deep, berry purple. Do not plant an Amur cherry anywhere that the fallen fruit will be an issue.

The leaves turn a lovely light yellow in the fall, and upon shedding its foliage, the true glory of the Amur cherry is seen—its bark. You would be hard-pressed to find another hardy tree with bark like this. It ranges from a rich, burnished copper to soft gold and is almost shiny in appearance—absolutely stunning!

Like mountain ash, however, it is extremely prone to frost cracking and sunscald. Unfortunately, these trees will often get to a decent size and immediately begin to decline. The branches are also weak and somewhat prone to damage—windstorms and heavy snowfalls can split these trees in half. As if that were not annoying enough, they are also prone to a fungal issue called shoestring disease, which often causes what looks like mushrooms to sprout at the base of the trunk and severely shortens their life. Although they can live to be as old as sixty years under good conditions, shoestring is so prevalent that the average lifespan of an Amur cherry now is usually about ten to fifteen years. Given how rapidly they grow and how easily they are propagated

from seed or cuttings, this is, I suppose, not such a big deal.

You will sometimes find seedlings in odd places, planted by the birds. If you are going to buy an Amur cherry from a nursery, it is recommended to buy a smallish one, as they can also be prone to transplant shock. Occasionally, if they are babied and pampered while they are young, Amur cherries can live much longer than they really should. It is worth checking out the row of Amur cherries growing in downtown Calgary: planted in 1925, they are just north of the LRT platform on 7th Ave. SW. When they were planted, there was plenty of sunshine and they were well cared for. Now they are surrounded by concrete and fairly shaded, and the leaves are often rather chlorotic-looking, yet still they persist and are in reasonably good health. Their fruit stains the sidewalks blue-violet every year, but the beautiful golden-red bark is enjoyed by thousands of passengers every day of the winter. These trees are close to 15 metres tall, and at more than eighty years of age, no one knows how much longer they will endure.

Prunus padus var. commutata (mayday cherry, bird cherry) I can't think of a single reason to recommend a mayday cherry, also known as mayday tree. Growing anywhere from 12 to 18 metres tall, the mayday is native to nearly every country in Europe all the way to Asia and Japan. It flowers quite early, and in many parts of its range it is flowering on May Day (May 1); hence, the name. This is the traditional day to decorate a May pole with ribbons and flowers. Mayday trees are extremely hardy, and they were extensively planted right across the prairies in the 1950s and 1960s. Nearly every neighbourhood in every prairie province could boast of several large examples of this tree in full glory during the 1970s. This led to many of today's gardening demographic having nostalgic connections to them, and thusly, there is still much demand for them, though I am trying hard to stomp this out.

Mayday is rapid-growing, which is good, but they also sucker extensively, which is bad. If you plant one, you will spend the rest of your life battling shoots, suckers, and water sprouts. Mayday is prone to transplant shock, and they can sometimes be difficult to establish. When they bloom, they bloom for all they are worth. The entire tree turns into an enormous, billowing white cloud. The flowers are beautiful, fragrant, and excellent forage for bees. The instant they are finished blooming, they rain down tiny, faded white-brown petals on *everything* for two weeks. Blooming, by the way, lasts for about fifteen minutes. (Okay, it's longer than that, but seriously, a maximum of seven to ten days.) That is, assuming that we do not have a killing frost while they are in bud. This happens every few years, and even old, established maydays cannot be expected to consistently flower well every single year, especially in the chinook zone.

When mayday are done blooming and done making a mess all over your entire yard, the fruit will develop. The fruits are slightly larger than that of the Amur cherry and produced more abundantly. Maydays drop their fruit all over sidewalks, cars, driveways, decks, and anything that might be beneath them. They are aided in this effort by birds, squirrels, and other small creatures. The fall colour of maydays is yellow, which I admit is nice, and they have very smooth, deep grey bark that makes the trunks and large branches resemble elephant legs, which also appeals to me. However, I think their flaws outweigh any contributions that they make. Profuse suckering combined with very messy petal drop combined with very messy fruit drop would be enough for me, but let me add to this.

Mayday is extremely prone to a fungal disease called black knot, *Apiosporina morbosa*, for which there is no cure. This

Mayday cherry.

disease both weakens and disfigures the tree. Black knot also affects chokecherries and pincherries and is very much present in the native populations of these trees. Black knot releases its spores during warm, rainy weather in the spring and is spread by birds, insects, wind, and infected pruning equipment. It causes large black knots to develop on the tree branches, mostly in late summer and early fall, and this both weakens the tree and kills the individual branches that it infects. There is no cure for this except to prune out infected branches well below the infection. Studies have also shown that serious fluctuations in moisture levels can make a tree much more prone to this disease. Few things in a prairie landscape look as horrible as a black knot–infected mayday tree in the middle of winter. It looks as though every branch is decorated with dog feces.

Have I still not convinced you? Let me keep going. If we should be lucky enough to get a heat wave in August, what immediately happens is an overwhelming aphid infestation in your mayday. Particularly if the tree is large, old, recently transplanted, or even somewhat drought-stressed, every aphid for kilometres around will come to feed on your tree. This leads many people to douse their entire yard in awful chemicals, and that is something I am very much against. Aphids will drop sticky, yucky honeydew everywhere, along with the staining fruits. This attracts wasps.

Oh, did I also mention that maydays are prone to being eaten by caterpillars? Let me be clear about this tree: *Don't plant one!* Serious flaws and various personality issues vastly overshadow any benefits or good qualities it has. I suppose if you have chosen to plant a mayday and my hatred for them hasn't convinced you otherwise, I might as well make you aware of the fact that although white is the usual colour, there is also a form with soft pink–coloured flowers that was introduced from Stockholm in 2002. In the last few years, 'Merlot' has been showing up in a lot of nurseries. It has foliage that ages from green to dark purple, and it is more compact than the species. Full size is about 7.5 metres, though it still has all of the flaws of its green-leafed brethren.

Prunus pensylvanica (pin cherry, fire cherry)

The pin cherry is a nice, small species of cherry native to North America. It can be found from British Columbia to Newfoundland and south all the way to Colorado and South Carolina. It is rapid-growing, totally intolerant of shade, and resentful of transplanting, which has somewhat limited its use in the nursery trade. This is really a lovely tree that is beautiful in all seasons. Single- or multi-trunked, the positively gorgeous bark ranges from orangey brown to a deep russet red. It is particularly striking in the winter months. The white blooms appear in May and are pleasantly fragrant, followed by drooping clusters of showy ruby-red fruits in late July or early August. Although most people find these very unpleasant raw, they make positively fantastic syrups, jellies, and jams. That is, providing the birds don't eat them before you do. Fall colour on these trees is vivid and long-lasting. A glowing burnt orange is the usual colour, but shades of red and gold are also common.

So why are pin cherries not more common than they are? Well, for one thing,

they sucker intensely, particularly if their roots are disturbed. They are susceptible to black knot, frequently resentful of transplanting, and they are not easy to propagate. Seed does not germinate reliably, and they do not always strike roots from cuttings. Having said that, two cultivars of this cherry can occasionally be found in the nursery trade. 'Mary Liss' was introduced from Alberta in 1937 and is both non-suckering and compact. It will not exceed 4 metres, whereas the species generally grows about 5.5 metres. 'Jumping Pound' was selected from a wild population near Kananaskis, Alberta, in 1936. It is more compact still, only 2.5 to 3 metres, and as it grows, it takes on a distinctly semi-weeping shape. It is particularly beautiful in the winter, when its slender branches are covered in hoarfrost. 'Stockton' is unusual for having larger double flowers. Pin cherries are hardy to zone 1.

Pin cherries were much used by First Nations people not only as an abundant food source but also as a medicine. The name *pin cherry* is derived from its use in killing pinworms and other intestinal parasites.

Prunus tomentosa (Nanking cherry)

Easily one of the most recognizable and common cherries on the prairies, this medium-sized shrub is easily and abundantly cultivated. Growing upward of 2 metres tall and just as wide, this is a dense shrub that makes for an excellent hedge. It is native to the Himalayas and China and is not troubled by any of the pest or disease issues that bother so many of its relatives. Hardy and adaptable, Nanking cherries do best in average, well-drained soil and they are extremely drought resistant once established, though fruit is much higher quality when moisture conditions are good. The flowers appear very early in spring and can be soft pink or white. They are both fragrant and extremely showy.

After flowering, the cherry bears small-ish, brilliant scarlet fruits that are delicious fresh and also make wonderful pies, jams, and jellies. If you do not claim the fruits, they are highly decorative in the garden and much appreciated by birds. The birds will also distribute the seeds via their droppings, so you may find Nanking cherries growing in peculiar places. They are even known to naturalize occasionally and can some-times be found growing along riverbanks or in clearings in the forest.

Although inconsistent, Nanking cherries will sometimes produce noticeable fall colours, ranging from pumpkin orange through dark yellow. They tend to bear large crops in alternate years, and they are both long-lived and low mainte-nance. They will establish themselves quickly and can be producing a crop in as little three years, even if they are grown from seed! Although red is the usual colour of the fruits, a black-fruited form is also sometimes cultivated. If you don't have room in your garden for a full-sized Nanking cherry, a semi-dwarf form called 'Petite Candles' is available. It grows only about 1 to 1.5 metres tall and just as wide.

Prunus virginiana (chokecherry)

Chokecherry just might be the most successful species in the whole clan. It is native to North America and can be found from British Columbia and all across the prairies to down into the United States as far south as California and New Mexico. It is an extremely rapid-growing, thicket-forming small tree or large shrub with non-showy white blooms in spring followed by beautiful, drooping clusters of highly astringent small fruits. Fall colour on these trees is often orange to red, with shades of usually very showy purple.

Chokecherries generally ripen in late August or early September and are very showy when hung with fruit. There are several naturally occurring variations of the chokecherry, with the *melanocarpa* variety being the most common. This means "dark-fruited." Indeed, the colour of the fruit is highly variable and ranges from nearly black through purple to a deep, garnet red. *Xanthocarpa* is far less common but is otherwise alike in every way except that it produces slightly sweeter, very pretty, bright yellow fruits.

Chokecherries produce huge crops of fruit and are a major food source for birds, small animals, bears, foxes, raccoons, skunks, and people. Many First Nations depended upon them and recognized that the fruit is much sweeter following a frost and even better after being cooked, which will sweeten them further. Almost all varieties will make excellent jams, jellies, and syrups. Although some people like them for wine, I would like to say from experi-ence that chokecherry wine is one of the worst things I have ever tasted.

Due to their heavily suckering tenden-cies, chokecherries are not much used in gardens except on farms and acreages as shelterbelts. A few cultivars have emerged over the years, but chokecher-ries are just as prone to black knot as the maydays, which discourages people from planting them, myself included.

Easily the most cultivated of all the chokecherries is an introduction from Bismarck, North Dakota, called 'Shubert' (also sometimes spelled 'Schubert'). This hideous monstrosity was selected from a wild population for its deep burgundy-coloured foliage. Rapidly growing to a height of 4.5 to 6 metres, this foul creature does as the mayday does and provides an ongoing barrage of suckers. The foliage emerges green and ages to a dark purple, usually turning red in the fall. It is a bit more resistant to black knot than green-leaved

'Schubert' chokecherry.

Chokecherry.

varieties, but that is hardly a recommendation. It also produces less fruit than other chokecherries but still enough to stain everything around it.

A number of "copycat" clones have appeared over the last few years, many claiming to not sucker as much—a claim I have found to be nonsense. Frankly, I cannot tell a 'Shubert' apart from 'Bailey's Select,' 'Midnight,' 'Mini-Shubert,' 'Sharon,' and 'Spur.' While a single specimen might be of value in the landscape, why do so many big-box stores, city planning committees, and cul-de-sacs insist that a purple-leaf chokecherry is the only tree available? Purple-leaf chokecherries are dark, sombre, light-absorbing, and really quite morbid when grown in mass quantities. One *might* be okay, but do you really want seventeen of these?

The only good reason to grow chokecherries is for fruit production or for wildlife. If you are looking for a yellow chokecherry, 'Spearfish' is a 1924 introduction from South Dakota that has done well on the prairies. 'Boughen's Yellow' was a 1930 introduction from Boughen Nurseries in Valley River, Manitoba. The fruit is large, showy, and produced abundantly. For black-fruited chokecherries, 'Garrington' is an introduction from Alberta that produces huge quantities of fruit. The Prairie Farm Rehabilitation Administration (PFRA) of Indian Head, Saskatchewan, introduced 'Pickup's Pride.' Originally discovered on the farm of John and Myrna Pickup of Broadview, Saskatchewan, this variety produces very large fruits with very small stones and it is extremely productive—among the best for using in the kitchen. 'Boughen's Chokeless' is a Manitoba introduction with notably less astringent fruit than other varieties and plenty of flavour. All chokecherries are hardy to zone 1.

Prunus x cistena (cistena sandcherry)

Although most prairie gardeners know this shrub, we rarely remember that it is indeed a cherry. Developed in South Dakota and introduced in 1910, this medium to large shrub is now grown in cold countries all over the world. Often treated more as a perennial than as a shrub, under good circumstances it will grow just over 2 metres and just as wide. In the harshest part of the prairies, it will usually winter kill to the snow line. This is just fine, as the best colour is on the newest growth and it grows very rapidly.

The foliage is a brilliant reddish purple, and the bright pink spring flowers sometimes appear before the leaves, sometimes together. It is sometimes grown as a pollen source for other cherries and plums. On occasion, it may even produce tiny inedible fruits. This is an excellent, low-maintenance shrub that adapts to most sites and soils, although it is intolerant of shade. It can be propagated quite easily from cuttings, but care should be taken not to crowd these plants, as they can be prone to powdery mildew.

Prunus spp. (plum) Plums are usually moderate- to fast-growing and quite easy to care for in the garden. There are lots of hardy and beautiful varieties to choose from. They require full sun and have a preference for fertile, well-drained soil with good moisture. Highly adaptable, most plums can be cultivated in any reasonable space. The flowers are very welcome in the spring, extremely beautiful, and can perfume an entire garden. The leaves are usually simple and oval, frequently becoming showy and fiery shades of red, orange, gold, and purple in the fall. The spines and dark, often exfoliating bark can create a beautiful silhouette in the winter months.

There are few pest or disease issues associated with plums, and once established they are reasonably care-free. Plums are usually propagated by grafting, though

The contrasting stamens on the white plum blossom really make them pop.

you can also grow the species from seed. A number of plums will sucker profusely if their roots are disturbed, and aphids can be a major nuisance, especially during a heat wave. Deer, rabbits, and mice will all eat plum trees, and birds will strip the fruit if you aren't diligent about netting. Most plums will begin to fruit well in the third or fourth year after planting and will fruit well for at least twenty or thirty years. They are self-fertile, but you will have much better fruit if you plant two different varieties in close proximity to each other.

Prunus americana (American plum)
One of the most important North American species is the American plum, which grows about 3 to 7.5 metres tall and hails from the eastern and central parts of the continent. It has dark brown, exfoliating bark and red or reddish-purple fruit with yellow flesh. Although not great for fresh eating, the large fruits are good for canning and cooking. They were much used by early settlers to the continent, as well as by First Nations peoples. Usually found in moist woodlands, the American plum can still be found in the wild in Manitoba and even Saskatchewan, though it is rare, and it is easily recognized by its intensely spiny branches. It is also quite showy in bloom. This species was essential in creating many of the modern hardy hybrids.

Prunus nigra (Canada plum) Equally important and often crossed with the preceding species is the Canada plum, also from the northeastern parts of North America. Usually a bit smaller and less spiny than the American plum, this beauty has shiny red to brown bark that ages to grey and becomes exfoliating. The fruit is red or yellow and quite large, and both of these trees are hardy to zone 3. They are even known to occasionally hybridize in the wild, making identification sometimes difficult. The Morden Research Station in Manitoba and the Brooks Experimental Farm here in Alberta developed hardy prairie plums, with many of their introductions still being available today. In the 1960s, the University of Saskatchewan

Double-flowering plum.

You know it's spring when the muckle plum is in bloom.

introduced more than fifteen new varieties, many of which can still be found in garden centres. Excellent varieties for eating include 'Bounty,' 'Brooks Gold' and 'Brooks Red,' 'Dandy,' 'Opata,' and 'Pembina.'

A selection of the Canada plum called 'Princess Kay' has been introduced by the University of Minnesota. Discovered as a chance mutation in the wild, this gorgeous variety reaches a height of just 3.5 to 5.5 metres and produces very showy, fragrant, double white blooms in great profusion. It may produce a few small yellow-red plums, which the birds will happily eat, but this is not the reason to grow it. In addition to the brilliant spring bloom, in fall this plum turns stunning shades of orange and yellow, and the very dark, purple-black bark and spines are especially striking against the snow in the winter. Full sun with ample moisture and good drainage suit it best. It tends to be slow-growing but deserves much wider use in our landscapes. This would make an excellent small specimen tree for a front yard.

Prunus triloba var. multiplex (double-flowering plum) The double-flowering plum is a beautiful shrub that was discovered in China about three or four hundred years ago and has been carefully selected and propagated vegetatively ever since. It is almost entirely sterile and produces an extravagant, incredible display of large, fully double bright pink flowers for about two weeks in spring. It often develops gorgeous orange or gold

colour in the fall as an added bonus. The problem with this shrub is that when it is in full bloom, it is so gorgeous that everyone covets it and immediately flocks to their local garden centre to purchase one. This shrub is actually very large, and few people have room for one, but they plant them anyway.

It will grow just over 2 metres tall on average, but sometimes as much as 3 metres. It is also much wider than tall, requiring anywhere from 2.5 to 3.5 metres of space. So what do people do? They prune them! They hack off branches and attempt to shape this plant into balls or cubes and goodness knows what else, and the shrub loses all of its natural dignity and beauty. The fact that the double-flowering plum puts up with this is an indication of how tough and resilient it actually is. If you want one of these shrubs, make absolutely certain you have the space for it.

Prunus nigra x Prunus tenella (muckle plum) Finally, we have the muckle plum. This is a hybrid between the Canada plum (*P. nigra*) and the Russian almond (*P. tenella*). Growing about 5 to 4.5 metres tall, this spectacular, small, sterile tree produces an explosion of hot pink flowers in very early spring. It is incredibly hardy and incredibly gorgeous, but it is also painfully slow-growing and prone to infestations from aphids. It is also difficult to propagate, which makes it expensive. Still, I would consider it to be well worth growing if you are looking for something unusual.

***Prunus tenella* (Russian almond)** This charming little shrub was very popular in the 1960s and 1970s, but sadly it seems to have fallen out of favour. What a shame! Growing to about 1.5 metres tall and just as wide, this hardy and low-maintenance shrub is the first thing to burst into bloom in the spring, sometimes flowering when there is still snow on the ground. The flowers are brilliant electric pink (or, rarely, white) and are produced in great profusion. Upon concluding its bloom, it is a dense, shapely shrub that often turns plum purple in the fall. Fuzzy almonds follow the blossoms, but these are bitter and not considered edible. Birds or squirrels will sometimes drop these seeds, and you may find tiny seedlings coming up here or there. They will also produce some suckers but not enough to be a nuisance. Grow it and you will love it. Russian almond wants full sun and well-drained soil. It is extremely drought-resistant once established and has no pest or disease issues.

Pseudotsuga menziesii (douglas fir)

When is a fir not a fir? When it's a douglas fir! Douglas firs differ from true species of fir, and, in fact, they are unique among conifers. Although we normally think of these as West Coast trees, a definite inland population can be found throughout Idaho and southwestern Alberta, with their most naturally occurring inland populations in Calgary and around the Nanton area. In Bowness Park, you can see douglas firs that are several centuries old. Douglas firs are large trees, and while they can be spectacular, they can just as often be scrawny, misshapen, and unattractive. Some very large, old specimens grow in Calgary, Canmore, and Lethbridge, but they are rarely remarked upon for their beauty. I wouldn't recommend planting one, but I would recommend enjoying them when you are out hiking in the mountains. Just because there is a hardy form of something available, doesn't mean it's something you want.

Pyrus spp. (pear)

It's surprising to most people that you can grow some pretty fantastic pears on the prairies. These are medium to large trees that want full sun and well-drained, fertile soil, but they can withstand significant drought once established. They explode into bloom in the spring with white flowers that resemble apple blossoms but without the fragrance. Fall colour on a pear is spectacular—reds, oranges, golds, and deep purples. The fruit is usually quite small but often good for canning and preserving. Excellent, surprisingly good varieties include 'Early Gold,' 'Golden Spice,' and 'Ure.' Pears take their time getting established, but they are well worth it.

'Early Gold' pear is a good choice—look how big they are!

Quercus spp. (oak)

Oaks have distinctive, simple leaves that are usually deeply lobed. They generally have wide-spreading canopies and are excellent shade trees. Male and female flowers are produced separately but on the same plant. They are pollinated primarily by wind, but insects also play a role. The seeds are very familiar: we know them as acorns. Oaks are well known for their long life spans (often several centuries) and their deep, carrot-like taproots. They favour rich, fertile soil, and while many are drought-resistant, all are better when water is available. As a general rule they are rapid growing when they are young, with growth rates slowing dramatically the bigger they get. They are resentful of disturbance, and if they must be transplanted, this should be done when they are as small as possible. Some oaks produce magnificent autumn colour, others hardly any colour at all, or at least inconsistently.

Quercus macrocarpa (bur oak) The bur oak is the hardiest oak known, ranging from Manitoba through eastern Canada and south all the way to Texas. It has ridged, scaly bark and will occasionally turn pale brown or gold in the fall, but usually there is little to no autumn colour. It is tolerant of pollution and poor soil and has virtually no pest or disease issues. It can grow anywhere from 16 to 36 metres tall and live for hundreds of years.

It is increasingly being planted in the chinook zone, and I find it to be a remarkable study in climate change. Fifty or sixty years ago, bur oaks simply did not grow here. They do not fare well with chinooks and would not establish well, suffering significant tip kill and dieback. Very, very few mature bur oaks exist here for that reason. However, the severity of our winters and the intensity of our chinooks have lessened in the past few decades, and this has allowed bur oaks to start to gain a foothold here. I always say if it's not bur oak, don't fix it!

Quercus ellipsoidalis (Northern pin oak) Bur oak is not the only oak you can try here. The northern pin oak, *Q. ellipsoidalis*, should not be confused with the pin oak, *Q. palustris*, even though these two species are quite similar. Native to the central and southern United States, this beautiful species turns a brilliant red in the fall and favours moist, slightly acidic soil. It normally reaches about 20 metres and makes a brilliant shade tree. More and more, this tree is showing up in prairie garden centres. Despite the fact that it is normally hardy only to zone 4, the University of Minnesota and Jeffries Nurseries in Portage La Prairie, Manitoba, have been doing some excellent work with it.

This tree occasionally adapts to locations that are colder and drier than it usually likes, and new cultivars are

Northern pin oak.

being selected from the very north-ernmost limit of its range, which is right around the Manitoba–Minnesota border. 'Majestic Skies' is a new cultivar that reaches 18 metres in height and is officially hardy to zone 3. 'Shooting Star' is similar but grows only 12 metres and turns brick red in the fall. There is definitely potential here, and no one has really experimented with them in the chinook zone.

Quercus mongolica (Mongolian oak)

The Mongolian oak is a beautiful spe-cies native to Mongolia, northern China, Siberia, Korea, and Japan. It resembles the bur oak, but the leaves have a bit of a different shape, and it usually turns warm yellow in the fall. Although it is capable of reaching 30 metres, 10 to 15 metres is much more typical. It is slowly but surely beginning to work its way into the nursery trade, but I should warn you that deer are fond of it too.

Rhamnus cathartica (buckthorn)

I'm including this plant here not because I want you to grow it, but because I don't want you confusing it with my beloved *sea* buckthorn. They are quite differ-ent things and, despite their common names, are not even related. Buckthorn is a spiny shrub introduced from Europe with glossy green leaves, spiny branches, and clusters of dark purple-black berries on the female specimens. These berries are mildly poisonous, which prevents them from being eaten. It has become a significant weed in many parts of Manitoba, Saskatchewan, and Alberta, and if you find it growing somewhere, I suggest pulling it out.

Rhododendron spp. and *Azalea* spp.

Sometimes people move here from British Columbia and assume they can just plant rhododendrons. I have news for you; you *cannot*. There are a few hardy rhododendrons that have been introduced from the University of Helsinki in Finland. There are also some hardy varieties such as 'Nova Zembla,' 'PJM,' and 'Roseum 2.' The University of Minnesota introduced the 'Northern Lights' series of azaleas, which are easily the hardiest azaleas in the world. However, hardiness is not the be-all and end-all of how a plant performs. To grow these shrubs, you need a sheltered, sunny spot. Partial shade is okay. Garden centre staff are fond of recommending them for full shade, but say no to this.

You also need a consistently moist, well-drained, acidic soil. There are very few gardens on the prairies that can offer this, and it's a lot of work to try to modify the soil for them.

They often show up at garden centres in full bloom in May when we are des-perate for colour. Don't be fooled. You need very specific growing conditions for them, and there's a reason you don't see them in every neighbourhood.

> If you are after "quick and easy," the rhododendron is probably not the shrub for you.

Ribes spp. (currants and gooseberries)

This group includes many species and hybrids. While they have nowhere near the popularity they once held, the great irony of this is that today there are much better selections available than forty years ago, when every garden was expected to have one. People often ask what the difference is between a goose-berry and a currant. Currants usually lack spines, and they produce many flowers and berries in a single cluster. Gooseberries are generally very prickly and produce both their flowers and fruits singly.

Depending on the variety, they will grow from 30 centimetres to 1.3 metres tall and just as wide. If you are planning to grow these plants, I recommend planting at least two varieties so you will get better crops—and give them lots of space. Although they are extremely drought-resistant once established, both will be much better garden plants if they are given ample water, particularly when they are fruiting. A humusy, fertile soil is appreciated, but they are highly adaptable and will get on just fine in most garden situations. Although currants and gooseberries can live to be fifty years old or even older, by that time, they are well past their best. These plants generally perform well for about a decade; then it's time to replace them.

Currants A number of currants are grown primarily for their flowers, and a few, such as the alpine currant, are sometimes used for hedging. All will produce a fruit of some sort, but a distinction is generally made between "edible" and "ornamental" varieties. All insist on being grown in full sun; if they are in even a light shade, they often become magnets for powdery mildew. Currant worms (which can defoliate mature plants over night!) are also problematic.

Black currants are little known in North America but much loved in Europe. They produce deep purple or black-coloured berries, often large, with a distinct flavour all their own. They are sweetest after a light frost, and although they can be eaten raw, they are usually made into jams, jellies, and any number of baked goods.

Black currant wine (called cassis) is considered a delicacy and is very expensive. Black currants can be substituted in any recipe that calls for blueberries or blackberries.

'Black Willoughby' is a very old variety of currant that was once much planted on the prairies. It is disease-prone and suckers profusely but has attractive

Golden currant autumn colours.

gold flowers in the spring and loads of plump, juicy berries later in the year. It has largely been replaced by better behaved, more vigorous growers, such as the compact 'Ben Nevis.' 'Ben Sarek' and 'Boskoop Giant' are also excellent producers, with good resistance to disease.

Red currants have a more tart, saucier flavour than black currants but are used in much the same way. They make a good substitute for cranberries, and even if you don't eat them, red currants are stunning in the garden. The fruits are almost translucent and hang in dangling, showy clusters. They look like a string of rubies. The birds make short work of these, so if you are planning to eat them, buy some bird netting. 'Red Lake' is an old cultivar that is still available and reasonably good, but 'Cherry Red' is better if you can find it. 'Redstart' is perhaps the most productive and certainly the showiest in the garden, but its disease resistance is low.

White currants are of the same species but produce grey-white to off-yellow fruits that are almost flavourless. Most people find them unappetizing to look at. I know I certainly do—who wants to eat a berry the colour of pus?

Gooseberries While gooseberries have long since passed their heyday and picking the damn berries usually requires getting your hands very scratched, there are few things in this world like a gooseberry pie. Depending on the variety and the growing conditions, the fruit can be very tart or pleasantly sweet. The colour is also variable, and some gooseberries will remain some shade of green when ripe and others will become dull red to dark purple.

'Pixwell' is an American cultivar with green fruit that has been around for years. It produces few thorns. 'Hinnonmaeki Red' was developed in Finland (where gooseberries are much loved) and has wonderful, very sweet, dark red fruit in early July. The fall colour is orange, and it also makes an excellent barrier plant. 'Thoreson' is perhaps the most prolific and not particularly thorny. The fruit is also delicious. 'Invicta' is vigorous, productive, and disease-resistant, as well as producing considerably larger fruit than the others.

Josta berries The josta berry is sometimes offered in garden centres, and it is a hybrid between a black currant and a gooseberry. The plants are vigorous and highly productive, producing large, juicy black berries that are better for fresh eating than either of its parents. They are also excellent for jams and jellies. Although officially hardy to zone 3, josta berries have not done well in prairie trials, even in the most sheltered of locations.

Rosa spp. (roses)

You better believe that you need some roses in your garden! So revered are they that when you go into a garden centre, they are often given their own section instead of being placed along with shrubs where they belong. Here's what you need to know to grow roses—you need full sun, rich fertile soil, and ample water. The real problem is trying to sort out all the different *types* of roses.

The easiest thing to do is to buy roses in the 'Parkland' or the 'Explorer' series.

'Morden Centennial,' one of the best Parkland roses available.

These are Canadian roses bred to grow in the Canadian climate. All you have to do for pruning is remove any deadwood in the spring and that's it. No extra winter protection, no worries about disease, no fussing or babying or pampering. These roses are solid and dependable and available everywhere. They are inexpensive and come in a wide assortment of colours, and there are even some good climbing forms.

"Old garden roses," such as the spectacular and much-adored 'Hansa,' is a good choice, as are the roses from George Bugnet of Legal, Alberta, such as 'Therese Bugnet' and 'Marie Bugnet.'

There are some great species roses, such as *Rosa glauca* with dark foliage and brilliant, showy clusters of fruit that are decorative in the winter. Quite a number of miniature roses are hardy if given good snowcover.

The roses you want to avoid are hybrid tea roses, grandifloras, floribundas, and David Austin English roses. Actually, that's not true. A lot of these roses are absolutely gorgeous and showy. David Austin's roses are some of the most exquisitely perfumed plants you can buy.

However, they are lacking in hardiness and care-free attitudes. If you want to baby, pamper, cajole, coddle, fuss, and fawn over your roses, plant these. If you want something disease-resistant, hardy, gorgeous, fragrant, and low maintenance, plant 'Parkland' or 'Explorer' roses.

Salix spp. (willow)

Willows are mostly trees, though a good number of them grow as shrubs. They require cold winters and are unable to cope with life in the tropics. They adapt to a wide variety of soils, including heavy clay, but they are unable to deal with drought. They are known for their exceptional growth rates and amazing ability to clone themselves. Cuttings root rapidly, and many of them also produce suckers and thereby become dense thickets.

Willow leaves are generally long and narrowly oval. They are so distinctive that we use "willowy" to describe both the shape and leaves of other species. In addition to growing rapidly, willows produce very tough, pliable branches that tend to be slender and fine-textured. They are well known for their ability to bend rather than break, and they are difficult to kill—few trees are more tenacious than a willow.

Perhaps one of the lesser-known facts about willows is that their root system tends to be both large and wide spreading, so they may pose a threat to sidewalks and driveways. If you attempt to uproot a smallish willow, you may be shocked to discover that its roots are often thicker than the branches it supports.

Willows are nearly all deciduous, although there are a few semi-evergreen varieties. Most produce excellent fall colour, usually yellow, and in the summer months, the leaf colour can range from dark green to blue-green or even yellowish, depending on the species. A few variegated forms exist. The flowers are cherished and can be quite showy. The pendant catkins appear very early in the year on bare branches as the much-loved "pussy willows" and are one of the first signs of spring.

Willows are prone to pests, and a few of them are used as hosts by several kinds of butterfly. You may find that willows are affected by aphids, caterpillars, leafminers, and spider mites, as well as occasional fungus issues. They make up for this by being early to leaf out in spring and holding their leaves well into fall. Deer, moose, and rabbits are fond of eating them, and they may need protection, especially when young.

Willows provide a nutritious and welcome source of pollen for bees. Male and female flowers appear on separate plants. Although willows do not produce huge amounts of pollen, they appear at a time when there are no other flowers competing so bees flock to them.

They are also short-lived; most of the largest willows have a maximum life span of around sixty years, though they can occasionally live to be as old as a century. The following willows are a collection of my favourites, but this certainly isn't an exhaustive list. I think all gardens should try to include at least one willow, even if it's a little one.

Salix acutifolia (sharp-leaf willow)

From cold places in Europe and Asia, the sharp-leaf willow has long been grown on the prairies as a shelterbelt and a windbreak. It is a very fast-growing tree with reddish-coloured new growth, dark bark, and usually yellow fall colour. It has better drought-tolerance than most willows but would very much prefer to be grown in places where moisture conditions are good. It reaches a mature size of 5 to 7.5 metres and nearly as wide. 'Blue Streak' is a good cultivar that has pale blue colouring on the twigs of the new growth. This species hybridizes freely, and much of what is now being sold as sharp-leaf willow is actually of hybrid origin.

Salix alba (silver willow) Also called the white willow, a reference to the wood, this is a rather amazing species that has been much used in willow hybridizing programs. Found throughout cold parts of Europe, Asia, and high altitudes in north Africa, it is a rapid grower that can reach 30 metres, although 15 metres is more average. This is a dense, billowy tree with blue-grey or green-grey foliage that has a soft and silky texture. It is extremely beautiful and very hardy, but is not commonly grown as it does not fare well in chinook zones. It has been planted in many places across the prairies both for shade and as a shelterbelt, though it does require moisture.

There are several naturally occurring variations of this species, and they can

Silver willow.

be found in the nursery trade. *Salix alba* var. *sericea* is a Siberian selection that is a bit smaller and slower-growing than the species, as well as being more silvery. It also has better drought-tolerance than the species and is less prone to littering. *Salix alba* var. *vitellina* is often called the golden willow. It has brilliant, golden-yellow twigs that are at their most showy in late winter and early spring. It grows quickly into a large tree, usually about 15 to 18 metres tall at maturity and up to 12 to 15 metres wide. Fall colour of the leaves is also showy (bright yellow), and in moist places on the prairies, it has been used as a shelterbelt and for shade.

The 'Flame' willow is an absolutely fabulous hybrid of unknown parentage, but it is believed that *Salix alba* is likely one of the parents. It is a rapid-growing small tree that grows 4.5 to 6 metres tall, with dense, dark green, glossy foliage. It turns a brilliant yellow rather late in the fall. The great attraction of this willow is the winter interest; the newest twigs are a fiery orange-red. They are exceptionally vivid in the winter landscape and are much loved by florists and flower arrangers. As it is the new growth that is most brightly coloured, flame willow will perform best if it is regularly pruned and clipped. It does best in full sun with evenly moist soil. It makes a nice small tree for a smaller yard or somewhat confined space.

Salix babylonica (weeping willow) Sadly, this iconic tree just isn't prairie hardy—zone 5 is pretty much the limit of its cold tolerance. What can you do if you really want a weeping willow but you live in a cold climate? Well, there are two selections that are worth investigating. 'Prairie Cascade' is a hybrid introduction from the Morden Research Station in Manitoba. It grows about 9 metres tall and wide, has brilliant golden stems, and as it ages, it develops a graceful, semi-weeping habit. Trials with this variety across the prairies have been mixed. It will often grow well for anywhere from four to six years and then suddenly experience extremely significant dieback. It does recover rapidly, but this can be extremely annoying if it's already a decent-sized tree when this happens. 'Northern Fountains' is a distinctly weeping form that was selected from the golden willow, *S. alba* var. *vitellina*. It has the same brilliant yellow bark and is extremely showy. It grows 6 to 9 metres tall and wide, and although not widely grown, it is worth investigating. It is hardy to zone 3 and possibly colder.

Salix brachycarpa This tree is not often cultivated, but there is a charming variety of it you should know about. 'Blue Fox' is dense and compact, rarely exceeding 1 metre, and is much more blue-silver in colour than the species. It also has much reduced suckering tendencies and makes for a marvellous little hedge. Hardy to zone 1.

Pussy willow The term *pussy willow* is often applied to any native willow that happens to produce catkins in early spring, and there are many French hybrid willows, many with a weeping habit, that have been introduced into the nursery trade with this common name.

If you grew up on the prairie and went to cut willows in bloom in the spring, you were probably cutting *Salix discolor*. This species grows in moist places throughout North America, everywhere from ditches and marshes to swamps and parklands. It is highly adaptable and highly variable, as well as being able to freely hybridize with most willows that grow near it. It is also a remarkable colonizer. It can be a medium-sized shrub or even a small tree up to 6 metres high. The brilliant brown-red stems are colourful and showy in late winter and early spring, often visible from a great distance.

The bright green leaves have paler undersides and usually turn bright yellow in the fall. The pearly grey catkins that appear on male plants in early spring are prized as much for their beauty as they are for their early appearance. In most places, this provides the first pollen source of the year for honeybees. Pussy willows are sometimes grown in gardens, but their suckering and demand for even moisture tends to put off most gardeners.

Salix exigua (coyote willow) This shrub is found throughout western North America and is particularly common in the waterways, creeks, streams, and river systems of Alberta. This is an extremely rapid grower that grows 1.8 to 2.7 metres tall and just as wide, with very long, fine slender leaves that are soft grey-green in colour. It favours cool night temperatures and warm days and turns a very bright, light yellow colour in the fall. It colonizes freely and is occasionally found in the nursery trade. Branches stuck in the ground root very rapidly. Coyote willow has been planted to control soil erosion and also makes an excellent substitute for bamboo. Use the suckering to your advantage, allowing it to form dense and beautiful thickets like it does in the wild.

Salix integra (Japanese willow) The Japanese willow is native to both Japan and Korea. It is a small, shrubby species growing around 1.5 metres tall and just as wide. It sometimes develops a semi-weeping habit with age. Although not particularly impressive in and of itself, there are two cultivars of it that have been heavily pushed in the nursery trade and can often be found at prairie garden centres.

'Hakura Nishiki' is a reasonably fast-growing little shrub reaching about 1 metre high, with intensely white variegated foliage that is most prominent on the new growth. Splashes of pink and coral appear in cool weather, particularly at the tips. It is often sold as a top grafted specimen or as a topiary. 'Flamingo' is very similar but even less hardy, though the pink colouring is much more prominent. Both of these willows will do best in partial shade, and hot, drying winds tend to leave them looking burnt and slightly scorched. They want ample humidity and moisture and do not recover well from abuse. Although officially hardy to only zone 4, they have done well in several prairie gardens with adequate mulch and winter protection. In any case, they recover quickly and grow fast even if winter does cut them back a bit.

Salix pentandra (laurel leaf willow)

Perhaps the most widely planted willow on the prairies is the laurel leaf willow. It is a rapid-growing species magnificent as a shade or shelterbelt tree. Native to cold parts of Europe and Asia, it has naturalized in North America. It reaches anywhere from 6 to 18 metres in height and just as wide, with deeply furrowed grey-brown bark and yellow-green twigs and branches. The long, lustrous leaves are a deep green that usually turn bright yellow in the fall.

Laurel leaf willows are exceptionally hardy, but they also drink exceptional amounts of water and are prone to dropping significant quantities of twigs and branches, particularly after a wind storm. If you plant one, expect to be raking a lot. It is also difficult to garden under or near a laurel leaf willow, as they will suck every last drop of moisture out of the soil. That said, they are an outstanding tree in the right place. They are not prone to suckering unless the roots are disturbed, so be careful about rototilling or digging near them.

Salix purpurea (arctic willow)

The arctic willow has something of a misleading name, being that it is actually native to cold places in Europe, north Africa, and Asia, right up into the Arctic Circle. It is a beautiful but rarely cultivated willow that grows up to 3.5 metres tall with blue-green leaves that turn a bright butter yellow in the fall. The twigs of the new growth are distinctly purplish, eventually aging to grey.

The variety 'Gracillis,' also called 'Nana,' is very common in the nursery trade and is a true dwarf. Accordingly, it is sold as dwarf arctic willow. I love this shrub! It normally grows about 1 metre tall and just as wide, but occasionally it can be nearly double that. It is much more fine-textured than the species and makes a marvellous little hedge or specimen shrub. As the best purple colour is on the newest twigs, it should be sheared or pruned regularly to encourage this. Given moisture and a sunny spot, dwarf arctic willow is extremely low maintenance and very beautiful. Every garden should make room for one of these.

Salix salicola (felt-leaf willow)

The felt-leaf willow is native to cold regions in the Arctic Circle. It has immense grey catkins and dull, grey-green foliage. It grows fast and eventually reaches a height of about 4.5 metres. It likely would have never gotten any recognition in the nursery trade but for a selection of it that was discovered in Athabasca Sand Dunes Provincial Park in northern Saskatchewan. It was named 'Polar Bear,' and while widely available, it is not planted much. It grows about 3 metres tall and twice as wide, with intense white-grey or silver foliage and huge catkins in the spring. It is an outstanding garden shrub, and though it prefers moisture, it is highly adaptable under garden settings. Older stems and branches sometimes die out for no obvious reason, but they are quickly replaced.

Sambucus spp. (elder)

Elders are not to be confused with alders, which are an entirely different group of shrubs. There are many species, but the most reliable one is probably the red-berried elder, *Sambucus racemosa*. Native to Europe, red-berried elders are occasionally found growing wild across the plains, as birds have spread the seeds in their droppings. There are more than twenty known species of elderberry, and while the blue and the black elders are well known for the medicinal properties of their fruit, they are not generally considered prairie-hardy. The red-berried elder, however, does just fine here and is quite tolerant of shade. When we see this shrub, it is usually one of the golden forms such as 'Goldenlocks' or 'Sutherland.' These are both fine shrubs, but just the standard, ordinary species form is not without its place.

To begin with, these large shrubs grow to their mature height of 2.5 to 3.5 metres quickly. They can easily reach full size within three to four years. They will grow in almost any soil, in sun or shade, and are extremely drought-resistant once established. The fruits of red elder are quite decorative and loved by birds but are mildly toxic to humans, causing nausea and stomach distress. The creamy white flowers in spring are also appealing, though they are not flashy. If there are any drawbacks to these plants, it is that they are not long-lived, lasting about ten years maximum, and that the weak, pithy branches can easily be broken during a storm. They are otherwise extremely versatile good choices for a prairie garden.

You will also find that two purple-leaf forms from a different species are increasingly available from garden centres. One is called 'Black Lace' and the other is called 'Black Beauty.' They have intensely smoky-purple foliage and pink flowers. They grow fast, and if you lived in Tofino, they would grow about 4 metres. Here, they suffer significant dieback, and I would not recommend them for an open, exposed area. Given shelter and good snowcover, they can be treated like perennials and will perform quite reliably. They will grow 1 to 2 metres in a season, which is more than adequate for most people, but don't expect them to flower.

Shepherdia spp. (buffaloberry)

Closely related to sea buckthorn, the buffaloberries are among the showiest fruiting shrubs native to the prairies.

Shepherdia argentea (silver buffaloberry)
The silver buffaloberry is well adapted to areas with dry, poor soil and produces attractive, silvery foliage and inconspicuous tiny flowers. These flowers give way to brilliant scarlet berries (though occasionally they are yellow) that are high in vitamin C and excellent for jams, jellies, and syrups. The berries are difficult to pick due to the extremely sharp and plentiful spines, but they are also very decorative. First Nations peoples used them to flavour buffalo meat; hence, the name. They can be used as a substitute in any recipe that calls for cranberries.

Buffaloberries are lovely, high in vitamin C, and good eating.

Like its relatives, buffaloberry is a good colonizer and one that requires ample room. They are untroubled by pests or disease, establish quickly, and are extremely drought-resistant. Anyone looking to discourage intruders need not look much further than this spiny shrub.

Shepherdia canadensis (Canada buffaloberrry, russet buffaloberry)
The Canada buffaloberry, also called russet buffaloberry, is much lower-growing, with dark green leaves with brownish undersides. Female plants produce stunning red berries that are loved by birds but can make humans mildly sick. It's not found in gardens very often, but it doesn't colonize the way its larger relative does and it stays quite a bit lower, usually growing around 1 metre tall and wide. Although rarely planted, it can grow in the hottest, driest sites with very poor soil and has no pest or disease issues. It's completely bulletproof, and it's very attractive.

False spirea.

Mountain-ash leaves are pinnate, meaning they have veins almost like a fern does.

Sorbaria spp. (False spirea, ash-leaf spirea)

This is a winner! Usually growing about 1.5 metres tall, it has white flowers loved by bees and handsome, lacy foliage that resembles mountain ash. It usually turns yellow in the fall, and it is early to leaf out in spring. An excellent colonizer for troublesome spots.

Sorbus spp. (Mountain ash)

Mountain ash should not be confused with the true species of ash (*Fraxinus* spp.), as they are not related. There are more than one hundred species of mountain ash and as many as fifty subspecies. There are also naturally occurring hybrids: some of which are fertile; some of which are not. The great diversity found here comes as a surprise to many people, and many prairie gardeners simply assume that all mountain ash are hardy. This is not so. A great many of them come from southeast China, coastal Japan, and lower elevations in the Himalayas, so many of them are only hardy to zones 4 or 5.

All the mountain ash have pinnate foliage, and while most of them are trees, a few of them are shrubby. All produce clusters of white or ivory-coloured flowers in the spring, and they are quite showy, although not long-lasting. This is actually a good thing, as many people find the fragrance of mountain ash to be somewhat unpleasant. They are cherished by gardeners all over the world for their beautiful smooth bark, gorgeous clusters of fruit, outstanding fall colour,

and ability to attract great numbers of birds and wildlife. They are also highly adaptable and easy to grow. Mountain-ash timber is occasionally used, but it is not particularly strong or desirable.

These trees are considered moderate to slow-growing, and they are not long-lived. The average life span of a mountain ash is about fifty years, and although they can live to be as old as seventy-five or eighty, this is unusual. As their name would imply, they are frequently found on slopes, cliffs, and ledges at moderate to high elevations, and as such, they are resentful of very high temperatures.

Remarkably, they are extremely tolerant of pollution. A moist, fertile soil with good drainage suits them best, but they are very drought-resistant once they are established. Although pests are uncommon (with pear slugs being an exception), there are a number of diseases and environmental issues that can affect the health of mountain ash. They can be highly prone to sunscald and frost cracking, particularly when they are young. In their native habitat,

SHOPPING WITH LYNDON

they are frequently understory trees, and there is almost always a buffer of shrubs and smaller trees growing around them, protecting them from this problem.

Chlorosis can be an issue, particularly on elderly trees growing in heavy clay soil. A number of cankers can infect mountain ash, and they can also be killed by fire blight. Although by nature they are shapely trees, mountain ash does not mind being pruned lightly as long as it is done when they are dormant.

Very tolerant of partial shade, mountain ash will grow fastest and be most happy in full sun, but as I said, they are adaptable. Mountain ash likes well-aerated soil, cannot tolerate standing in water, and will suffer if grown in extremely windy or dry sites.

Sorbus americana (**American mountain ash**) Perhaps the most widely grown species of mountain ash is the American mountain ash. It comes from the eastern half of North America and grows about 6 to 9 metres tall. It is multi-trunked as often as it is single-trunked and produces bright green leaves with grey-green undersides. The fruit is brilliant red, and autumn colour is usually golden through yellow through orange. The dark, reddish-brown bark is quite lovely in winter, as are the black buds. Several cultivars have been developed, perhaps the most noteworthy of which is 'Red Cascade.' This is a very compact form, reaching about 7.5 metres and producing exceptionally large clusters of brilliant red berries.

Sorbus aucuparia (**European mountain ash**) The European mountain ash is also widely grown, and there are many cultivars. In the wild, it ranges across northern Europe, throughout the British Isles, and west all the way through Russia, Siberia, and northern China. It was sacred to the ancient Celts, and they called it rowan, a name that remains to this day. The word *rowan* comes from the word *rune*, meaning "sacred" or "having magical significance." It was widely regarded as being powerfully repellant of evil, and this tradition carried on well

after Great Britain was settled. It was much planted in churchyards, cemeteries, and other important places to repel witches, ghosts, and the occult.

Reaching 6 to 12 metres, the European mountain ash is a fine specimen or shade tree. The fall colour ranges from orange through red or even purple and, like its American relative, can either be single- or multi-trunked. 'Cardinal Royal' is a very upright, vigorous form with unusual scarlet-orange berries that are quite large.

There are several interesting varieties available. *Fastigiata* is the columnar variety of mountain ash, growing about 6 metres and just under 2 metres wide. It is quite slow-growing but beautiful. It makes an excellent and unusual substitute for the ubiquitous Swedish aspen. *Pendula* is also slow-growing; this is an unusual weeping form that some people find grotesque. *Variegata* has softly golden variegated foliage, but it is not very vigorous (or hardy), and *xanthocarpa* has strange, yellow fruit.

'Blackhawk' is an excellent, highly recommended form that is narrow and upright when young, becoming somewhat broadly pyramid-shaped with age. It is a very vigorous grower that fruits well even from a young age, growing about 9 metres tall. Both the orangey-red fall colour and fruit displays are outstanding.

Sorbus aucuparia var. *rossica* (**Russian mountain ash**) The Russian mountain ash is more slow-growing and more upright than the species, and the fruit clusters are also larger. As anyone who has cultivated these trees will know, the birds distribute the seeds in their droppings and they germinate easily. A few even consider this a "weed tree."

This species has widely naturalized across North America and can be found growing in nearly every province and territory. Contrary to popular belief, mountain ash fruit is not poisonous. Although extremely bitter and unpleasant to humans, the fruit are high in vitamin C and quite nutritious. After they have been sweetened by several frosts, some people will make mountain ash jelly. The Finns have long used mountain ash fruit in their winemaking, both for enriching other flavours and for making the brew especially intoxicating.

Sorbus decora (showy mountain ash) Long considered the most desirable and hardiest species, the showy mountain ash is well deserving of all the accolades it receives. Ranging from Greenland and Iceland into much of the northeastern corner of North America, including southeastern Manitoba, this species is rather slow-growing but worth waiting for. Reaching as tall as 9 metres in height under cultivation, it is often much smaller and shrubbier in the wild. It produces huge clusters of stunning red or orange fruits and has perhaps the longest-lasting and most incredible display of autumn colour of any species. Depending on weather, the colour can range from red to gold to orange or anything in between, often with strong shadings of purple. It is absolutely magnificent and hardy to zone 1.

Showy mountain ash.

Sorbus x thuringiaca (oak leaf mountain ash) As mountain ash will often hybridize in the wild, there are a few hybrids in cultivation that also should be examined. The oak leaf mountain ash is a cross between *S. aucuparia* and the much less hardy *S. aria*. It is fairly slow-growing but eventually reaches 9 to 12 metres in height. The leaves are strangely oak-like and highly attractive. Fall colour is usually orange or yellow. Small red fruits are attractive but not produced as profusely as other mountain ash.

Sorbus scopulina (western mountain ash) The western mountain ash is native from British Columbia east through Saskatchewan and north though the Yukon and Northwest Territories. It is a major food source for birds and is known to hybridize with the American mountain ash. Usually multi-trunked and reaching 3.5 to 6 metres tall, this species is occasionally cultivated. It likes significantly more moisture than most of its relatives and can even handle soils that are too wet and heavy for other mountain ash. It also has a preference for higher elevations. The fruits are large, bright red or orange and produced in great abundance.

Sorbus reducta (shrubby mountain ash) The shrubby mountain ash is seldom found in cultivation but perfectly hardy. This little charmer only grows about 1 metre tall and suckers extensively to form colonies, making it unsuitable for a confined space, but this takes time. The flowers give way to red or pinkish fruits. Autumn colour ranges from red through yellow. It is native to western China, Tibet, and Nepal.

Sorbus sitchensis (sitka mountain ash) One of the other shrubby species (albeit a large shrub) is the sitka mountain ash, which grows about 4 metres tall. Fruit ranges from red through almost purplish, and it is native to British Columbia, the Yukon, and western Alberta. It is reasonably common in Kananaskis and both Banff and Waterton Lakes National Parks.

Spirea spp.

Spireas are in the rose family, and like the potentilla they have become so overused as to be shunned by many gardeners. This is unfortunate, because many spireas are very pretty. They tend to be low, fine-textured shrubs, and their flowers attract bees and butterflies. The Japanese spireas bloom all summer, and many of them have spectacular foliage. They want full sun and good drainage, and they are drought-resistant once established. They are also fast-growing and pest- and disease-free. Japanese spireas include the popular 'Gold Flame,' with its gold foliage including red new growth and pink flowers; 'Gold Mound,' which is compact with golden foliage; 'Magic Carpet,' much like 'Gold Flame' but more intensely coloured and wider than tall; and 'Little Princess,' which forms a perfect dome covered in lavender flowers all summer.

Spireas make excellent little hedges and are perfect housewarming gifts,

Spirea bumalda.

especially for new gardeners. The bridal wreath spireas flower in early summer and include many cultivars, such as 'Renaissance,' 'Swan Lake,' and the three-lobed spirea. They have gorgeous, arching branches that give them a fountain-like shape and produce a fantastic show of white blooms. Many of them also have excellent golden fall colour. Spireas are well worth cultivating, lending themselves well to low-maintenance, bee-friendly gardens.

Symphoricarpos spp. (snowberry)

Snowberries are a good example of berry-producing shrubs that can be worth growing, but you do *not* want to be eating the berries as they are both unpleasant and poisonous. Closely related to honeysuckles and weigela, there are seventeen species of snowberry and all but one of them is native to North America. The plain green leaves are not especially interesting, and the tiny pink flowers are neither showy nor particularly noteworthy, but the flowers give way to fruits of varying size that are often white and will stick out of the snow all winter; hence the name snowberry.

Symphoricarpos occidentalis (western snowberry) This shrub is native to much of North America in a variety of habitats and spreads aggressively by means of underground runners. It is not

especially showy but is valuable because it will grow in places where no other shrub will. Sun, shade, moist, dry, rich, or poor soil do not make any difference to it. The greenish berries age to a dull white.

Symphoricarpos albus (white snowberry) White snowberry is similar to the western snowberry but a bit less aggressive and generally grows a little taller, usually around 1.3 metres. It has wiry stems of white berries that can be interesting in the wintertime if they are planted in a prominent spot.

Symphoricarpos orbiculatus (coralberry) The coralberry is native to the eastern USA and Mexico. It can grow up to 2 metres tall and produces dark green leaves with reddish tints in the fall and hard white berries that age to a deep red.

Although widely regarded as being hardy to zone 3 and adaptable to many different growing conditions, the coralberry has not fared well in trials on the prairies. Though it tends to survive, it also suffers serious tip kill and dieback here. 'Amethyst' is a new cultivar with vivid, fuchsia-pink berries instead of red. It is a vigorous grower but has not yet been widely tested and is much less shade-tolerant than the species.

Much loved in Holland and Germany, snowberries are entering what could be considered their golden age, with plant breeders looking at them with interest.

The Dutch in particular have been doing a lot of work hybridizing these shrubs, and I expect many new hybrids to be hitting the market in the next few years. Unfortunately, many of the hybrids that *have* been hitting the market are only hardy to about zone 4. 'Snow Flurry' produces very pure white berries, quite large, and in great profusion. It is more or less useless in a prairie garden, as is the gorgeous 'Marleen' (with deep lavender-plum coloured berries instead of the usual white.) A variegated snowberry has also been introduced, and it has failed miserably in all its prairie trials.

Syringa spp. (lilac)

Lilacs have been grown on the prairies since the 1920s and with good reason! They are extremely hardy, beautiful, and low maintenance. Lilacs are also highly variable, ranging from 1 metre dwarfs to small trees, such as the Japanese tree lilac. The flowers are fragrant and loved by butterflies, as well as being fabulous for cutting. There is also a wide range of colours to choose from: white, purple, pink, violet, soft yellow, burgundy, mauve, to even a few bicolours. Lilacs are long-lived and showy. They will do best in full sun with good drainage and should be planted where the fragrance will be most enjoyed. The French lilacs and the Preston lilacs are perhaps the best suited for the average

prairie garden, but you would be hard-pressed to find a lilac that isn't reliable and lovely.

Lilacs will last for generations. They are drought-tolerant once established and capable of withstanding extreme cold, wind, and generally adverse growing conditions. Be sure to grow them in full sun if you want them to flower well, and lilacs that are fertilized and pampered a little bit will appreciate it.

We all know and value lilacs for their intense, powerful fragrance. The old-fashioned French lilacs have the strongest scent, but some of the Preston lilacs are also noteworthy. French lilacs have smooth, almost heart-shaped leaves and a tendency to sucker. They also have larger flower clusters than the Preston lilacs. 'President Grevy' (blue-purple), 'Madame Lemoine' (white), and 'Congo' (dark purple) are all outstanding lilacs for scent. 'Sensation' is a glorious purple-white bicolour that is also strongly scented, and 'Beauty of Moscow' has double, light pink blooms with a strong scent.

If you are seeking a Preston lilac, which I recommend because they are beautiful and non-suckering, I really like 'Miss Kim.' This is a semi-dwarf lilac that only grows 1.2 metres by 1.2 metres, and produces bright pink, strongly scented blooms in great profusion even from a

French lilac.

very young age. It is also one of the few lilacs to develop fall colour and usually turns an intense plum-purple in the fall.

Lilacs are a fantastic nectar source and will draw bees, butterflies, hummingbirds, and sphinx moths.

Thuja spp. (cedar)

I've already talked about cedars being either sensational or disastrous in the chinook zone, but if you want to grow them, don't buy them from a big-box store. Buy them from a garden centre and find out where they were grown, as that will tell you a lot about their hardiness. 'Brandon,' 'Emerald Green,' 'Skybound,' 'Techny,' and 'Wareana' are good choices. The globe-shaped 'Little Giant' usually does poorly in the chinook zone, though it succeeds easily in other parts of the prairies. Grow them in rich, moist soil as sheltered from the wind as much as possible and make sure you water them in well before freeze-up. Also keep in mind that you can do

everything right and that cedar might live for twenty years or more … and then an especially bad chinook might come along and kill it. It happens.

A hardy cedar is lovely, especially in the winter when greenery is uncommon.

Tsuga spp. (hemlock)

Oh my goodness, no. You just move straight to Port Moody if you want hemlocks.

Ulmus spp. (elm)

Earlier I talked about dutch elm disease (DED) and how remarkable it is that Saskatchewan and Alberta were largely able to defend these trees from certain death.

***Ulmus americana* (American elm)** The American elm is the largest species of elm native to North America, with a mature height of 25 to 30 metres. It has beautiful soft yellow to golden fall colour and a magnificent spreading shape. It is native to southeastern Saskatchewan all the way to the East Coast and south nearly to Georgia and Florida. It has been extensively planted in parks, along boulevards, and on farms and acreages. It is also the species that has been most devastated by DED. American elms have large, shallow root systems, and although they do best in moist, fertile soil, they are also exceptionally drought-tolerant.

In addition to DED, they are prone to a number of bacterial infections, aphids,

and cankerworms. High winds and storms can cause breakage due to the great weight of the branches, and fallen elms can cause immense damage. A few cultivars have been developed, but it is largely just the species that is grown.

Maturing at 12 metres, 'Brandon' is a somewhat more compact selection that came from Manitoba many years ago. 'Valley Forge' was released in 1995 and has excellent resistance to DED. It is important to remember that there are no kinds of American elm that are immune to DED, but several are much less likely to be infected by it. 'Lewis & Clark' was released by the University of North Dakota in 2004. It was selected from the only elm left standing after a severe outbreak of the disease more than fifty years ago. 'St. Croix' was selected by the University of Minnesota after the same outbreak. This elm was found in the Minneapolis neighbourhood of St. Croix. Nearly every elm in the city was

Though we may take them for granted, elm-lined boulevards no longer exist in most places anymore.

dead but for this one century-old specimen in this elderly area of town. It was subsequently named and introduced and has done very well in trials across the continent.

Assuming that they are not taken down by disease, American elm trees are exceptionally long-lived. Their life span is about two hundred to two hundred and fifty years, but under ideal growing conditions, they are known to live even longer. Prior to DED, elms that were three hundred or four hundred years old were not that uncommon.

Ulmus davidiana var. *japonica* (Japanese elm)

The Japanese elm has been widely tested and evaluated as a possible replacement for the American elm, despite the fact that it is not as large or as vigorous. It reaches about 9 to 12 metres, and although officially hardy to zone 3, it tends to suffer a fair bit of dieback in very cold regions. 'Discovery' is a selection of it introduced from the Morden Research Station, with attractive yellow fall colour and virtually no seeds. It definitely has potential.

Ulmus pumila (Manchurian elm)

As soon as I mention the Manchurian elm, I can actually sense gardeners across the prairies bristling. Native to Russia, Siberia, northern China, Mongolia, and Korea, this tree reaches 6 to 9 metres but tends to be shrubby and low when growing conditions are harsh. It occasionally turns soft yellow in the fall, and was extensively planted across the prairies in the 1920s and 1930s in shelterbelts, hedges, windbreaks, and even cities.

It is largely resistant to DED but unfortunately is a much poorer tree than *U. americana*. It is prone to breakage and storm damage, and produces copious amounts of seeds, all of which germinate. It is a dreadful and persistent weed. Having said that, it is much faster-growing than many species of elm and has been used extensively in the development of new and disease-resistant cultivars.

Viburnum spp.

The plants in this genus are commonly called cranberries, but they should not be confused with the cranberry of commerce (*Oxycoccus* spp.), even though their fruits can be used in much the same way. These plants range from small to very large shrubs, all of which want a sunny spot and moist, well-drained soil. Aphids are the only real issue, especially on young plants. Although they will tolerate partial shade, they will be much nicer in a sunny spot.

Viburnum lantana (wayfaring tree)

The wayfaring tree is a large shrub that is vastly underused on the prairies. It never fails to amaze me how few people actually *know* about wayfaring trees, and how fewer still plant them. Hailing from northern Europe and northwest Asia, wayfaring trees are well suited to our growing conditions. They are exceptionally hardy, not troubled by pests or disease, and give much while asking little.

Like nearly all species of *Viburnum*, a rich and moist soil is essential. Once established, wayfaring trees are capable of surviving considerable drought, but this is by no means ideal for them and they should be watered regularly if you want them to look nice. They are also exceptionally tolerant of alkaline soils and can even do well in fairly heavy clay.

Very dense and beautiful, wayfaring trees can reach anywhere from 3 to 4.5 metres high and 4 to 6 metres wide, and they will fill in a large space quite nicely, though admittedly are not fast-growing. The handsome leaves are velvety upon emerging and become smoother and darker green as they age. The white flower clusters are profuse and showy. They are also longer-lasting than many other species. The clusters of fruit start out orangey red and slowly age to blue-black. They are edible and very attractive-looking. If all this weren't enough, did I mention the very nice fall colour? Long-lasting and pretty, the leaves become a dark purplish-red late in the season.

If you don't have a lot of space, the cultivar 'Mohican' (introduced in 1956) makes a good addition to most yards. It is far more compact (2 to 3 metres tall and wide) and somewhat faster-growing than the species. 'Variegata' has intense creamy-splashed foliage and is also available, but personally I don't find it very attractive. If you want something beautiful, hardy, and endlessly delightful, you really do need a wayfaring tree.

Viburnum lentago (nannyberry) The nannyberry is such a lovely small tree or large shrub that I wonder why it is so rarely seen. I suspect we would grow nannyberry in greater quantities here if it were more drought-tolerant. The leaves also droop slightly, and some people dislike how this looks. Either way, I think the nannyberry should be accorded a certain level of respect, as it is beautiful, hardy, and surprisingly uncommon.

A native of damp, cool soils on the edges of woodlands, nannyberry can be found growing wild throughout the eastern half of our continent. Mature height is usually around 4.5 to 5.5 metres, but heights of 9 metres are not unheard of. It produces lush, oval green leaves that have a certain shine to them and are quite beautiful. Creamy-coloured, fragrant flowers in spring are also very attractive. This is one of the best things you can plant to attract birds. They will positively flock to your place to eat the blue-black fruits. Some people put netting on them to keep the birds away since nannyberries also make excellent jams and jellies. The flavour is similar to that of raisins. They are high in vitamin C and very nutritious.

The main reason to grow nannyberry is the fall colour. Usually the first shrub to change colour in the fall, the display is long-lasting, and though not the same every year, it is always beautiful. A deep plum purple is the most common fall colouration, but it can vary from red through purple, often with hints of pink as well. The berries themselves go through a stupendous colour change—starting out greenish and becoming yellowish, then pink, then red, then purplish black.

Not prone to pest or disease problems, there is only one real restriction with growing nannyberry—it can't tolerate dry soil. Give it a rich, humusy soil with good moisture retention, but good drainage is also critical. Nannyberries will survive in much poorer soil but will hardly flourish. A rich diet is essential to help them meet their full potential. It's also important not to disturb the root

Nannyberry.

system once they are established—this can cause suckering, which creates problems. Once you've seen one in full fall regalia, you'll definitely want one.

Viburnum opulus (European cranberry) The European cranberry is a hardy, well-known species found throughout northern Europe and parts of Asia. It is the parent of many hybrids but also very similar to the North American *Viburnum trilobum*. A vigorous and fast-growing species, it can reach as tall as 4.5 metres and produces light, thin branches with smooth greyish bark. The large leaves are handsome and darker above than below, with lacy clusters of pretty white blooms that become bright scarlet fruits. Full sun or partial shade suits it fine provided that it has ample moisture and highly fertile soil. This species is completely intolerant of dry soil and will promptly die if planted in a windy, exposed site with inadequate water.

It is also exceptionally prone to damage from aphids. For whatever reason, certain strains of aphids are attracted to these plants and tend to feed at the tips and the undersides of the leaves. The plant reacts to this by producing extremely distorted, twisted leaves that make the plant look disfigured or like it has been sprayed with herbicide. This, in fact, makes the shrub so ugly that it induces vomiting. So likely is this to occur that I don't even bother planting them anymore. One should be aware of this potential problem before purchasing!

Several cultivars, hybrids, and selections from this species have been introduced. Some of them are very much worth trying, but others not as much. A golden-leafed cultivar called 'Aureum' has been developed, and it does best with at least partial shade as it tends to scorch in full sun. There is also the dwarf form of European cranberry, *V. opulus* 'Nanum,' which originated in France in 1841. Commonly available in nurseries and garden centres, this form almost never flowers and even more rarely produces fruits. It is a slow-growing, extremely compact shrub growing about 0.75 metre tall and 1 metre wide. It makes a dense green globe of maple-like foliage that occasionally becomes bronze or reddish in the fall. It makes an excellent hedge.

By far the most popular variation of this plant is the snowball bush, *V. opulus* 'Roseum,' also listed as 'Sterile.' Believed to have originated in Europe in the sixteenth century, this cultivar is indeed sterile. No fruit is produced, but the flowers are perfectly round, snow white, ball-shaped clusters. A snowball bush in full bloom is breathtakingly beautiful! It makes an excellent companion for lilacs, as their bloom times overlap and they do well in similar conditions.

Although some years the snowball bushes do have dieback on the prairies, they are mostly hardy and do well in most locations. Some shade from the hot afternoon sun seems beneficial, and they dislike a windy site but seem to be fairly adaptable. They make long-lasting cut flowers and some years develop orangey-red or gold fall colour. They are worth planting at least once in your horticultural journey.

Viburnum trilobum (American highbush cranberry) Previously known as *V. americanum*, this is one of the best known in the genus and is widely cultivated. There are several good reasons to add this to your list of "coveted shrubs." This is a dense, bushy shrub reaching up to 3 metres tall and usually slightly wider. The broad, handsome leaves are three-lobed and usually some terrific shade of orangey red or scarlet in the fall. It grows reasonably fast, does well in sun or shade, and adds considerable interest to the yard. The lacy, showy white circles of bloom that appear in the spring are wonderful in themselves, and they become a large crop of somewhat sour scarlet berries that make fabulous jams and jellies. The fruit is retained into winter if unpicked, and the greyish bark is not unattractive. Fabulous for attracting birds, if you can give highbush cranberry a prominent site in rich, damp soil, it is well worth your time to do so!

A great number of cultivars have been introduced, and nearly all of them are worth growing. 'Alfredo' is said to be an improved form, but I cannot tell a difference between it and the species. 'Bailey's Compact' is justifiably popular. It grows just over 2 metres tall and slightly wider and consistently produces dark red fall colour. It is an excellent bloomer and produces large crops of fruit. 'Wentworth' is another vigorous and hardy strain that is worth growing for the same reasons.

If you're looking for something different in a cranberry, two cultivars are also worth seeking out. 'Garry's Pink' is like the species in every way, but instead of the normal white flowers, the blooms on this one are a pastel pink instead. 'Xanthocarpum' is a cultivar of viburnum that produces deep golden yellow instead of red fruit. It makes especially interesting-looking jelly. Grown together with the red-fruited form, they are very striking in the winter landscape.

Highbush cranberry is less common than it once was, likely due to problems with aphids, but healthy plants in good soil are prone to infection than those under unsuitable growing conditions. Aphids aside, these plants should still be considered for a spot in your yard.

Weigela spp. (weigela)

Closely related to honeysuckles, weigelas are beautiful flowering shrubs from cold parts of Asia. They want fertile, moist soil with good drainage, and they dislike windy locations. Their main flush of bloom is early summer, though they may flower off and on throughout the summer. They are much loved by hummingbirds. Although there are a few dozen cultivars available, not all of them are hardy.

Weigela blooms may be red, white, or pink in colour and are very showy. One excellent and hardy cultivar is called 'Centennial.' Developed in Manitoba, this is easily the hardiest of all the weigelas and will reach 1.5 to 2 metres in height, flowering right to the tips. The flowers are bright pink and highly attractive. In addition to hummingbirds, they will also attract bees, and they flower over a long period. 'Centennial' does tend to get quite woody and twiggy with age and will therefore benefit from a hard pruning every few years. 'Minuet' and 'Rumba' also do well here.

Do *not* be sucked in by any of the variegated weigelas. Though pretty, they are not going to do a whole lot for you here. This is equally true of the purple-leaf cultivars such as 'Wine and Roses,'

which garden centres bring in full-sized and in full bloom. It's hard to resist, and I understand that, and maybe you'd like to try them just once. That's fine. If you treat them like tea roses and mulch them really well, sometimes they survive. 'Red Prince' is an especially dazzling form that I have bought more than once—and regretted more than once. Feel free to experiment, but if you want one that survives, you want 'Centennial.'

Weigela is another lovely flowering shrub. You should plant one.

Acknowledgements

I have many people I need to thank! I have, in many ways, lived an extremely charmed life. I am grateful for all the friends and lovely people who have invited me into their homes, hearts, and gardens. I am humbled by the love that surrounds me, and I am overwhelmed by all the ways that people have gone out of their way to make me feel loved, welcome, and like I belong. For a prairie boy who spent most of his life feeling like he did not belong anywhere, I am enormously appreciative of the people who went to great lengths to disabuse me of this notion.

I need to thank my publisher and my editors, of course, because this would not have been possible without you believing in me. Thanks to Vanessa, who did her best work by pushing me to write *my* best work. If this book is even remotely readable, it is because Vanessa took what I had written and found a way to polish my words and make them glow. THANK YOU!

This book was written in Calgary, Canmore, Lethbridge, Vancouver, Nanaimo, and Tofino. Deep gratitude and big love to Angela Dillon, Brandon Makhan, Diana Zoe Coop, Jordan Bowie, Jay Weiler, and Paula Duncan for opening their doors to provide me with quiet places to write, sunshine and laughter, and a safe place to sleep.

I have to thank my mom, Val Penner, for loving me so fiercely and always encouraging me to chase my dreams. Thank you for being proud of me, praying for my safety, and teaching me to believe in myself. Thank you to Grandma and Grandpa Wiebe, who have put up with my bad attitude and frustration over the years, fed me and given me money, hugged me and blessed me, and saved me in every way that a person can be saved. Mom and Grandma, you are the reason I am a gardener. You read to me when I was little and taught me to love the garden and the earth. This book could not have happened without the two of you. To my sisters, Jamey and Kim, who both surprised me by reaching out to me this year and who carried me in ways I am sure they are not even aware of.

Beth Towe of Waterton Lakes National Park, you are an inspiration and a true friend. Thank you for all you have done for me and all you have done for the wildest and most beautiful place in Canada. Moira Watson, you were the first person I told about this book. Thank you for being so ridiculously excited for me. Kristin Smysniuk, thank you for sticking around. We've been together a long time. You and me and the Dixie Chicks will always be a winning combination!

Thank you, Rebecca Baron, for making Boychuk Greenhouses so much fun and for your friendship and endless devotion to Michael Bublé! Colin and Diane Atter of Plantation Garden Centre, thank you for employing me, keeping me paid/fed/entertained for the last five years, and being supportive when I left. I wish you much continued success. Denis and Lynae Dufresne, thank you for coffee, laughter, and music, but mostly for your friendship. Lori Campbell, you have been a true friend and a beacon of light. Megan Evans, it has been so much fun hanging out with you, teaching with you, and laughing with you. You have been so supportive of this book and have ensured that I didn't starve or come undone while I was writing it. Thank you for being fabulous! Katie Songer, thank you for countless nights out, being hysterically funny, lending me money when I'm broke, understanding the value of a good squash, appreciating a good pumpkin, and being my sugar mama. You will always be one of my most favourite people.

Leslie Halsall, here it is, girl. "Our" book deal! We've been friends for eternity—through darkness and through light. You are one of the people who has kept me hanging on. You have supported me, loved me, encouraged me, and pulled me through. If not for you, I would not be here to write this book at all. I owe you a debt of gratitude I could never hope to repay. This book exists because of you.

Finally, Miss Madison Scheinler. I am so sad that you can't be here to celebrate this book with me, but I know how proud of me you would have been. I felt your presence on every page, and I felt your company as I sat up writing into the wee hours of the morn. Thank you for being my muse. Thank you for a friendship that transcends time and space and book deals. I will see you again—there are not many things in life I am sure of, but this is one of them.

Finally, many thanks to all of *you*. Of course I can't mention *everyone* here, but you know who you are. I have great friends and great clients, and I am so grateful. For all of you who have been there with me from the start, I thank you. Thanks for listening to me on CBC, coming to my gardening classes, reading my blog, and sending me your messages of hope and encouragement and support. Thank you for buying this book. Thank you for being interested in a better, more garden-filled world.

I hope that this book will be a help to you, that it will entertain and educate you, and that it will be a reference you turn to again and again. I hope this book will make an impact and lead to better gardens and a deeper appreciation of this amazing world. Lastly, I'd also like to thank myself, for being crazy enough to even attempt this.

Photograph credits

Photographs listed by page number below with l: left, r: right, c: centre, t: top, b: bottom if needed.

David Arsenault: 43: l; 133; 134: 224: l; 229

Annelise Doolaege: x

Akemi Matsubuchi: vi: l; xii; 13; 14; 17: c; 18: r; 19: tr; 19: cl; 20; 21; 28; 37; 38; 39: r; 41; 46; 49; 52; 53; 55; 59; 64; 80: r; 83: l; 84: t; 85: b; 91; 93; 114, 117; 132; 137; 138; 139: l; 140; 142; 144; 145; 147; 148; 149: l; 151; 152: r; 153; 157; 158; 162: r; 163: l; 164; 165: l; 167; 169; 170; 171; 172; 173; 174; 176, 177; 181; 182; 184: cr; 187: b; 188; 189; 196; 200; 207; 208; 211: l; 212; 218; 220; 224: r; 226

Justine Murdy: 130; 152: l

Lyndon Penner: vii: l; vii: c; ix; 9; 17: t; 17: b; 18: l; 27; 43: r; 51: t; 56; 68: t; 80: l; 83: tr; 83: cr; 143: c; 159; 160; 163: r; 166; 168: b; 178; 180; 194; 197; 199; 204; 213: r; 214, 215; 223; 230; 233

Katie Songer: 11, 116; 120; 139: r; 141; 149: r; 156; 161; 162: l; 168: t

Grant Wood, University of Saskatchewan: 6; 12; 19: tl; 24; 25; 29; 39: l; 40; 42; 48; 51: b; 62; 66; 68: b; 69; 73; 74; 77; 79; 82: b; 84: b; 85: t; 86; 88: t; 89; 90; 92; 94; 98; 99; 100; 101; 107; 108; 111; 113; 136; 154; 155; 165: r; 179; 185; 186; 190; 201; 202; 206; 213: l; 217; 227; 231

Vanessa Young: vi: r; vii: r; 22; 61; 72; 76; 82: t; 82: c; 88: b; 96; 143: t; 175; 184: tl; 187: t; 193; 198; 203; 211: r; 228

Plant Lists

Plants that produce edible fruit, berries, or seeds
apple, apricot, buffaloberry, cherry, cranberry, currants, gooseberry, nannyberry, plum, prensepia, saskatoon berry, sea buckthorn, walnuts.

Plants that do well in partial shade
ajuga, astilbe, barrenwort, bergenia, bleeding heart, blue poppy, brunnera, bugbane, chokecherry, columbine, corydaylis, cranberry, dogwood, dwarf balsam fir, ferns, fritillaria, globeflower, hepatica, heuchera, hosta, hydrangea, lady's mantle, lady's slipper, lamium, ligularia, masterwort, mertensia, mockorange, monkshood, narcissus, periwinkle, pulmonaria, rodgersia, sweet woodruff, viola.

Plants that can handle deep shade
ferns, hosta, goutweed, lady's mantle, lily of the valley, periwinkle, primula, pulmonaria.

Plants that make good cutflowers
allium, aster, astilbe, beebalm, bleeding heart, coralbells, echinacea, fleabane, forsythia, gaillardia, delphinium, globeflower, globe thistle, goldenrod, ligularia, lilac, lupines, mockorange, monkshood, penstemon, peony, phlox, poppies, rudbeckia, shasta daisy, yarrow, wild indigo.

Plants that add fragrance
apples, cherries, daphne, honeysuckle (some), hostas (some), lavender, lilacs, lilies (some), mock orange, phlox, plums, roses (some).

Plants that bloom early in the year
bergenia, cherries, creeping phlox, daffodils, forsythia, hepatica, honeyberry, marsh marigold, pasque flower, plums, primula, Russian almond, squills, tulips, willows.

Plants that bloom late summer/fall
aster (fall), bugbane, chrysanthemum, echinacea, goldenrod, grasses, sedum, rudbeckia, Russian sage.

Plants for winter interest
birch, cranberry, echinacea, evergreens (e.g., spruce, pine, fir, juniper, and cedar), globe thistle, grasses, hawthorn, hydrangea, mountain ash, sea buckthorn, sea holly.

25 favourite annuals
bachelor's buttons, calendula, California poppy, clarkia, four o' clock, fuchsia, gazania, geranium, heliotrope, impatiens, kochia, lavatera, lobelia, marigold, morning glory, nigella, portulaca, rudbeckia, safflower, salpiglossus, salvia, sunflower, sweet pea, thunbergia, zinnia.

Index